THE
COMPUTER USER'S
SURVIVAL GUIDE

THE
COMPUTER USER'S
SURVIVAL GUIDE

Joan Stigliani

O'Reilly & Associates, Inc.
103 Morris Street, Suite A
Sebastopol, CA 95472

The Computer User's Survival Guide
by Joan Stigliani

Copyright © 1995 O'Reilly & Associates, Inc. All rights reserved.
Printed in the United States of America.

Editor: Linda Lamb

Production Editors: Jane Ellin and Kiersten Nauman

Printing History:

October 1995:   First Edition

This book is printed on acid-free paper with 85% recycled content, 15% post-consumer waste. O'Reilly & Associates is committed to using paper with the highest recycled content available consistent with high quality.

ISBN: 1-56592-030-9

[   ]

To the meadows and redwood forests of Boulder Creek
for their inspiration
and the rhythms of Santa Cruz
for moving it through

May computer users everywhere
their friends, families, peers, and associates
be healthy, comfortable, relaxed, and free of injury

Table of Contents

Preface

If you use a computer regularly, you're probably concerned about how it might be affecting you—with good reason. Computers have drastically changed the way we do office work, and brought about new working conditions that pose health risks to a large number of people. The terminal at your desk changes the surface you read from, how you sit, how you move (or don't move), how much light you need, how much radiation you're exposed to, and how fast you have to work.

You are probably more interested in the specifics of how computer work affects *you*:

- Is your headache from tension? From eyestrain? Do you have to put up with it or is there something you can do?

- Is the slight numbness that you're feeling in your fingertips something to worry about?

- Will you get carpal tunnel syndrome?

- Will you get cancer? Have a miscarriage?

- Is stress an inevitable part of your job? Is there any time for slowing down or taking a rest?

- Will your eyesight deteriorate?

The Computer User's Survival Guide examines the health questions you face. It gives you background about how bodily systems work, how computer work affects those systems, and what you can do about it. Risks to your health will vary with the kind of equipment you use, how long and intensely you use a computer, the physical layout of your office, your work habits, your general health, and so on. From the information and suggestions here, you can craft a response to your situation.

About the Audience

This book is written primarily for computer users themselves. It assumes that you have some interest in your health, and that you'd like to have more control over the health risks in your workplace. Some simple changes can make a significant difference in your health.

This book is also useful for business people who need an overview of the risks faced by computer users: managers, those working in human resources or personnel, members of company safety committees, and so on. The changes that we talk about in *The Computer User's Survival Guide* are more easily achieved if your business is supportive of employees' health. As you read, compare the recommended work environment to your own. Remember that if something is "on the books" but not adhered to, it doesn't count. For example, if you have rules for a ten-minute break every two hours, but the atmosphere of a department is such that no one takes breaks, your employees are at risk.

This book is also written for those already working in the occupational health field, such as ergonomics consultants, occupational therapists, physical therapists, massage therapists, and occupational safety nurses. Depending on your profession and experience, you probably already know a lot about specific issues, for example, the musculature of the arm, or the proper use of input devices. *The Computer User's Survival Guide* broadens your view of the risks to your clients, and emphasizes the interrelatedness of bodily systems and solutions.

Parents and teachers can use this book to help children use computers safely. Children are resilient, but their growing bodies are still affected by fatigue, wear and tear, eyestrain, poor posture, and radiation exposure. Any bad computing habits they acquire become deeply ingrained. Kids learn by example. If the adults around them use computers safely and practice good work habits, kids are more likely to do the same.

Who's Responsible for What?

When there's an occupational health epidemic, there's a tendency for everyone to lay the blame elsewhere. Injured individuals blame their employer and the equipment; employers blame the workers and the equipment manufacturers; and so on. For computer-related health problems, everyone is responsible to some degree—individuals, employers, equipment providers, and the government.

Individuals are responsible for their technique and work habits:

- Set up your work area so you're comfortable.

- Learn how to adjust your furniture, and how to use the hardware and software.

- Pace yourself on the job and take your breaks.

- Develop good habits of working, sitting, and using your eyes.

- Exercise and take care of your health.

- Take the health-related training programs your employer offers.

- Report symptoms early.

- Work with your employer to secure good working conditions.

Employers are responsible for providing safe and reasonable working conditions:

- Focus on prevention. Make changes to the workplace and job design that are beneficial to employees' health. These might seem expensive or disruptive at first, but will pay off over time.

- Provide a variety of ergonomic furniture, computer equipment, and software. Train workers how to use them.

- Provide health-related training programs, and have health checks every three to six months to detect problems early.

- Define job responsibilities and goals.

- Set reasonable working hours, breaks, and vacation time.

- Provide employees as much autonomy and flexibility in scheduling as possible.

- Provide a workplace free of chemical and environmental toxins.

- Design a workplace that accommodates workers and their tasks.

- Work with employees (and unions and trade associations) to develop solutions beneficial to everyone.

Manufacturers are responsible for creating adjustable, comfortable, and easy-to-use products:

- Incorporate ergonomic developments into the design of computer equipment, software, furniture, and accessories.

- Produce lines of ergonomic furniture in the same style and fabrics so employers can provide a choice of furniture with the same interior design scheme.

- Train the sales force in ergonomic principles so they can help customers choose appropriate equipment and furniture.

The government is responsible for protecting the well-being of the work force:

- Support research in all areas of computer health and safety.

- Develop and enforce standards and regulations that protect the health and safety of computer workers.

This book concentrates on the changes that you can make in your own work environment: the things that are under your control.

In most instances, the changes that you can make will be enough to reduce health risks substantially. You also will want to work toward a safer workplace in partnership with your employer, whether through your department, a human resources or personnel department, a safety committee, union, or trade association.

How to Use This Book

The Computer User's Survival Guide is divided into five parts:

- Part I, *The Basics*

- Part II, *Repetitive Strain Injury*

- Part III, *Eyestrain*

- Part IV, *Stress*

- Part V, *The Potential Risks of Electromagnetic Fields*

The topics in *The Basics* are there because they relate to all other health risks and systems. Positioning, setting up your work area, problem solving, body awareness, and general health affect RSI, eyestrain, stress, and risks from radiation exposure.

If you are interested in only a single health risk right now—such as eyestrain or radiation—read *The Basics* and then the part that deals only with that health risk. However, if you already have a painful repetitive strain injury, go immediately to Chapter 11, *Treating the Injury*.

Within each part, there are one or more chapters that describe the health risk, and one or more chapters that describe what to do about it. The background chapters are meant to give you an understanding of what's going on in your body, so that you can tailor solutions to work for you. You can skip the background material if you want to accept our general suggestions without knowing the reasons behind them.

We'd Like to Hear From You

You can contact us to make suggestions for future editions of this book, or to inquire about sales information:

> O'Reilly & Associates, Inc.
> 103 Morris Street, Suite A
> Sebastopol, CA 95472
> (800) 998-9938 (in the US or Canada)
> (707) 829-0515 (international/local)
> (707) 829-0104 (fax)

email address: *nuts@ora.com* or *uunet!ora.com!nuts*

For information on volume discounts for bulk purchase, call O'Reilly & Associates at 800-998-9938 (U.S. and Canada), or send email to *linda@ora.com* (*uunet!ora.com!*).

For companies requiring extensive customization of the book, source licensing terms are also available.

Acknowledgments

This book would not have been possible without the help and support of the many people who shared their expertise and encouraged me along the way. I offer my thanks and gratitude to all of them.

To those who helped keep the project going and carry it to completion—at O'Reilly & Associates, Linda Lamb, Steve Talbott, Tim O'Reilly, Clairemarie Fisher O'Leary, Kiersten Nauman, Chris Reilly, Kismet McDonough-Chan, Sheryl Avruch, Mike Sierra, Seth Maislin, Nancy Priest, Jane Ellin, and Edie Freeman. Jaye Schlesinger for her illustrations. Lynne Oberlander, MA, OTR, for her review.

To my family and friends for their constant support, especially Lillian Swanstrom, Kay Stigliani, Cheryl Skinner, Jack Burness, Linda Heuman, Heidi Dielmann, Priscilla Sawa, Ann Driscoll, Leslie Leland, Cristina Falcoski, Danny Duck, Mary Petruchius, and Ruth Greene. And to Janet Egan, friend, mentor, and writing coach, for encouraging me to keep writing.

Special thanks to Caroline Rose, *RSI Network* newsletter; Kristin Barendsen; Carina Chiang; Judy Doane, San Francisco RSI Support Group; Gary Karp, Onsight Technology Education Services; Mona Bernstein, MPH, Environmental Health & Safety, Lawrence Berkeley Laboratory; Uli Schwaninger, MD; Eileen Vollowitz, physical therapist, Back Designs, Inc; Bruno Marti; Per Erik Boivie, Swedish Confederation of Professional Employees (TCO); Rick Mehaffey, DC; Eileen Bracken Carter, CMT; Marion Moore, yoga instructor; Nona Viro, CMT; Lark Carroll, educational kinesiologist; Jane Williams; Steve Turner, National Writers Union; and Ken Ceder, Ott Light Systems, Inc.

To those who shared their experiences and knowledge—Rik Ahlberg; Deborah Bennett; Steve Elias; Collins Flannery; Jerry Halberstadt; Joan Lichterman; Jonathan Luskin; James McCormick; Roy Nierenberg; Gary Owens; Jerry Peek; Beatrice Terranella; members of the *San Francisco RSI Support Group*; online contributors to the newsgroups *sorehand, c+health, boston-rsi, sci.med.occupational*; contributors to the *RSI Network* newsletter; and many others.

To many health care professionals, ergonomists, and industry experts for their invaluable interviews and suggestions—Andrew Barnes, Safe Computing; James Barrett, Applied Learning Corporation; Ellen Behrens, University of California at Davis Disability Resource Centre; Russel Coillot, Jr., Professional Ergonomic Solutions; John Pelgye Douthit, OMD; Deborah DeWeese, PT; Bert Dumpé, Ergotec Association, Inc.; Maggie Graf, Swiss Federal Institute of Technology; Kathleen P. Hawk, EMF issues consultant; Rolf Ilg, Fraunhofer-Institute for Industrial Engineering (IAO); Pete Johnson, University of California at Berkeley Ergonomics Laboratory; Elizabeth Klein, OTR, CHT, CWA, CalARM Hand Rehabilitation Associates; John Lamp, Comcare Australia; Thomas Läubli, MD, Swiss Federal Institute of Technology; Claudia Leonhardt, Biofeedback-Center Stuttgart; Ruth Lowengart, MD, MSOM, Orthopedic Medicine and Occupational Health private practice, University of California at San Francisco School of Medicine Assistant Clinical Professor; Walter Lips; Rui Xiong Mai, OMD, Boston Chinatown Acupuncture Center; Steve Marshall, The Ergonomics Lab; Judy Matsuoka-Sarina, OTR, CHT, Occupational Therapy, San Jose Medical Center; Dheena Moongilan, AT&T Bell Laboratories; Linda Morse, MD, MPH, FACOM, Repetitive Motion Institute, Valley Medical Center; Marino Menozzi, Swiss Federal Institute of Technology; Karl Nyman, MD, ophthalmologist; Stephanie O'Leary, MS, OTR, Computer Evaluation and Learning Lab, Department of Veterans Affairs; Ilana Parker, PT; Bill Parlette, TechAid Development AG; Rich Pekelney, Kensington Microware Limited; Samuel Pesner, OD; Margaret Phillips, MS, OTR, FAOTA, Occupational Therapy, San Jose Medical Center; Vern Putz-Anderson, PhD, National Institute of Occupational Safety and Health (NIOSH); Louis Slesin, *VDT News;* Wm Michael Smith, PhD, psychologist; Walter Stulzer, Swiss Federal Institute of Technology; and Stephen Tamaribuchi, RSI consultant.

Thanks also to Allen Dobney and Dee Cravens, Radius Inc.; Carol Fitzgerald, Kensington Microware Limited; Tana Brinnand, MouseMitt International; Carolyn Workinger and Virginia Bonto Brown, BioElectric Shield Company; Gudrun Pettersson, TCO Information Center; Cathy Bergman-Venezia, The EMR Alliance; Leif Södergren, Association for the Electrically and VDT Injured; Robert Ingle, Ingle International, Inc.; and Shirley Lunde, Kinesis Corporation.

PART

I

The Basics

There are specific health risks for computer users—repetitive strain injury, eyestrain, stress, and radiation exposure. No matter what risk you're trying to avoid, certain general principles apply:

- Problems rarely exist in isolation. For example, sitting with your head forward because of eyestrain can hurt your neck, compress your lungs, and raise your level of stress.

- Problems often result from a combination of factors—your physical work environment, job stress, the way you work and use your body, and your general physical condition.

- You are not meant to sit still. You are meant to move and switch positions. You can find a range of neutral body postures to switch between so that you can be comfortable all day long.

- You are able to identify health problems only if you're aware of your body and the signals it's sending. Since computer work tends to take you "into your head," you'll have to put some effort into this awareness at first. Full, diaphragmatic breathing is one way to quickly get in touch with your body.

- You will help prevent repetitive strain injuries, eyestrain, and stress if you balance computer work with exercise, stretching, and rest.

CHAPTER

I

Where Do You Begin?

No problem can be solved from the
same consciousness that created it.
—ALBERT EINSTEIN

Our usual mode is to seek a single fix for a single problem, to match symptoms and solutions one-to-one, to apply the exact same solutions across the board for everyone. For health problems related to computer work, this approach is unsuccessful more often than not. There are too many variables—the hardware, software, furniture, lighting, job demands, working conditions, corporate culture, the individual doing the job and what that individual does at home. What creates symptoms in one person may or may not create the same symptoms in someone else. Likewise, the same symptom can result from different causes in different people.

We've gone on a long time addressing our health complaints piecemeal. Glare screens for eyestrain, wristrests for wrist pain, stress management workshops for burnout. So far, it hasn't really worked. People still get eyestrain, repetitive strain injury is on the rise, and high stress is a major occupational hazard.

Long-term solutions come when you change your view of the problems. Computer work affects us biologically through the visual, musculoskeletal, and nervous systems. It also affects our psychological and emotional states. These are all interrelated. The health of one system influences the health of the others. Effective solutions take them all into consideration.

Know What You're Looking For

Health effects from computer work range from specific complaints, such as eyestrain and repetitive strain injury, to general discomfort and malaise. Stress and its related ailments are known problems, and many people are concerned about the immediate and long-term influence of electromagnetic fields on health and well-being. If you work on a computer only a few hours a day, you may never experience discomfort or injury. When you work about four hours a day or more, there are some problems to watch out for.

Muscle Soreness and Fatigue

General muscular aches and pains, back pain, chest pain, numbness or pain in the legs and feet are common complaints. They are typically the result of poor posture, which could result from a variety of conditions. The chair may not fit or be adjusted for you, the setup of your equipment and furniture may take you out of good posture, or you may have habitual ways of sitting and moving that your body doesn't like. To find the source, look first at your posture and the setup of your work area, described in Chapter 2, *Get Comfortable*, and Chapter 3, *Customize Your Work Area*.

Neck, Shoulder, Arm, Wrist, and Hand Pain

Any pain, discomfort, or vague but disquieting sensations in the neck and entire upper limb, from the shoulder blades to the fingertips, require your immediate attention. See Chapter 11, *Treating the Injury*. These indicate a possible repetitive strain injury (RSI), which, unless you take care of it early, has the potential to take from you the use of your hands. There is usually no single cause of repetitive strain injury, but several factors coming together, including posture, the setup of your work area, the pace of work, and your typing technique.

Eyestrain and Visual Distress

Eyestrain, the most widespread complaint, can result from glare and bad lighting, flicker and blurry images on the screen, straining to see, or using eyeglasses with the wrong prescription. Because of its strong influence on posture, eyestrain may be the source of muscle tension in the neck, shoulders, and upper back, areas in which RSI often originates. It also increases tension in the head and face, which contributes to headaches.

Stress-Related Disorders

High levels of stress are related to a variety of internal disorders and diseases, and can affect your emotions and behavior. Aside from the general stresses of life, you may also experience stress from certain aspects of your job, such as electronic performance monitoring and the pace of work. Stress can also come from elements of the physical office environment, such as noise, poor air quality, and, possibly, electromagnetic fields. The longer you sustain high stress levels, the more susceptible you are to muscle soreness, headaches, eyestrain, and RSI.

Environmental Sensitivities

Some people have suffered skin rashes, possibly from exposure to electromagnetic fields (EMFs). Increasing numbers of people have become hypersensitive to EMFs from various sources in the office and general environment. Chemicals, glues, cleaning agents, and other substances in the office may also trigger allergic reactions.

Headaches

Headaches are often the result of muscle tension and nerve irritation in the neck, especially at the base of the skull, which could result from eyestrain, stress, or posture. Headaches may also be reactions to indoor air pollutants and odors, noise, flickering light, dust, and dry air.

The Possibility of Life-Threatening Conditions

Increased risk of miscarriage from proximity to computer monitors has been a concern since the late 1970s, and there is still no definitive answer. The issue has become more complicated as we learn more about the effects of electromagnetic fields, and consider exposure not just from computer monitors, but from other sources in the office as well.

A relatively new concern is an increased risk of cancer. In offices where increased incidences of certain cancers were reported, people may have been exposed to strong electromagnetic fields from building wiring, computer equipment, and other sources. This exposure has been suggested, but not proven, as a cause, and investigations into the situation are far from complete.

Take a Holistic Approach

Holistic medicine aims to treat the body as a whole, instead of as a jumble of separate parts. Computer work involves the hardware, software, furniture, work area, job, and you. It's a dynamic system, and you are the crux of it. All the other parts should be adapted, adjusted, and optimized for your comfort. That's what ergonomics is all about—fitting the task, the tools, and the work environment to you, not the other way around.

Fixing One Problem Often Eliminates Other Problems

Problems don't usually exist in isolation, and, typically, one problem brings several others with it. For example, office lighting that creates glare affects how your eyes feel and how you sit, which can make your body sore and tense, and influence how well you do your job. Taking away the glare can reverse the

Why Not Sit with Your Head Forward?

The muscles in your face tense up, contributing to eyestrain and neck tension. The tissues at the base of the skull become compressed, leading to headaches.

The muscles in the upper neck and shoulders tighten as they strain to hold up your head, causing stiffness in the jaw, neck, and shoulders.

The tightness of the neck and shoulder muscles may put pressure on the nerves and blood vessels that serve the arms. This can decrease circulation, compress the nerves, and increase your risk of RSI.

The rounding of the shoulders and back overstretches and weakens the back muscles, and causes the chest to collapse. This leads to backache, inefficient breathing, and poor circulation.

The slump in the lower back alters its natural curve and increases the pressure on the ligaments and discs in the spine, decreasing the flow of nutrients to the discs and causing aches and stiffness.

The abdominal muscles can become weak and soft, and the internal organs can be compressed.

The arms bend more at the elbows and wrists, further increasing your risk of RSI.

The hips bend more, cutting off circulation to the legs and feet, possibly resulting in numbness and pain.

effects. Speeding up the pace of work increases both stress and the physical demands on your eyes and hands. Slowing down eases the strain on both.

Physical discomfort often comes from two primary sources—holding your head forward toward the screen, and not having good postural support for your body. Both are common, and frequently go together. As the head comes forward, the whole body slumps forward, away from the back of the chair. The resulting rounded posture has repercussions throughout the body. (See Figure 1-1.) Correcting this posture fixes many problems. When you move your head back, the body follows. The back straightens and releases tension as it rests on the chair. The head is supported by the spine, the shoulders stay back, and the chest opens. The angles of the elbows, wrists, and hips open up. Your body feels better, and you reduce eyestrain, muscle tension, and your risk of RSI.

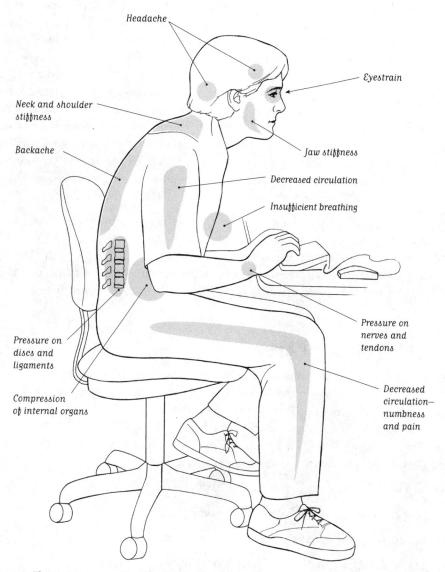

Headache

Eyestrain

Neck and shoulder stiffness

Backache

Jaw stiffness

Decreased circulation

Insufficient breathing

Pressure on nerves and tendons

Pressure on discs and ligaments

Compression of internal organs

Decreased circulation— numbness and pain

Figure 1-1. The repercussions of sitting with your head forward

Solutions Are Often Multifaceted

To correct a problem, you have to find its source. Frequently, there's more than one. Whether your complaint is blurry vision, a headache, or a pain in the wrist, you have to look beyond where it hurts to find possible causes in the equipment, the setup of your work area, your job, or your habits and workstyle. The solutions, then, are found in some or all of those places, and they may not be the same for everyone.

If you're uncomfortable because you sit with your head forward, you need to know *why* you are sitting that way. The monitor may be too high or too far away, so you can't see it well. The screen characters may be blurry or small or hard to read. You might be trying to see around glare or reflections on the screen. Your glasses might not be the right prescription, or you might be using conventional bifocals and tilting your head back to see through the bottom of the lenses. Your work might require exacting visual tasks. You might be tired as a result of working long hours. The chair might be uncomfortable or improperly adjusted. You might be so involved in your work that you unconsciously go closer and closer into it. Or you might sit that way out of habit. To correct the posture, you might need to reposition the monitor, get a screen with better resolution, change the lighting, get different glasses, or get some rest.

Wrist pain may also have several causes. It might come from bending your wrists back when you type. But what's the source of the bend? Is it a habit you've acquired, or is the keyboard too high and far away? Maybe it's both. The first impulse may be to get a wristrest, when what you really need to do is change your typing technique and the position of the keyboard. A wristrest might help or it might not.

Start Where You Are

What you create at the computer requires the combined effort of mind and body. Whether you are writing code or entering data, your body has to be comfortable so ideas and thoughts can flow clearly onto the screen. The basics in these first chapters lay the foundation for comfortable computing. Together, they improve your overall comfort and give you the tools to prevent injury, discover health problems early on, and heal quickly when you're hurt.

Whatever your situation, implement the basics first:

- Learn how to get comfortable with good posture.

- Set up your work area so you can stay comfortable.

- Practice body awareness to detect aches and pains early on.

- Learn good breathing patterns to reduce stress and strengthen your system.

- Take care of yourself with exercise, stretching, nutrition, and relaxation.

The basics are fundamental to dealing with general aches and pains, RSI, eyestrain, and stress—the main problems that stem from computer work. As you read about these specific complaints, you'll find the basics integrated into the suggestions for prevention and recovery.

There's one exception—if you have acute pain in the hand, wrist, arm, or shoulder, stop what you're doing, seek medical advice, and treat the pain (see Chapter 11).

Don't Buy Anything Until You Know What You Need

Go through the next chapters using your existing equipment and furniture. If you can't set yourself up comfortably by adjusting and repositioning what you already have, and you can't find any way to modify it to make it work, then consider buying something new.

Look at the way you use your equipment—your hands may hurt because of the keyboard design, or because of your typing technique. If you improve your technique and your hands still hurt because the keyboard design keeps them in an awkward position, consider getting a new keyboard. By practicing body awareness and following the guidelines for posture and customizing your work area, you'll discover what purchases you need to make, if any.

Make Changes over Time

As you learn the basics, you'll find out what changes you need to make. Your main priority is to get comfortable through posture and the arrangement of your work area, so concentrate on that first. Make one or two changes at a time, testing them as you go. Give yourself time to get used to them. Note which problems you've solved, and which remain.

Some things may not be completely under your control. You may need help rearranging your work area, or you may need your manager's approval to change your work schedule, or to purchase a new chair or keyboard. Selecting equipment takes time, and then you have to wait for the equipment to arrive. In the meantime, do what *is* under your control, especially practicing body awareness and changing habits that perpetuate discomfort. Don't wait—no one else is going to do it for you. Even small changes can make a big difference.

2

Get Comfortable

Getting comfortable means working with good posture. Sure thing, you say, straightening yourself to match the image you've seen of "good posture" for computer work—spine bolt upright, elbows, knees, and hips at strict 90-degree angles, feet on a footrest, your body locked into place. That stiff image is so ingrained that we've come to think of it as correct. There's something uninviting about that way of sitting, though. It looks tense, constrained, and unnatural. After a few minutes of it, you probably slip back into your usual way of sitting.

This chapter deals with posture by itself, not in relation to your desk and computer equipment, so you can learn how it feels to sit comfortably without external constraints. Chapter 3, *Customize Your Work Area*, helps you set up your work area to keep that comfortable posture.

Good Posture Is Something You Feel

Good posture is not so much something you measure from the outside, but something you feel from the inside. It's not about being fixed in one position. It changes with what you're doing. It depends on your body type, size, and flexibility. It's not limp or passive, but relaxed and comfortable—your muscles aren't stiff or tight, your mind is alert, and your body is in a position that promotes circulation and eases strain on the muscles, joints, and spinal discs.

It's Neutral

The term *neutral posture* refers to our natural anatomical posture, the lineup of our bones, joints, and muscles when they are in their most balanced position. It is our most comfortable posture.

NASA offers us a dramatic example of neutral posture in weightlessness — the position that the body, when given the choice, returns to and rests in (Figure 2-1).[1] NASA found that without the effect of gravity, the body not only goes to this posture automatically and maintains it indefinitely, but also that if a person tries to stay in or is confined to any different posture, the result is discomfort, fatigue, and inefficiency. In neutral posture, the muscles, tendons, and ligaments are in balance, the internal organs have more room and function more efficiently, and circulation is better. The body likes it.

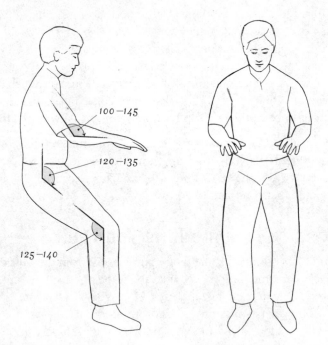

Figure 2-1. Neutral posture in weightlessness

It's Relaxed and Stable

To maintain the relaxation of neutral posture in gravity, you need stability. This means your chair supports your body, arms, and legs so you don't have to rely too much on your muscles to hold yourself in place. You also need to have your equipment set up so that it's within easy reach. If you have to hold your arms out all day to use your keyboard or mouse, or if you need to tilt your head or bring it forward to see your work, your muscles don't get a chance to rest. Chronic muscle tension develops in your neck, back, shoulders, and forearms that can lead to discomfort, pain, and injury.

If you feel tension when you sit in a posture for more than a few minutes, then it's probably not neutral. Sitting in slumped, awkward, or non-neutral posture for a few minutes may feel good in the short term, but you need neutral, relaxed postures for enduring comfort.

It's Dynamic

The body thrives on movement, but computer work is sedentary and constrained. Whether the task is fascinating or boring, you're pretty much stuck sitting in a chair, hands on the keyboard or mouse, eyes on the screen. There is some variation when you answer the phone, look through your papers, or jot down a note, but once you settle in to the computer task, you're in that basic position, and that's where you'll probably stay.

Good posture is active. When you change tasks, change position. Recline slightly or sit upright for computer work, and sit forward with your upper body supported for desk work. Stand up or lean way back when you're thinking or talking on the phone. Think of these postures as being on a continuum, from reclined to standing—you can choose from the whole range (see Figure 2-2). Find the positions you like and switch between them. Make minor adjustments throughout the day. Keep moving—when you stop, your body suffers.

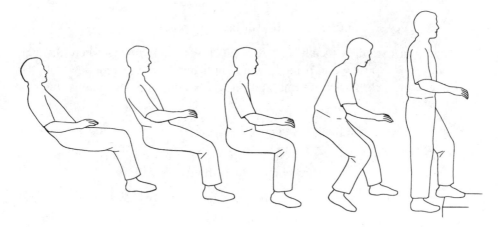

Figure 2-2. The posture continuum

exercise and bodywork, but the ̇̇̇ ̇̇̇ ̇̇̇ body is right now. Concentrate not on exact angles and measurements, ̇̇̇ ̇̇̇ what's comfortable and neutral for you.

Neutral Body Posture

When you sit in neutral posture, the angle made by the thighs and torso is open and relaxed, the shoulders are relaxed down and back, and the chest is open, not collapsed. A neutral thigh-torso position is about halfway between the extremes of bending over and arching your back when standing, or in the middle of the range of motion of your spine. Eileen Vollowitz, physical therapist and founder of Back Designs, Inc., advises that this angle is somewhere between 115 and 145 degrees for most people. Some people are more comfortable with tighter angles of approximately 90 degrees, or even less. Flexible people tend to have a greater range of neutral body postures. When you adjust your chair and experiment with different postures, keep the thigh-to-torso angle in your range of comfort.

Neutral Head Posture

As much as possible, keep your head balanced over your spine, somewhere between the extremes of having your head pulled way back or pushed far forward:

- Stand up or sit comfortably with your back supported.

- Find your extremes. Gently pull your head way back, noting where the strain starts. Then push your head forward, noticing how the muscles feel. (Use only your neck muscles to pull and push, not your arms. If there is *any* pain, stop.)

- Let your head relax back into its usual place.

- Pull your head up slightly from the back of the neck, or imagine your body being suspended by a string coming from the top of your head.

- Let your shoulders drop down and your neck muscles relax. Pull the chin in slightly.

- If you feel strain, back off until your muscles feel relaxed. That's your neutral head position.

Why We Need Movement

Movement is the driving force of the circulatory system. The pumping of the heart moves blood through the body, and the movements of the arms and legs help the heart with its task. Movement helps you breathe more fully, so you get more oxygen into your blood. Fresh blood coming from the heart brings oxygen and nutrients to the muscles, bones, and internal organs. As the blood flows through, it carries away the naturally occurring metabolic waste products created by the muscles and body processes such as digestion and respiration. Without movement, the blood stagnates.

Movement helps the muscles, tendons, and ligaments stay flexible and strong, so they can support the bones and provide a wide range of motion. Moving helps the muscles maintain their natural pattern of contraction and relaxation. When the muscles contract, the blood vessels inside the muscle are compressed, and the blood carrying the waste products is squeezed out of the muscle. When the muscles relax, the oxygen and nutrient-rich blood can come into them and the depleted blood is washed away, carrying with it the ache- and pain-causing lactic acid and metabolic wastes.

The discs in the spinal column also depend on movement. Discs are not nourished directly by the blood flow, but through a passive mechanism of diffusion and fluid exchange between the discs and the surrounding tissue. Changing positions among reclined, upright, and forward postures encourages this process by changing the pressure on the discs. Sitting upright increases pressure, which pushes fluid and waste products out of the discs. Reclining eases the pressure, letting the discs soak up fresh fluid and nutrients. Discs need changing pressure—a continually compressed disc can't soak up fluid, and it dries out.

When you sit too long in one position, especially in an awkward position, the back, shoulder, and neck muscles holding you in place get overused and tight, while the muscles in the buttocks, thighs, and abdomen get weak and soft from lack of use. Your lower back might hurt. Your feet might swell or go to sleep. Your thighs and buttocks can become numb, painful, or sore from lack of circulation, and sometimes even the skin can hurt. The spinal discs get compressed, your joints become strained and stiff, and you feel tired, uncomfortable, and stressed.

If you have developed a naturally forward head posture from years of reading, desk work, or computer work, your neutral head posture may still be slightly forward. That's okay—just avoid sitting with your head in either of the extreme positions. You may eventually want to change that posture through exercise and bodywork, but that's a different issue.

the muscles, and ~~~~
use a conventional keyboard.

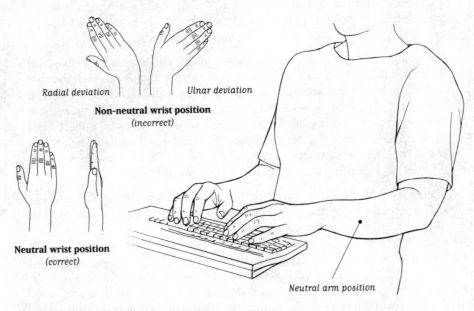

Radial deviation   Ulnar deviation

Non-neutral wrist position
(incorrect)

Neutral wrist position
(correct)

Neutral arm position

Figure 2-3. Neutral arm and wrist positions

If you hold your arms out as in weightless neutral posture, the joints are more relaxed, but the muscles and eventually the joints become strained unless they have proper support. As you hold your arms out, the elbows also go out, and the wrists have to bend even more to type, unless you have a split keyboard.

To feel the difference between arm positions, try this:

- Relax your arms at your sides, palms turned into your sides.

- Keeping your wrists and upper arms in the same position, lift just your hands until your elbows make about a 90-degree angle.

- Look at the position of your hands, wrists, and arms. Your wrists are in line with your forearms and not quite vertical, your thumbs are up and in the same plane as the index fingers. The palms face in. This is your neutral wrist posture when your arms are relaxed at your sides.

- Starting in that position, hands lifted, watch what happens when you raise just your elbows out to your sides. The wrists stay in line with the forearms but are closer to horizontal. The palms and thumbs face down, and the wrists are further apart from each other. This is closer to neutral arm posture in weightlessness.

Whether you relax your arms down to your sides or have your elbows further out, you must both support the weight of your arms *and* maintain neutral wrist posture when you type. Ultimately, your arm position depends on your body position and on the type of arm support and keyboard you use.

Support Your Body

An adjustable, ergonomic chair supports neutral postures, allows you to move and change positions frequently, and prevents you from sitting in extremely bad postures. Sometimes people balk at the idea. *An adjustable chair? They're so expensive!* A company might spend thousands of dollars on computer equipment for an employee, but when the same person requests an adjustable chair, expense suddenly becomes an issue. A person might spend extra money for a particular automobile just to get a more comfortable driver's seat, but won't spend extra money for an office chair, even though that chair probably gets more use.

The chair by itself won't give you good posture, but a good chair encourages your efforts. For people who already have an injury, either from computer work or something else, the right chair can keep a short-term injury from becoming chronic. It can make the difference between working in pain or in comfort, or even between working and not working. A new chair can easily be cheaper than a round of visits to a doctor or therapist. One person with a new chair describes the change:

> I just got an adjustable chair that is actually comfortable. I'll probably need to fool with it more over the next few days, but right now, my back feels supported, my quadriceps do not feel uncomfortably stretched, my circulation is not cut off at the knees, and my arms even feel better since I adjusted the armrests. I might be in chair heaven right now.

Selecting a Chair

No single chair is comfortable or suitable for everyone. If you're shopping for a chair, go to a place with a well-trained staff and allow time to find one that fits you well. If your company provides a a variety of chairs, try them all before you choose one. If possible, have someone knowledgeable help you decide which chair is a good match. Chairs often come with instruction booklets that describe their features and adjustments.

distance

- *Comfort*. The backrest contours match the natural curves of your ... seat distributes your weight evenly, has a rounded front edge, and is about two inches wider than you. It allows a space of about 1 to 3 inches between the front edge of the seat and the back of your knees.

- *Stability*. The chair supports your weight and has a sturdy, five-pointed base with smooth-moving castors that make it easy to move and swivel.

Choose a chair that supports the tasks you do and the postures you find comfortable. You may not need full adjustability or extra features. If you never sit in forward postures, you don't need a chair that supports them. If you don't use extremely reclined postures, you don't need a headrest. Depending on how you decide to support your arms, you may not need armrests.

For more information on finding a chair that fits, see Appendix A, *Equipment Selection Guide*.

The Basic Adjustments

Practice adjusting the seat height, the backrest height, and the seat-to-backrest angle until the adjustments feel easy and natural to make.

- Lower or raise the chair so your feet are flat on the floor. Your feet shouldn't dangle and your thighs shouldn't come up off the seat.

- Sit with your bottom fully on the seat pan, and your low and middle back against the backrest.

- Adjust the height of the backrest so its contours follow your spinal curves.

- Adjust the tilt of the seat pan and the angle of the backrest so your thighs and torso are in neutral position. Try various combinations of seat tilts and backrest angles.

- Relax into the backrest and let the chair support the weight of your torso. This is critical.

- Relax your shoulders and find your neutral head posture.

- For now, just rest your arms in your lap. Arm support is discussed in the next section.

Get in the habit of adjusting your chair throughout the day to accommodate how you feel and what you're doing—don't just adjust it once and leave it that way. When you leave work, raise your chair up so you have to adjust it the next morning.

If You Don't Have an Adjustable Chair

If you can't adjust your chair, see how different postures feel in the chair you have. At the very least, you should be able to lean against the backrest and still get close to the keyboard and mouse. Stand up, move around, and stretch frequently. Try alternating chairs every 45 minutes or so.

A non-adjustable chair may be acceptable if it's comfortable and you spend only an hour or two a day at the computer. A variety of cushions and supports are available that make non-adjustable chairs more comfortable. Sometimes even a rolled-up towel can help as a lumbar support for your back. For regular computer use, however, you really need an adjustable chair.

You may be sitting in an adjustable chair and not even know it. Many therapists have had clients who for years never realized their chairs could be adjusted. A chair that feels uncomfortable may simply be adjusted for someone else.

Be careful with kneeling chairs (also known as balans chairs). They tend to immobilize your legs, and if they don't fit properly, can put too much pressure on the knees and shins. They can be good for reading or writing at a slanted desk, but aren't practical for computer work because they don't support upright or reclining postures. Use a kneeling chair only part-time or during breaks, alternating it periodically with a different chair.

Support Your Arms

Whatever arm position you use, arm support is important for offloading the weight of your arms from your neck, shoulders, and back while you work. Without it, tension builds throughout the upper limb, from the hand on up to the shoulders and neck. According to Vollowitz, lack of proper arm support is a major cause of injury.

There are three main types of supports—armrests attached to the chair, forearm supports that attach to the desk or keyboard tray, and wristrests for keyboard and mouse use. You may want to use different supports for different postures.

Whatever type of arm support you use, consider these factors:

- *Arm supports should be adjusted so they hold the weight of your arms with your neck and shoulders relaxed and your wrists in neutral position.* Supports that are too high can cause you to raise your shoulders and tighten your

may want a wristrest.

- *Never rest your wrists, forearms, or inside of the elbow on a hard surface or a sharp edge.* Doing so can constrict blood flow and put pressure directly on nerves and blood vessels. A non-absorbent hard surface can contribute to swelling if moisture accumulates under the wrists or forearms. Put padding on hard surfaces. Wrapping foam or bubble-pack around hard armrests and covering it with cloth can protect your forearms and elbows.

- *The support should be made of comfortable, non-allergenic materials.* Certain fabrics or materials might cause skin irritation or physical discomfort, and some have chemical odors that may be irritating.

Armrests

Armrests on a chair can be helpful for upright and reclined postures, and should be adjustable for height, depth, and distance between them. They shouldn't bump into your desk or interfere with your arm or body movements. Adjust the armrests so they are close to your body and just barely touch your elbows when you type. You should be able to relax your arms onto them and keep your shoulders down and free of tension.

Wristrests

Wristrests can be used both as arm support and as a guide for keeping your wrists in neutral position when you type or use the mouse. The thickness and length of the wristrest must match the device you're using it with—thicker keyboards require thicker wristrests. The wristrest should be deep and soft enough to support your wrists and protect you from hard surfaces and edges. Narrow ones may not be adequate, and deep ones may put too much distance between you and the keyboard, causing you to reach for the keys. Wristrests that are too high or low can cause you to extend or flex your wrists too much.

Forearm Supports

Static or mobile forearm supports that attach to the desk or keyboard tray provide a resting place for your arms through the forearms, especially in upright postures. Forearm supports that don't fit can interfere with speed and accuracy. If they're too high, they can increase tension in the neck and shoulders. The movement of mobile, articulating supports should be smooth and allow your arms and hands to float over the keyboard. A stiff mechanism can increase the amount of force you need to exert.

Support Your Feet

Footrests are often recommended when you have to raise the chair, usually because the keyboard or desk can't be lowered. A footrest can be helpful, but having your feet on the floor is always better. You use your feet to move and turn in your chair, and to balance you when you change postures. They need a lot of room to do that. People change foot position frequently, sometimes alternating one foot forward and the other back, or resting them on the chair legs. Footrests are cumbersome, and you often end up kicking them out of the way or using your feet to drag them back into place.

Make every effort to adjust your furniture and equipment so you don't have to use a footrest, even if you have to improvise. Raise your chair and use a footrest only if there is really no other solution. Letting your feet dangle can cause back problems. Letting the seatpan cut into the backs of your thighs cuts off circulation and can cause numbness in your legs. Twisting your feet around the chair legs or resting them there for a long time can also cause discomfort.

Choose a footrest that is sturdy, high enough, and wide enough for both feet to have some room to move around. The platform tilt should be adjustable. Two phone books taped together side by side can function as a temporary footrest.

Move Through the Postures

Move. Change posture. Move some more. Change posture again. Stand up and stretch. All day long. At least once an hour, or even better, every 20 minutes or so. Shift your body frequently.

At first, it may seem like you're spending all of your time just switching positions or jumping up out of your chair, to the point where you might think, "But if I do this all the time, how will I ever get any work done?" You will. You'll feel more comfortable during the day, and your mind will be more relaxed. It may take some getting used to, but it's worth the effort. Considering that you'll probably be more efficient at the end of the day, and will probably lose less time for health reasons, you could even come out ahead. If good posture doesn't help you relieve aches and pains, you may have other problems that require consultation with a health care provider.

Reclining

Reclined postures are popular. Most computer users will lean back if they can adjust their chair and arrange their work materials to allow it. Reclining is well-suited to tasks that involve primarily screen work, such as writing and programming, though a slight recline can be comfortable for data entry and word processing, depending on how you set up your documents.

Reclining with good lumbar support is the most relaxing position for the back—it puts the least pressure on the discs and causes the least amount of muscle tension.[2] By leaning onto the backrest, you transfer part of the weight of the torso onto the backrest and let it do the work. Vollowitz notes that in a reclined posture, the discs can expand, which actually increases body height.

The thigh-to-torso angle for reclined postures is roughly between 100 to 135 degrees. If you recline more than about 110 degrees, support your head so the neck muscles aren't strained. Some chairs have or can be fitted with neck or head supports. If you have a back or neck injury, check with your health care provider about using them. If you recline too far, your head may come forward to see your work, which can also strain your neck.

Experiment with different degrees of reclining. You may prefer to recline less in the morning and more in the afternoon, or to recline a lot while talking on the phone or thinking, and just a little while typing. As you adjust the chair, be sure the lumbar support is in the right place, as the position may vary with the adjustments.

Sitting Upright

Upright postures are the ones we typically find recommended in articles, pamphlets, and brochures about computer work. We often have to sit upright because it's the only way we can line ourselves up well with the keyboard and work materials. It can feel good to sit upright—it makes you feel active and energetic. The thigh-to-torso angle for upright postures is about 90 to 100 degrees.

If you spend a lot of time in upright postures, be sure you recline slightly into the backrest. The same studies that found reclined postures to be the most relaxing found that upright postures are the least relaxing for the back—they caused the most muscle tension and put the most pressure on the discs. Sitting upright with no back support for a few hours actually causes people to lose several centimeters of body height because of disc compression. This effect is less pronounced for sitting upright with a low back support and in forward sloping chairs.

Sitting Forward

According to Vollowitz, forward postures *with upper body support* are actually more relaxing for the back muscles and better for the discs than sitting upright. Without that support, either through your arms or some sort of torso support, sitting forward can be extremely stressful.

Sitting forward is a good intermittent position for desk work or taking a break to relax or think. It's better for tasks that require only one hand, since you need at least one arm to hold your upper body weight. Slanted work surfaces are helpful for this. Sitting forward is not so suitable for computer work because you can't use your arms to type and support your body weight at the same time. Some chairs have a backrest that swings around to become a "frontrest" you can lean on, leaving both arms free to work.

If you sit forward for any length of time, use a chair with a forward seat tilt to help you maintain neutral body posture. Depending on the tilt mechanism, you may also need to raise your chair height. For short periods, it's okay to tighten up your hips and give them some variety of motion, or to sit on the edge of your chair. *However, don't sit forward without upper body support for more than a few minutes at a time.*

Standing

Standing is another good intermittent posture, as long as you can raise your work surface and equipment enough to keep your arms and head in neutral position and to stand upright without twisting your spine. Stand with both feet flat on the floor, and shift your weight frequently from one foot to the other. Resting one foot on a footstool or rail may be better for your lower back. Change the position of your feet often.

Standing may not be comfortable for long periods of computer work unless you can support your arms well enough to stabilize the upper body. For handwriting, use a slanted work surface and use one arm for support.

Other Postures

Take a walk down the hallway at work (or in any office building), and notice how people sit. Some are actually sitting comfortably and fit well in their chairs. Some people slump way down, practically sitting on their lower back, and some are poised on the edge of their chair. Others seem to prefer a skewed posture,

change positions,

reach sometimes for movement and variety—just don't ...

If you sit one way long enough, you get used to it, even when it starts to be uncomfortable. You accept the discomfort and pain out of habit, and may not even realize you hurt. There's a difference between being comfortable because you're sitting well, and being comfortable because you've sat that way for so long that your body feels funny sitting any other way.

Avoid the following positions, especially for long work sessions:

- Head jutting forward, turned to the side, or tilted up or down

- Upper back slouched forward

- Shoulders slumped or raised

- Chest collapsed

- Arms unsupported and extended away from the body

- Elbows unsupported and held out away from the body

- Resting the soft side of the elbow on a hard surface

- Wrists bent or angled to either side

- Base of the palm or wrist pressing down on the edge of the desk while typing

- Forearms or wrists resting on a sharp edge, especially while typing

- Legs or feet dangling

- Legs crossed

- Feet twisted around each other or the chair legs

- Toes or feet propped up on the chair castors

- Spine twisted

- Sitting unevenly on the pelvis—for example, because of something in a back pocket

- Sitting forward in the chair with your upper back on the backrest and a hollow between the chair and lower back

- Sitting on the edge of the chair

- Holding the body stiff and rigid

- Writing on the desk, either to the right or left of the keyboard, while reaching over the keyboard tray

- Transcribing from documents on a table, without a copyholder

Posture and Laptop Computers

Laptop computers pose special problems for posture. In some ways, they exacerbate all the problems of regular computers. For several years, we've known that keyboards and screens must be separate so they can be positioned correctly. Many laptop or portable computers don't have detachable keyboards, and some don't have the option of connecting a separate screen. When the keyboard is at the right height, the screen is too low. The head comes down and forward, your shoulders round in, your chest collapses.

It's almost impossible to use a laptop with neutral postures. Their small size can force you to scrunch up to use them. While conventional keyboards are sometimes too big for people with small hands, laptop keyboards can be too small for people with big hands. If you use a laptop, take a lot of breaks, move around, and find the most comfortable position possible.

3

Customize Your Work Area

Good posture is the basis for comfort, and the setup of your work area is the basis for maintaining good posture. Too often, we make ourselves fit into the work area instead of making it fit us. This is never a good idea. The typical result is that we're forced to work all day in awkward, uncomfortable positions that leave us susceptible to general aches and pains, repetitive strain injury, eyestrain, and mental stress brought on by physical tension and discomfort. In an optimal work setup, you have plenty of room to move, you can see your work clearly without strain, and the things you use most are within easy reach.[1]

With enough space, you can move freely in unconstrained postures. You have room under and around your desk so you can easily move your legs, change positions, and get in and out of your chair. You also have enough room on your work surface to get to your work materials without obstructions.

When your screen and work materials are placed so you can see them clearly with your head in neutral posture, your body will also stay in neutral posture. Where you look, your head follows and takes the body with it. If you put your head forward to see better, you slump forward and lose the support of the backrest. Pulling it back too far creates muscle tension in the neck, shoulders, head, face, eyes, and jaw. Twisting your head twists your neck and spine.

Your body follows your arms, too. The further you extend them forward, to the side, or behind you, the more you take your body out of neutral position. When your keyboard, mouse, and other equipment are positioned well, you don't have to reach, and your arms and body stay in neutral posture.

shifts in posture may not req...

Figure 3-1 shows how you and your equipment fit together for reclined, upright, and forward postures.

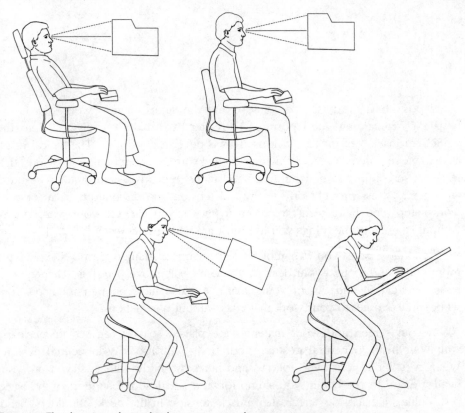

Figure 3-1. The changing relationship between you and your equipment

For forward postures, your feet should support your weight without having your knees excessively bent. Alternate having one foot forward and one back. For desk tasks, raise your work surface so you can rest your arms on it without slumping and without raising your shoulders towards your ears. Use a slant board or tilt your work surface. For typing, tilt the keyboard and mouse to match the angle of your arms. Do not support the body weight on the arms or hands. You may need a torso rest for typing.

Ideally, we would all have desks that let us adjust the height and position of the keyboard, mouse, monitor, and writing surface independently, smoothly, and efficiently. Then we could adjust our equipment as easily as we adjust our chairs to move through the day. As it is, we spend a lot of time improvising solutions.

If you share a work area, adjustable furniture is vital. A short person working at an area set up for a tall person continually reaches up or out for everything; a tall person working in a short person's area works hunched and cramped all day. With adjustable furniture and equipment, both could be comfortable. For shared work areas at home, adjustability allows a good set up for both children and adults.

Some employers provide adjustable furniture, but many of us have our computers set up on non-adjustable desks that are much too high because they are designed for doing paperwork and to fit average-sized men. Even modular furniture is usually set up at the same height in every office, and your facilities department may not be anxious to change it once it's installed.

Without adjustable furniture, changing the position of your equipment to match your posture requires more effort—you'll probably need a keyboard tray, a monitor stand, a copyholder, and a few improvised solutions. These should be sturdy, easy to use, and, preferably, adjustable. The keyboard tray should fit both the keyboard and mouse. If it doesn't, you'll need a separate tray or other way to keep the mouse at the same height as the keyboard.

Often there is no way of making ongoing height adjustments for the keyboard and monitor, even if you have a keyboard tray or monitor stand. In this case, set everything up to fit the posture you spend the most time in. When you change positions, use a rolled-up cloth or piece of foam to change the angle of the keyboard if you need to, and use the monitor's tilt and swivel mechanism (most have one) to change the angle of the screen.

Position Your Equipment

Start by clearing out the space under your desk. You need plenty of room to stretch your legs and move in your chair without banging your knees or feet into things. Store those extra boxes, papers, and bags of stuff somewhere else.

Then make these basic adjustments, described in detail in the following sections:

- Sit in your favorite posture with your feet on the floor. This is your reference point.

- Position the keyboard and mouse to promote neutral arm and wrist posture. If you tried everything you can think of and still can't find a way to get them low enough, then raise the chair and use a footrest.

The Keyboard

The keyboard placement described here is for conventional, flat keyboards. Some new keyboard designs may require different positioning, though the principles are the same—set it up to match your neutral wrist and arm posture (see Figure 3-2).

Figure 3-2. Positioning the keyboard

Many keyboard trays have a fixed height and simply move in and out like a drawer, but some adjust for height and tilt. The tray should be easily adjustable and no part of it should interfere with your leg movements or bump into your knees. Any wrist support built into the tray should be padded.

- *Place the keyboard directly in front of you so your hands are centered over the main keys.* If you center the keyboard as a whole in front of you, your hands will be off to one side to use the main keys, and your wrists will go out of neutral position. If you use the numeric keypad more than the main keys, position the keyboard so the hand that uses the numeric keypad stays in neutral.

- *Lower or raise the keyboard to match your neutral arm posture.* Your arm should be relaxed with your wrists at about elbow level or a little below, and roughly parallel with the home row on the keyboard. If you can't get the keyboard low enough, you'll have to raise your chair and use a footrest.

  Sit with your hands relaxed in your lap. Raise them slightly as if to type, in neutral position without reaching. Place the keyboard just under your hands and adjust the tilt so your wrists stay neutral. You may want it almost flat or in a negative tilt for upright postures, and tilted slightly towards you for reclined postures.

  If you don't have a keyboard tray that tilts, prop up the keyboard with a thin piece of foam or a rolled up cloth. Some keyboards have feet; be careful using them, as they tend to tilt the keyboard too far toward you, and may force you to bend your wrists back to type, especially for upright postures.

- *Bring the keyboard close enough so you don't have to reach for it.* Hold your hands in front of you as if to type. Notice the amount of tension in your arms, and then rest. Raise your arms again, holding them out in front of you a little further, and a little further. Note where your arms tense up and your body leans forward to follow the reach. Back off to where your arms are relaxed and your torso rests on the backrest. This is the furthest away you can have your keyboard comfortably, but closer is better.

- *Position your wristrest, forearm supports, or armrests so your arms can relax in the position you just found.* See Chapter 2, *Get Comfortable*, for details.

The Mouse, Trackball, or Other Pointing Device

Whether you use a mouse, trackball, or other type of pointing device, *never place it where you have to extend your arm to use it.* This is extremely hard on your arm. The muscle tension it causes under your shoulder blade, in your neck, and all down your arm can be painful and may lead to RSI.

If you use the mouse more than the keyboard, give its position first priority.

- *Place the mouse or trackball at the same height as the keyboard.* When you move your hand from the keyboard to the mouse, you may have to reach a little, especially if the mouse is on the same side as the numeric keypad. Keep the mouse as close to you as possible to minimize the reach. (See Figure 3-3.)

Figure 3-3. Positioning the mouse

- *Don't set the mouse where it's too high and far away.* That position is simply too risky. If the keyboard tray doesn't accommodate the mouse, use a separate mouse tray or improvise a way to keep the mouse lower and closer to you—don't set it up on the desk.

- *Try using the mouse on the opposite side of the numeric keypad.* This keeps the mouse closer and balances the workload of the right and left hands. Using the same hand for both the numeric keypad and the mouse overloads that hand.

- *Try placing the mouse pad at about a 20-degree angle.* Some people find this position makes mouse use easier and more comfortable.

The Monitor and Hardcopy

The optimal position for your screen and documents lets you see your work clearly *and* keep your head naturally relaxed over your spine—not pushed forward, pulled back, or turned continually up, down, or to the side:

- Whatever you look at most—screen or documents—is directly in front of you.

- The monitor is at about arm's length.

- The part of the screen you look at most is between eye level and about 20 degrees below.

- The screen and documents are about parallel to your face.

The size and clarity of the screen characters, glare, the quality of light in the office, and your own visual abilities also affect how well you see your work and may affect the placement of your monitor and documents. First, set them up as described here. If glare interferes or you can't see the screen well enough, refer to Part III, *Eyestrain*, for solutions.

Use a copyholder to bring your documents into the same visual plane as the screen so you don't have to twist your head down to see them. If you're working from a notebook or book that doesn't fit on a copyholder, prop up the top so it isn't lying flat. If you use a task light for your documents, set it up so it shines only on the documents and not on the screen.

Monitor stands let you adjust for height, angle, and distance. They are available mainly for small and mid-sized monitors. If you need to adjust for height and don't have a stand, improvise with old phone books or something similar. Most monitors swivel and tilt.

Put Whatever You Look at Most Directly in Front of You

Place the monitor directly in front of you if your work involves looking only or mainly at the screen. Put your papers on a copyholder to one side, or between the keyboard and the screen. If you have a shallow desk and a big monitor, resist the temptation to put the monitor to the side and angle it toward you. Use a keyboard tray or improvise some sort of desk extender to add depth to your work surface so that you can face the monitor full on.

If you look primarily at hardcopy and less at the screen, put the copyholder in front of you, and the monitor either behind the hardcopy or to the side.

For work that involves looking back and forth equally between the screen and hardcopy, put both the copyholder and the monitor in front of you or set them up side by side in front of you. If you have two monitors, you will also need a compromise position, depending on which monitor you look at most and how often you need to refer from one screen to the other. Consider separating the monitors and having two worksites; make sure that you can sit comfortably at both.

For any compromise position, switch the side the hardcopy or screen is on periodically so you don't develop the habit of looking only to one side. Whatever is off center, angle it slightly towards you slightly. Move both your head and your eyes when you look to the side, using gentle, relaxed head movements. Avoid stiff, jerky, or abrupt movements.

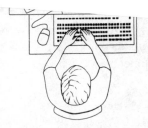

For looking mainly at the monitor.

For looking frequently at both monitor and document, or mainly at the monitor.

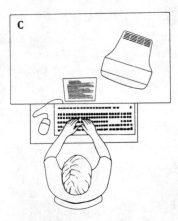

For looking mainly at the document.

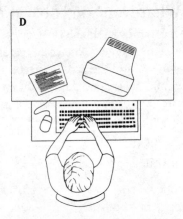

For looking frequently at both monitor and document.

Figure 3-4. Positioning the monitor and documents

Put the Monitor at Arm's Length

Keeping the screen at arm's distance or more relieves the visual strain of constant close work, gives your eyes room to relax, and reduces tunnel vision—the further away the screen is, the less it dominates your visual field. The monitor should be no closer than about 18 inches, and no further away than about 36 inches (see Figure 3-5). You may need to bring the screen forward for reclined postures, and push it back for upright postures.

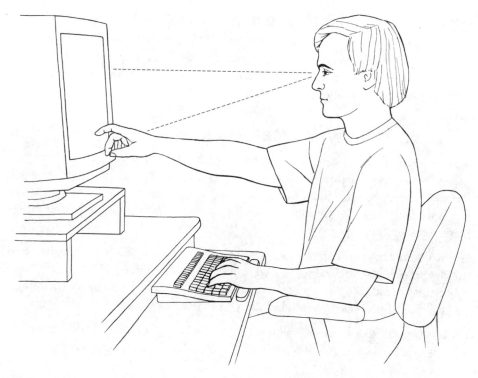

Figure 3-5. Adjusting the monitor distance, height, and angle

If you can't see the screen clearly at arm's length, you may need to adjust the screen's focus or character size, or you may need to get glasses prescribed specifically for computer work (see Chapter 14, *Take Care of Your Eyes*).

Put the Main Part of the Screen Slightly Below Eye Level

Because monitors vary in size, and software programs use different parts of the screen, you have to position the height of your monitor according to where on the screen you most frequently look. You should be able to read the screen with your eyes relaxed, looking straight ahead and slightly down, without tilting your head.

Sitting comfortably, look straight ahead towards the screen. Scan it, noting which part of the screen you look at most. Adjust the height so this area is in the most comfortable place for your eyes—typically between eye level and 15 or 20 degrees below (see Figure 3-5). Some people prefer to look down more. If your chin is thrust forward, the monitor is too high.

If you look at all parts of the screen equally, get in neutral posture and place the monitor so your nose points to the center of the screen.

Arrange Your Work Materials

Where you place your telephone, calculator, notepad, manuals, and other work materials depends mainly on how often you use them. Put the items you use most in a semicircle around you, within comfortable reach. Keep your immediate work area uncluttered and unobstructed by printers, disk drives, and other equipment. Set them up out of your way.

When you do have to extend your arm to use something, don't stay in that position for long. Bring it close to you when you use it, and then put it back. Putting some things further away so you have to stand up and go to them encourages you to take a break. Don't reach behind you to use something or to pick it up.

Place heavy books or manuals you refer to often on your desk or on the middle shelves of a bookshelf. Avoid reaching over shoulder level for heavy books.

Writing and Reading Materials

Using a slantboard or a slanted desk will probably make you more comfortable for reading and writing. Slantboards angle your materials toward you so you don't have to bend over so far to use them. They also provide arm support for forward postures. A thick three-ring binder, a clipboard across a drawer, or a pillow can substitute for a slantboard in a pinch.

To jot down a few notes as you type, bring your notepad as close to you as possible. Use a clipboard to lean back in your chair and write.

Hang your whiteboard low enough on the wall so you don't have to reach above shoulder level to write on it.

The Telephone

If the phone is an integral part of your job, keep it close to you, especially for dialing. Some people like to put the phone on a moveable stand to free up space on the desk and make dialing easier. If you don't use the phone much, consider keeping it further away so you have to get up to use it.

Use a telephone headset or a speaker phone if you use the phone a lot, particularly if you type or write and talk on the phone at the same time. Cradling the phone between your head and shoulder can create serious aches, pains, and structural problems in your neck and spine. Gripping the phone can increase tension in the hand and aggravate symptoms of RSI.

Fit into the General Work Environment

The setup of your immediate work area is fundamental to your comfort, but you are influenced by the larger office environment as well, whether you work in a cubicle, in an open room with several other people, or in an office with a door.

As you set up or modify your own work area, be aware of how the general environment influences your well being, and what factors you can change:

- *Office lighting* has a profound effect on your eyes and on how you feel. It's important to eliminate glare and reflections, and to find the right brightness and quality of both ambient (overall) and task (specific) lighting. (See Chapter 16, *Work in the Right Light.*)

- *Noise* from people or machines can be distracting and stress-provoking. Set up printers, photocopiers, and noisy equipment at a distance from your work area. (See Chapter 15, *Create a Visually Comfortable Environment* and Chapter 20, *The Health Risks We Wonder About.*)

- *Air quality* directly affects your health and well-being. Dust, dryness, and indoor air pollution are problems in many office buildings. Certain plants help clean the air, and humidifiers and air filters can help. The building's ventilation system should be well-maintained, and filters in printers and office machines should be changed regularly. (See Chapter 15 and Chapter 21, *Protect Yourself.*)

- *Color and visual variety* have a more subtle effect, but can make a difference in your mood and in how your eyes feel. Use colors that don't create glare or imbalances in the office lighting, and put things you like to look at on your desk and on the walls. (See Chapter 15.)

- *Exposure to electromagnetic radiation* is increasingly being recognized as a health concern in office buildings. Many experts now recommend an approach called *prudent avoidance*—taking reasonable steps to reduce your exposure while scientists continue to explore the issue. (See Chapter 21.)

CHAPTER

4

Be Aware of Your Body

Computer work is almost entirely cerebral. Most of the time we're in our heads, thinking about what's happening on the screen, oblivious to what's happening beyond our brains. We can go on like this for hours, ignoring the body's signals. You emerge from this work depleted, stiff, sore, exhausted, even stunned. It's no wonder—the whole time you barely moved, didn't eat, hardly glanced away from the screen, and maybe didn't even stop to use the bathroom.

The more you forget about your body, the more likely you are to be surprised by pain. With eyestrain and stress, recovery is fairly straightforward and quick, but a severe repetitive strain injury is more complicated and can take months or more to heal.

Body awareness is the key to avoiding injury in the first place, to catching injuries early, and to recovering quickly if you're already injured. It helps you tune in to discomfort and pain so can you stop before you hurt yourself. You start to recognize habits that lead to pain so you can change them. You become conscious of how your body interacts with your furniture and equipment so you know what fits you well and what doesn't, and whether any aspect of your work setup is causing the problem.

Practice Body Awareness

Being aware of your body simply means paying attention to physical sensations, pleasant, unpleasant, and neutral, and recognizing them for what they are. All you need is the conscious decision to shift your attention away from your mental activity and towards your body.

related disap-

ning—moving your attention through all the area physical sensations you find there. Scanning your body is also an excellent way to reduce stress.[1]

Long Body Scan

Do this lying down comfortably on your back in a quiet place. Cover yourself to stay warm. Take as long as you like, anywhere from about 15 to 45 minutes.

Close your eyes and breathe calmly, just noticing the breath going in and out. Let your body sink into the floor or cushion, totally supported. Imagine you are floating. Feel the blood flowing through you.

Notice your general energy level. Are you exhausted? Lethargic? Wired? What does that feel like physically?

Let your face and eyes relax, easing the tension around your head. Feel your face smooth and fresh. To enhance the relaxation, smile a tiny bit, turning up just the corners of your mouth.

Turn your attention to the sensations in your body. Are there any areas that take longer to relax, that are tighter than others? Keep breathing with your attention on the tight part. Stay with it for a few breaths, noticing the qualities of the tension. Let that area relax.

Scan your whole body, starting with the left leg. Move your attention slowly up through your toes, foot, leg, and pelvic area. Then scan your other leg from your toes up the leg, and then go on through each part of the torso. Scan one arm at a time from your fingertips up to the shoulder and around the shoulder blade. Go on to the neck, throat, jaw, eyes, face, head. As you pass over each area, notice the varying sensations of relaxation, comfort, tension, soreness, achiness, numbness, tingling, or pain. Breathe in and out from that area a few times, let go of the sensations, and move on.

Finish by turning your attention back to your breath for a few minutes. Let it flow freely and calmly. Stretch and get up slowly.

Begin by doing some long body scans at home to get the idea. Then practice five-minute body scans a few times a day at work. Eventually, you can do quick scans throughout the day while you work—they'll help you know when it's time to rest.

Five-Minute Body Scan

Do this five-minute body scan a few times a day, sitting in your chair. Before you start, stand up, stretch or shake out your body, and drink some water.

Relax into your chair in a comfortable posture with your hands resting in your lap and your feet flat on the floor. If you keep your eyes open, face away from the screen.

Breathe calmly, feeling the chair support your whole body, relaxing your face, eyes, neck, shoulders, arms, and back.

Scan your body from your feet up to your torso, and then from your hands up through your wrists and forearms to your shoulders, neck, eyes, and head.

Along with the physical sensations in each area, notice how your body feels in the chair. Is it well-supported, comfortable, or uncomfortable? How do your thighs feel against the seat? How does your lower back feel?

Ask yourself what you need. Are you thirsty, hungry, sleepy, tired?

Breathe into and out from any areas that are tense, letting them relax.

Finish by returning your attention to your breath. Stand up and stretch.

Do quick body scans as often as you like throughout the day—even a minute or so is helpful. Either stop working and put your full attention on it, or learn to scan with part of your attention on your work and part on your body. Breathe calmly and scan quickly for signs of discomfort. Let any tense or sore areas relax. Stand up or move around in your chair, and stretch or massage any areas that need it. Take a short break if you need one.

If you become aware of recurring aches or pains in the same area, such as your hands, wrists, forearms, shoulders, or neck, pay special attention to them. Stretch and massage them frequently. Watch how you type or use your arms or how you hold your head to see where the problem is coming from. You'll quickly become aware of the habits or conditions that are bringing on the pain.

Learn New Habits

We all have habitual ways of doing just about everything—moving, walking, sitting, seeing, typing, working, eating, thinking. Usually we're not aware of their

- Staring at the screen

- Not blinking

- Pounding on the keys

- Gripping the mouse tightly

- Sitting in awkward postures

- Holding your breath

Changing habits requires your intention to change, your awareness of when you're repeating the old habits, and some effort to learn the new ones. At first, you have to practice consciously until the new habits become ingrained. How long the process takes depends on how entrenched the old habits are and how much attention you give the new ones. It could take only a few weeks or much longer.

Use body awareness to discover habits that might be causing you trouble. If you have several, start with one or two of the most problematic. As your awareness increases and you experience the benefits of the new habits, changing the rest becomes easier.

Take Regular Breaks

Human beings are not designed to do the same task all the time, whether the task is physical or mental. Computer work chains your brain to the task and your body to the equipment. Without adequate pauses to rest, the mind loses its clarity and sharpness, and the body suffers wear and tear. You become less productive and more prone to injury.

Give yourself some variety, and take short, frequent breaks throughout the day. Rest your hands and eyes for a few seconds every few minutes. Stand up and stretch for a minute or two every 20 minutes. Take 10 or 15 minutes every hour or two to walk around, have a snack, talk to your co-workers, or exercise. Change activities. Switching from concentrated work to straightening up your desk or making a few phone calls changes your body movements and refreshes your mind.

The more your job depends on continuous typing and mouse work, the more resolute you need to be about taking breaks, and the more often you need to take them. *Don't work through your breaks.* If your job has a formal break schedule, typically 15 minutes every two hours or less for intensive computer work, take those breaks *and* your own few-second or few-minute breaks. Pause frequently for as long as it takes to close your eyes, rest your hands in your lap, and breathe in and out three times. Those short breaks won't hinder your work. In fact, they'll get you through the day with much less stress and fatigue.

Through our own experience and recent research, we are finding that taking more breaks makes us more efficient as well as more comfortable. One study showed that for data entry work, increasing the number of breaks actually sped up the work and improved the work quality.[2] Many people recovering from repetitive strain injury can attest to the effectiveness of short, frequent breaks. Try it and decide for yourself the benefits.

Work Reasonable Hours

People often experience considerable pressure to work long hours, whether it's to meet a deadline, to do required overtime, or to satisfy their own internal compulsion to work hard. You may find yourself working consistently more than eight hours a day, spending most of those hours working intensively on the computer, taking work home with you on evenings and weekends, and somehow never getting around to taking your vacation. Eventually, something will give, and it probably won't be your job demands. Chronic overwork wears you down, increases stress, makes you vulnerable to injury, and generally interferes with your life outside your job.

Try not to do more than four or five hours a day of continuous computer work. This is not to say your schedule should be exactly the same every day—this would be too monotonous. Work goes in cycles, and so does your energy. Pace yourself accordingly. Mix computer work with other activities to dispel its intensity. After working long hours for a period of time to make a deadline, take time off, or at least take it easy for a while to recuperate. Take at least one full day off every week, and take your vacations and holidays.

Never Work Through Pain

When you work through pain, your mind may ignore it, but your body does not. Your body compensates as long as it can, lulling you into thinking nothing is wrong, until one day it reaches a breaking point and you're struck with a serious injury. The injury seems sudden, but actually it was a long time in the making—you just didn't notice it.

dangerous — ~~~~~~~ ~ ~~~~~~
cause of the pain right away, and using medication for short-term intervention.

Use Your Eyes Well

The way your eyes feel directly relates to how the rest of you feels. When your eyes hurt, your stress level goes up and muscle tension increases. Staring continuously at the screen, not blinking, squinting, and straining to see are detrimental not only to your eyesight, but also to your posture and general comfort. Chapter 14, *Take Care of Your Eyes*, describes several ways to keep your eyes feeling good.

Use Good Keyboard and Mouse Technique

Hand/arm technique is a major factor in repetitive strain injury. If your technique includes gripping things tightly, pounding on the keys, or extending and stiffening your fingers when you type or click, change these habits immediately. Chapter 10, *Good Hand Technique Reduces Your Risk*, gives you some suggestions.

Use Good Posture and Body Mechanics

Habitual poor posture and awkward body movements influence eyestrain, stress, repetitive strain injury, and your general comfort. Learn the dynamic, relaxed, neutral postures described in Chapter 2, *Get Comfortable*.

If your movements are uncomfortable or seem to be causing you aches or pains, consider learning how to move your body differently. One way to learn is through bodywork such as Alexander and Feldenkreis techniques, Trager, somatics, or other methods. Another way is to practice an exercise system that includes body alignment and efficient movements, such as yoga or tai chi.

Breathe Fully

Breathing is such a simple act that we often overlook its contribution to our well-being. We don't realize that we have habitual ways of breathing that can perpetuate stress, eyestrain, muscle tension, repetitive strain injury, and physical and mental fatigue. People commonly hold their breath in or out, or breathe so shallowly that the exchange of air in the lungs is never complete. These breathing habits limit the amount of oxygen you get, inhibit circulation, and allow toxins to build up in the blood, muscles, and organs.

Good breathing is a universal tonic—it's good for what ails you. Awareness of your breathing enhances awareness of physical sensations and calms the mind. Practicing good, full breathing is easy, helps you stay healthy, and promotes healing when you're injured. For details, see Chapter 5, *Breathe*.

Understand Pain

Pain can be subtle or excruciating. It can build slowly and become an unwelcome longtime companion, or it can pounce on you with the ferocity of a demon. Either way, strong pain colors all aspects of your existence, and demands attention.

Aches and Pains Are Often Interconnected

Although we often think of our aches and pains as being separate, they don't exist in isolation. When one area is tense, the surrounding area tends to become tense. If you have a pain on one side of the body and start to favor it, another part of the body kicks in to compensate. That part in turn becomes stiff or tired from overuse, and the body gets off-kilter. If the corresponding muscle groups on both sides of the body are out of balance, they pull unevenly on the skeletal system, causing further imbalance, pain, and possible injury.

An Injury in One Place Can Cause Pain in Another

Sometimes pain or discomfort originates in one place and is felt in another. This is called *referred pain*. An injured muscle or irritated nerve in your neck, for example, can refer pain or discomfort to your hand, palm, or fingers; an injured nerve in your low back can send pain to your thigh or your toe. An injury to the shoulder might be felt in the forearm. You might not even feel the pain at the point of injury at all, which complicates diagnosing or isolating the pain.

The places where we injure ourselves the most—the neck, shoulder, forearms, and low back—are the areas that most often refer pain. For more information on this topic, try Ben Benjamin's *Listen to Your Pain*. A more technical and extremely thorough text is *Myofascial Pain and Dysfunction: Trigger Point Manual*, by Janet Travell and D. Simons.

Pain Can Be Difficult to Diagnose

Sometimes when computer users complain of pain, they are faced with disbelief. Friends who don't work with computers, or even other users who aren't experiencing pain, sometimes can't understand why you're hurting. After all, there's no

When pain is deep, location. Even physicians sometimes may not accurately diagnose. from chronic muscle tension or a sudden increase in muscle tension may also be difficult to pinpoint. This pain is usually due to prolonged or increased stress, and can either be generalized or sharp and specific.

Sometimes we think we have muscle pain, but the problem is coming from somewhere else. A heart attack can feel like muscle pain in the arm below the shoulder, a stretched ligament might feel like muscle soreness, and a disc problem in the neck might manifest itself as a muscular ache in the arm or shoulder blade.

Chronic Pain Can Affect Your Emotional Well-Being

Acute pain is a severe and immediate call to action. Pain that goes on for a long time can be frustrating, disheartening, and difficult to treat. The dull, elusive ache gets deep inside, evading your attempts to comfort it. Chronic pain can wear down your good spirits and optimism, and lead to depression.

There are many approaches to understanding and treating chronic pain, but no definitive method. You may find that bits and pieces of several methods are helpful, which means that chronic pain sufferers often find themselves going from treatment to treatment, seeking relief. Much has been written about treating and living with chronic pain. Check the sources in the Suggested Reading list, and browse the health and self-help sections of your local library and book stores. Some hospitals have pain or stress reduction clinics that teach people how to manage chronic pain.

CHAPTER

5

Breathe

The breath connects the mind and body. When your mind is calm, your breath is slow and deep and the body relaxes. With anger, excitement, stress, and fear, the breath is faster and shallower, you breathe from the chest, and your whole body becomes tense. When you're sad or depressed, you sigh and your energy slumps.

Good breathing relieves muscle tension, eyestrain, and stress, improves sleep, memory, and concentration, and generally strengthens your entire system. It fills the blood with oxygen. Its smooth rhythm supports the pumping of the heart, improving blood circulation, digestion, and all body processes. Fresh blood flows through the body, bringing oxygen and nutrients to the eyes, brain, muscles, tissues, and organs, washing away toxins and metabolic wastes. These processes keep you strong and help you heal when you're sick or injured.

Paying attention to your breath concentrates your mind, brings you back to your body, calms you when you're stressed, and energizes you when you're tired.

Your breath could be your most powerful tool for staying comfortable at the computer.

Learn How You Breathe

The way you breathe is always changing, reflecting your physical, mental, and emotional states. The breath regulates itself naturally, changing speed and rhythm during physical exertion, stress, or strong emotion, and returning to deep, even, belly breathing when you're back to normal. Unfortunately, we often breathe in ways that interfere with this process.

When you're trying to make a deadline or are just absorbed in your work, you can easily develop irregular breathing patterns, like holding your breath in or out,

Normal, relaxed ~~~~~~~~~ moves the breath in and out from the abdomen. This is the ~~~~~. breathe most of the time. To find out how you breathe, try this:

- Sit or lie down comfortably with one hand on your chest and one on your navel. Breathe as you normally do, without consciously changing your usual pattern.

- Note how the breath moves your hands. Does the chest hand or the belly hand move up with the inbreath and down with the outbreath? Do both hands move at the same time?

- Is your breath shallow or deep? Do your hands move up and down a lot as you breathe, or are they almost still?

- Watch the speed and rhythm of the breath. Is it fast? slow? smooth? steady? jumpy? irregular? hard? soft? Do you hold your breath in or out? Does it flow in and out in a regular pattern?

- Did your breathing change during this experiment?

Try Different Ways of Breathing

We have the same power to regulate our breathing as we do to interfere with it. Replacing irregular breathing patterns with belly breathing boosts your clarity, strength, and energy. Consciously breathing to a specific part of the body reduces tension and relaxes the muscles there. Coordinating the breath with body movements increases flexibility and enhances the benefits of any exercise.

Breathe from the Belly

- Sit or lie down comfortably. Put your right hand over your navel and your left hand on your upper chest.

- Breathe into the area around your stomach and navel. Most of the movement is in the upper abdomen, with a slight movement in the lower part of the chest, and no movement in the upper chest. The right hand moves up with the inbreath, and down with the outbreath. The left hand is still.

- Continue breathing this way, slowly, softly, without effort. Breathe smoothly and evenly, with no pauses or abrupt changes in speed. Let the outbreath be slightly longer than the inbreath, both flowing without interruption.

- Notice how you feel after breathing this way for a few minutes.

In the morning when you wake up and in the evening before you sleep are good times to practice this way of breathing. Do it at work whenever you think of it or when you need to take a quick break. The more you do it, the sooner it'll come naturally.

Breathe to Stretch Your Chest and Back from the Inside

- Sit comfortably at your desk with your feet flat on the floor. Clear a space in front of you. Take off your glasses, lay your arms down on the desk, lean over and rest your head on your arms. Close your eyes, breathe to the belly and let your upper back muscles relax.

- Take a few long, full breaths, inhaling to the back of the lungs. Fill them completely. Feel the ribcage expand towards your back, and the muscles in the back and between the ribs relax. Inhale and exhale completely.

- Then breathe a few times to your sides in the same way. Feel the rib cage expand under each arm, letting the muscles at your sides relax.

- Sit up slowly, and relax into your chair in neutral posture with your back fully supported. Breathe into the front of your chest a few times, expanding and opening the chest and shoulders.

Stretch and Breathe

- With your arms relaxed at your sides, stand with your feet about hip-width apart, or sit straight but comfortably in a chair with no arms.

- Turn your palms away from your body. Inhale and lift your arms up so your palms face each other over your head.

- Turn your palms out and exhale completely as you bring your arms back down to your sides. As you exhale, blow the air out through your lips.

Any time you exercise, coordinate your breath with your movements. In general, inhale to expand your body, and exhale to contract it. When holding a stretch, breathe smoothly and evenly. Exhale to lengthen the stretch.

Breathe to Relax

Taking a few conscious breaths whenever you think of it can help you relax. Anything can be a reminder. Breathe before you answer the telephone, at the end

6

Take Care of Yourself

You can't expect to stay healthy and comfortable for computer work, or anything else, if you don't take care of yourself. As with much of our behavior, how well we do this comes down to time, priorities, and habit.

Rather than encouraging good health habits, the momentum of computer work often undermines them. All your good intentions to exercise and eat well get washed away. Even the most diligent people can have trouble maintaining their exercise routine or outside activities when they're drawn into their work.

Exercise, stretching, eating well, and relaxing are all necessities, and all take time and attention. The less time you give them, the more you lose them as habits. Inertia sets in—the less you do, the less you want to do. As you get increasingly out of shape, you become more unhappy and more susceptible to injury and illness. Your body suffers and your work feels like drudgery.

If your good health habits have fallen by the wayside, pick them up again little by little. Don't expect to change everything all at once. At the very least, walk, stretch, eat well, and get out and have some fun.

Exercise

Walking, internal exercise, and aerobic exercise all counteract the negative effects of your sedentary, cerebral work. Walking gets you moving and is easy to incorporate into your day. Internal exercise enhances body awareness, builds strength and flexibility, and calms you. Aerobic exercise is energizing. It gets your heartbeat up, releases built-up tension, builds strength and stamina, and gets you completely out of office mode.

- *Don't do too much too soon.* be forced. If you've been sedentary for a long time, consider getting shape through walking and internal exercise. These exercises condition you gently while you work up to more vigorous routine.

- *If you're injured or have a known health problem, check with your care provider before you begin a new exercise program.* Doing certain movements or exercising in the wrong way can aggravate injuries, especially repetitive strain injury, back problems, or neck problems.

- *If you feel sharp or shooting pains, don't do the exercise.* Any pain from exercise should be the good ache of well-used muscles, as after a workout, or the pleasant tenderness of sore muscles when they are massaged.

Walking

Walk as much as you can. Create opportunities for it. Use public transportation or park the car some distance from where you're going. Take the stairs. Walk to your co-worker's office instead of using the phone. Walk around the block or the building on your break. Walking by yourself gives you space to clear your mind and time to reflect and think about the events of the day. Walking with a friend or colleague is a good way to converse and exercise at the same time.

A walk can be what you want it—a leisurely stroll or brisk exercise. Both have their merits. Wear supportive shoes to protect your back and let you move more naturally. For more on walking as a sport, check the physical fitness section of your local library or book store.

Internal Exercise

Any system that emphasizes awareness of the breath, body movements, and energy flow in the body can be considered an internal exercise. Yoga and tai chi are the most ancient and well-known disciplines.

Their movements systematically stretch, contract, and relax the muscles, promote circulation to all the organs, and coordinate breathing and movement. They condition the body slowly, increasing strength and flexibility. This makes you less prone to injury when you work or do other sports. Because they focus your attention on what's happening inside your body, they relax the mind as they relieve muscle soreness and fatigue.

The best way to learn yoga or tai chi is by taking classes regularly. A class once a week is helpful, though you'll make more progress and feel the benefits sooner if you go twice a week or more. Learning on your own through books and videos is possible, but more difficult, especially if you're a beginner. In a class with a skilled teacher, you'll learn the movements correctly from the start and have the social support of the other students to keep you motivated.

Aerobic Exercise

Pretty much any vigorous exercise will do you good—swimming, dancing, racquet sports, volleyball, soccer, running, aerobic walking, hiking, bicycling. Choose whatever gets your heartbeat up, gets your whole body moving, and gives you pleasure. Do it two or three times a week for at least 20 minutes. Exercise by yourself or with a partner, take an exercise class, or join a team. Bicycling to work builds exercise into your daily routine.

Stretches

Much of computer work requires our muscles to be continually contracted. The muscles never relax enough to release the wastes that build up and let fresh blood soak in. To compensate, they shorten and become stiff, losing elasticity and flexibility. Continuous contraction of the muscles in the hand and forearm is a major contributor to repetitive strain injury. Stretching is essential for keeping your muscles flexible and resilient.

Stretch before and after each work session, and as much as you can throughout the day. Use smooth, easy movements. Breathe evenly, and exhale when you extend and lengthen the stretch. Hold the stretch for a few breaths and take it further. *If you feel pain, back off.* Don't do any stretch that causes pain.

Try the basic stretches presented in Figures 6-1 through 6-3 and see how you like them. There are more stretches for the shoulders, arms, and hands in Chapter 10, *Good Hand Technique Reduces Your Risk.*

Self-Massage

Massage is relaxing and therapeutic. It improves blood circulation, muscle condition, bone strength, and lymph flow, with many positive effects. Massage increases the exchange of nutrients to all tissues and organs, reduces swelling, increases flexibility, decreases pain, muscle fatigue, and soreness, increases body awareness, and promotes healing.

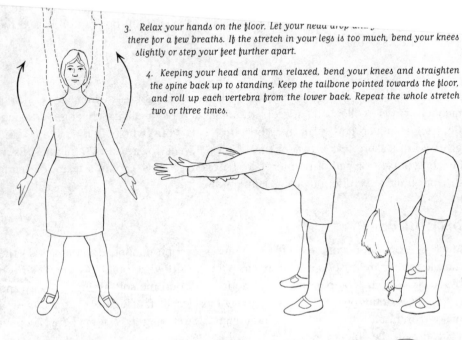

3. Relax your hands on the floor. Let your head drop and stay
   there for a few breaths. If the stretch in your legs is too much, bend your knees
   slightly or step your feet further apart.

4. Keeping your head and arms relaxed, bend your knees and straighten
   the spine back up to standing. Keep the tailbone pointed towards the floor,
   and roll up each vertebra from the lower back. Repeat the whole stretch
   two or three times.

Stretch the Upper and Mid Back

1. Move your chair away from your desk. Sit comfortably with you
   feet flat on the floor and your legs a hand's width or so apart.

2. Bend your upper body forward and rest it on your legs, your
   head hanging loosely between your knees. Let your arms hang
   down by your legs. Let go of the tension from your upper back,
   shoulders, neck, face. Soften the muscles as you breathe to
   the belly. Imagine all the tension falling away from your body
   to the floor. Stay there a few breaths or sit up when you're
   ready.

Try the stretch in a different way to open the hip joints at the
same time. Sit on the edge of the chair with your feet wide apart.
Lean your upper body forward, and rest it between the legs. Keep
the weight down through the feet.

Figure 6-1. Stretch your whole body

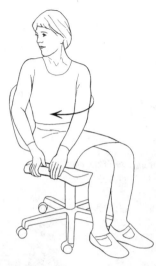

Stretch the Waist and Sides

1. *Move your chair away from your desk. Sit fully in the chair with both hips flat on the seat and your feet flat on the floor.*

2. *Turn your upper body to face one side. Hold the seat or the armrest with both hands, and keep your feet on the floor.*

3. *Slowly twist towards the side of the chair using your hands on the chair and the movement of your belly to twist. Twist until your waist can't turn anymore. Don't twist too far.*

4. *Hold the twist, relax into it, and breathe. When you're ready, twist to the other side.*

Stretch the Neck

1. *With your head in neutral position, slowly tilt your head to one side. Let the ear drop towards the shoulder, easing into the stretch. Breathe a few times, feeling the stretch in the side of the neck. Raise your head slowly back to neutral position. Stretch to the other side, ending back in neutral.*

2. *Slowly drop your head forward, letting the chin fall towards the chest. Feel the stretch in the back of the neck and across the shoulders. Relax your face, jaw, and tongue, and breathe into the stretch. Bring your head slowly back to neutral position.*

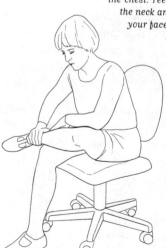

Open the Hips

1. *Sit comfortably with your feet on the floor. Cross the left leg over the right, with the left ankle just above the right knee and your right hand holding the ankle.*

2. *Put your elbow on the left knee and lean forward. Keep the back straight—don't hunch. Hold the stretch and breathe into it. After a few breaths, do the stretch on the other side.*

Figure 6-2. Stretch your waist, sides, neck, and hips

2. *Put your hands on the doorframe at shoulder height with the elbows back. Step one foot forward into a comfortable lunge position. Lean into the lunge, feeling the stretch in the chest muscles and in the calf of the back leg. Hold it about 30 seconds, breathing calmly. Switch legs and repeat the stretch.*

Try the stretch with your hands at ear height and again at chest height. When your hands are higher, let the entire inside of the forearm rest against the doorframe.

Figure 6-3. Open the chest and stretch the calves

Regular massage from a professional massage therapist can increase your base level of comfort and help keep your body resilient. Choose someone who is well-trained and has experience with computer users. Massage should be a pleasant experience. You may feel discomfort when the therapist finds sore spots, but this should never cross over into sharp or intense pain. Breathing into the area while it's being touched aids the massage and reduces the soreness. Skilled practitioners are sensitive to this issue and will ask whether or not the pressure they're using is appropriate. Stop any massage that hurts too much.

Massaging yourself isn't quite as relaxing as being massaged by someone else, but it definitely eases tension and makes you feel better. See Figures 6-4 and 6-5 for some self-massages you can do at work. Self-massage tools can help you reach the shoulders, back, and between the shoulder blades. These are often available in health care supply catalogs and natural food stores.

Nutrition

Your muscles, bones, and immune system need to be strong to withstand the physical demands of computing, and to counteract the effects of stress from the job and the physical office environment. By paying attention to what you ingest, you can make your entire system more resilient.

Stimulating Massage for the Whole Body

Stand comfortably with your feet about shoulder width apart.

Cup your left hand loosely and pat the right shoulder and chest, continuing down the outside of the arm from the shoulder to the hand. Come back up the underside of your arm using the back of the hand, and then go down your side with the cupped palm. Stimulate the left side of the body in the same way, using the right hand. Using the palm side of both hands, pat down the legs from thighs to ankles and top of feet, and come back up the back of the calves using the back of your hand. Use the thumb side of your hands for the back of the thighs, buttocks, and lower and middle back as high as you can comfortably go.

Place your palms on your lower back, your fingers towards the spine and thumbs to your sides. Rub your palms in a circular motion all over your lower back, kidneys, and middle back. Feel the warmth from your palms soothe and relax the muscles.

Rub your palms gently over your face, head, neck, chest, stomach, abdomen. Enjoy the warmth and touch of your palms.

Eat regular, simple meals made from fresh, whole foods. As much as possible, eat organically grown fruits and vegetables, and avoid processed foods that contain a lot of chemical additives. Avoid foods loaded with sugar, salt, and fat, and go easy on caffeine, alcohol, and soft drinks. Drink plenty of water throughout the day.

Certain vitamins and minerals, such as vitamin B_6, potassium, calcium, and magnesium, may benefit muscles and nerves. The antioxidant nutrients—vitamins A, C, and E; beta-carotene, and the trace mineral selenium—may be useful for stimulating the immune system to protect against various diseases, as well as for preventing and recovering from repetitive strain injury. Vitamin E and selenium may help protect against the harmful effects of free radical molecules; there is some speculation that exposure to electromagnetic radiation increases the number of free radicals in the body. You may want to consult with an herbalist or nutritionist to find foods, herbs, or supplements that work well for you.

You also need plenty of natural light to maintain your biological rhythms and body processes. Natural sunlight stimulates the pineal and pituitary glands, which regulate your biological systems and affect your moods. If you stay in your office all day, especially one with no windows, you may not be getting enough natural light. Get outside at lunchtime or during breaks, even for a few minutes a day.

strong, circular motions with your thumb. To ~~straighten~~
hands, hold the fingertips against the back of the head.

3. Pull your ears down and away from your head,
   starting from the middle of the ear and working
   down to the earlobe.

4. Tap your fingers gently all over your head,
   including the face and the base of the
   skull, and down the neck and shoulders.

5. Scratch your scalp vigorously with
   your fingertips.

6. Gently pull your hair, starting from the
   hairline and moving back to the base of the skull.
   Grab your hair by sliding your fingers into it and
   making a fist close to the scalp. Tug away from the
   scalp with an up/down motion.

Neck, Shoulder, and Arm Massage

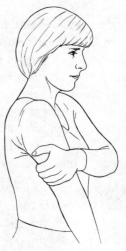

1. Raise your left arm over your head, fingers
   pointing up. Bend the elbow and let the
   palm rest on the back of the neck. Cup
   your hand around the neck, palm
   centered over the vertebrae, heel of the
   palm and fingers on either side.

2. Starting from the bottom of the neck
   and moving up to the base of the skull,
   squeeze your neck between your fingers
   and the heel of the palm. Use the whole
   hand, not just the fingertips and thumb.
   Keep as much of your palm and fingers
   in contact with the neck as you can to
   relax and warm the muscles.

3. Drop the elbow, and put your left hand on
   your right shoulder. Cup your hand over the muscle and squeeze it
   between your fingers and the heel of the palm, moving up and down
   across the shoulder. Continue massaging down the arm to the wrist.

4. Do the massage again with the right arm.

Figure 6-4. Head and face massage

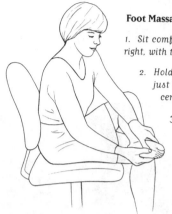

Foot Massage

1. Sit comfortably with your feet on the floor. Cross the left leg over the right, with the left ankle just above the right knee.

2. Hold your left foot in both hands. Starting at the ball of the foot just below the toes, press in strongly with both thumbs down the center of the foot to the heel. Do this a few times.

3. Squeeze and pull each toe.

4. Squeeze the whole foot, top and bottom, between the fingers and base of the palm of each hand. Move the massage up the calf if you want to.

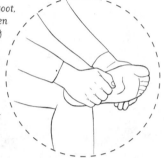

5. Holding the foot with your left hand, make a loose fist with your right hand and gently tap the entire bottom of the foot. To finish, rub down the foot with your palm.

6. Repeat the massage for the right foot.

Figure 6-5. Foot massage

Rest and Relaxation

Spending long hours at the computer is hard work for both your body and mind, even when you enjoy what you're doing. To maintain and enhance creativity, mental clarity, and physical comfort, you need a certain amount of time away from it. People aren't designed to do exactly the same activity all the time, mental or physical. We do best when we vary our body movements and give the mind enough space to get perspective on our work, our social interactions, and the course of our lives and careers.

At one level, resting and relaxing simply mean taking it easy, maybe lying around the house for a day, reading, napping, listening to music, hanging out with friends. It also means adding diversity to your life, balancing the need to make a living with the more intangible human needs for companionship, art, music, beauty, inner development, and intellectual pursuits that may not lead directly to new job opportunities. Resting and relaxing, whether passive or active, recharge your physical and mental reserves and keep you connected to the people around you and the world you live in. Rest and relaxation can bring a freshness and energy to your work and life that you may not have known you were missing.

PART

II

Repetitive Strain Injury

If you don't learn anything else about RSI, know:

- The most effective thing you can do to prevent or treat RSI is to listen to your body. Practice deep breathing, take breaks, and check in with yourself. Stay conscious—don't lose yourself in your work. Notice pain and other symptoms. Observe how you sit, how you type, how you work, and when you relax and stretch muscles.

- Almost everything can affect your risk of RSI: your equipment, your position at the desk, how tightly you grip a pen, how you hold your fingers to type, how much you use a mouse, whether your jaw is clenched, how well you can see the screen, how you hold your head, what your hobbies are, how much you exercise, how heavy your briefcase is, whether you ride a bicycle or motorcycle . . . everything.

- Treat RSI early—that's when it's easiest to reverse.

- Because RSI is related to so many factors, you can make any number of small and large changes to help prevent or recover from RSI. Once you are injured, recovery can be a long process, with a lot of detective work.

7

RSI Is Real

Repetitive strain injuries are invisible injuries. You get them when you do the same movement again and again while you are busy paying attention to something else. The initial signs of injury are subtle and easy to ignore, especially when you are working intently. It hurts, but you can still work. By the time the symptoms are bad enough to stop you in your tracks, you've done serious damage. You may have finished your project on time, but you've sacrificed your arms and hands in the process and greatly impaired your ability to do similar projects in the future.

RSI does not have to be debilitating. It is often preventable, and if treated early, is usually reversible to a great degree. The longer you've had the symptoms, the harder they are to treat, and the injury becomes a challenging, frustrating, and even enigmatic problem for both you and your health-care provider. With RSI, everyone loses. A severe RSI can cause you partial or permanent disability, and force you to change careers, limit household activities, and abandon loves and hobbies. In the words of one RSI sufferer, "it's all-encompassing." You lose your livelihood and pleasures. Your employer loses you.

Why Us, Why Now?

Many people are bewildered by the dramatic increase in RSI. People who get it don't know what hit them. People who don't have it don't understand why so many others do—they've been doing the same thing for years and *they* don't have it, so why should anyone else? Yet colleague after colleague arrives at work in splints, or goes out on disability.

RSI is not a new occupational injury. In 1717, Italian physician Bernardino Ramazzini described as a workplace hazard "certain violent and irregular motions

Until recently, computer workers seemed to be _____ in the 1980s, when office workers in Australia experienced an epidemic of hand and arm injuries that became known there as repetitive strain injuries, a term we are now familiar with. Australia has curbed the problem through prevention and early intervention,[2] but now increasing numbers of computer workers in the United States, Europe, Japan, and all over the globe are getting injured. Awareness is growing, and people are now more likely to report their symptoms. With more cases have come advances in diagnosis, and the problems are now better documented. By 1993, RSI accounted for 60% (302,400 cases) of all occupational illnesses reported in the U.S., up from 14% (20,200 cases) in 1978,[3] before computers became common in the workplace.

Computers are now the common denominator for all sorts of jobs and tasks. What once involved a variety of postures, movements, tools, and materials is now accomplished by sitting, typing, and clicking. At least some aspect of almost every activity—communication, art, entertainment, finance, business, research—can now be done online. As the number of people using computers increases, more and more of the population is affected. RSI is a cumulative disorder, and typically develops over time. Perhaps we've reached a critical mass of people who have worked at computers long enough to develop it.

There are many workplace factors to consider as well. Significant increases in stress and the pace of work, a trend towards jobs that require repetitive keyboard and mouse use, lack of training in the use of computer equipment, software, and furniture, poorly designed keyboards and mice, and an increasingly out-of-shape workforce are some of the major contributors to RSI.

Who Pays the Price?

RSI has a high cost to everyone involved. Disabled individuals face a drastic cut in income, and may have to pay medical bills not covered by insurance. If you're severely injured, your job opportunities are limited and the quality of your life is diminished.

Businesses are estimated to spend billions of dollars each year on RSI. The National Council on Compensation Insurance estimates that a single RSI case costs, on average, $29,000. This doesn't consider losses due to lowered productivity and lost work time.

Preventing RSI is far cheaper than curing it, both for individuals and for businesses. Individuals can prevent costly injuries with time and attention: modifying work areas, changing work habits, dealing with injuries promptly, and asking for support from employers. If you are self-employed, especially if you have no disability insurance, spending the money and time needed to create a safe and comfortable office insures the longevity of your career and livelihood.

Business can prevent injuries and lessen the severity of injuries that do occur by providing ergonomic equipment, furniture, and training. This prevention might cost anywhere from a few hundred to a few thousand dollars per person. Many businesses resist spending money on prevention, even as growing numbers of their employees get injured, claiming the initial costs are too high and they will be forced to cut jobs. This attitude is economically short-sighted and causes many people to suffer needlessly. The $290,000 it would cost to compensate 10 workers with RSI could provide 300 workers with almost $1,000 each for prevention.

Who Is Getting Injured?

Anyone who uses a computer regularly can get RSI. Some people can work on computers for years before they notice an injury. Others notice symptoms after weeks or months of computer work. And the lucky ones never get symptoms at all. Though RSI affects some of us more than others, there is no hard and fast rule about who will get it or when. The demographics of RSI sufferers are neither well documented nor well understood.

Top Performers and People in High-Risk Jobs

The people who are most likely to get RSI are for the most part *not* dissatisfied, unproductive, malingering workers looking for a way out of an unpleasant job, though some sufferers may indeed be angry and disgruntled. RSI sufferers are often the top performers—the ones who work the extra hours, skip breaks, put in the extra effort to do a good job, make a tight deadline, or take on additional responsibilities. They are loyal, skilled, and valuable employees who tend to work through the pain, and often suffer tremendously when the deadline is over. RSI deals them a crushing blow, stopping them short in mid-career, leaving them with limited use of their hands and few outlets for their creative energy.

On the other hand, you don't have to be an overachiever to get RSI. Reasonably productive workers in stressful, fast-paced work environments are at risk, too. Workers in telecommunications, telemarketing, airline reservations and sales, data entry, word processing, and clerical positions have been hard hit by RSI. In the

furniture that women use to g— —
women are more likely to do repetitive keying in awkward postures.

The role of hormones in RSI remains largely unexplored. We do know that female hormones promote flexibility, so women's ligaments might have a tendency to over stretch. Other muscles and tendons then strain to take over a supporting role that they weren't designed for. Judy Matsuoka-Sarina, OTR, CHT, describes these muscles and tendons as being like cables on a bridge: once one cable gets stretched out, the others have to take up the slack. They can compensate for a while, but over time, the entire structure is weakened. Since women's hormone levels decrease with age, these over-stretched tissues become less flexible and more prone to injury.

Finally, working mothers may be more at risk than women without children. Many working women still perform the greater share of household responsibilities, leaving them with less time to relax and recuperate from the stress of the workplace. Physically demanding childcare and house cleaning can include motions that aggravate tendons and ligaments already strained from working with keyboards and mice. Dr. Thomas Läubli has observed that of women who work part-time, those with children tend to be more susceptible than those without.

Young People

As the body ages, it becomes less resilient to wear and tear. Yet a growing number of young people are affected by RSI, perhaps corresponding to the growth of the personal computer industry, the increasing presence of computers in schools and homes, and the popularity of computer games. Problems in children seem to stem not so much from excess keyboarding as from playing computer games. Children are easily absorbed in their computer activities, and need help monitoring themselves. College students and people in their twenties often approach their work with boundless enthusiasm, spending hour after hour in front of their computers. They may have already spent several years working on computers, possibly accumulating microtrauma from a very young age.

Prevention Is the Solution

The best way to deal with RSI is to prevent it, and to act early if you do get it. From the Australian experience, we know this works—because of preventive and early detection measures, their rate of injury and re-injury is very low, and most of those who do get injured recover almost completely. The earlier you catch it, the easier and cheaper it is to treat, and everyone is better off.

If you're not injured, don't be complacent. Examine your work area and your work habits to see if the conditions for injury are present. Follow the suggestions here and in Part I, *The Basics*, so you can stay free of RSI.

At the first signs of injury or re-injury, take action. If you do it soon enough, you may not even need to see a doctor. A computer-industry consultant in his 40s noticed discomfort in his wrists and elbows, and within a short time traced it to his typing technique and his bicycle. He immediately improved his typing habits and changed the handlebars on his bicycle to reduce vibration and pressure on his wrists, and his pain went away.

If you need medical treatment, remember that it's an important *part* of recovery. To be successful, treatment must be accompanied by changes in your workplace, your job, and in you. Awareness is essential. Test the treatments you pursue and the changes you make in movement, behavior, and ergonomics by noticing your body's reaction to them. Only you know what your symptoms are, how bad they feel, and what they respond to. If the pain and discomfort diminish, you're doing something right.

The biggest obstacles to early intervention are denial and disbelief. At the personal level, these attitudes lead you to ignore pain until you've done serious damage. At the management level, they create a tense, antagonistic atmosphere in which injured workers are afraid to speak up. If supervisors, managers, or even fellow employees think that these injuries aren't real and exist only in people's heads, then injured people are not likely to report early symptoms for fear of losing their job or being perceived as slacking off. Instead, they will mask their pain as long as possible to avoid repercussions.

The end result is a serious injury that is detrimental and costly to everyone involved. Disability is far more expensive than early intervention, and has a severe impact on your life. An injury that might be taken care of with simple ergonomic and behavioral changes and a few medical treatments often becomes a major ordeal requiring months or years of medical care and more complicated workplace accommodations. By establishing programs for prevention and early detection, companies can create an atmosphere of cooperation where people are encouraged to report early symptoms, and everyone works together to remedy the problem.

CHAPTER
8

The Nature of the Beast

RSI isn't always perceived as an occupational injury. Symptoms often come on after work, at night, when you wake up, or when you're doing something completely unrelated to your job. The connection between the job and the pain is not always clear. You seek treatment for the pain you felt when you opened a jar; the doctor treats the symptoms and may or may not relate them to your work or hobbies.

Everything you do at and outside of work can contribute to injury. Sometimes RSI may be due to pregnancy, heredity, or pre-existing conditions, such as neck injuries. You need to look not only at the physical forces acting on the body, but at the context of the injury as well. Environmental, social, and personal factors all play a part. Yet the primary cause may well be related to the activity you spend the most time doing. For many of us, that means computer work.

RSI is hard to pin down. Symptoms disappear from one place and show up again somewhere else. One injury can lead to another. It's not uncommon for a diagnosis to change over time. Your first thought may be that the doctor is incompetent and didn't diagnose the problem correctly from the start. Misdiagnoses do happen—some doctors are more skilled than others—but before you jump to that conclusion, consider that RSI does move around in the body. People often suffer from more than one injury at a time, and symptoms change or disappear as you improve your situation through ergonomics, better work habits, modifying the job, and taking care of yourself. Diagnosis is a continuing process.

As much as we would like to match certain activities with certain pains and injuries, it's not always possible. It's true that some ways of using your body put you more at risk. Some types of pain also tend to accompany specific problems, such as the pins-and-needles sensations and numbness associated with nerve damage,

What It Feels Like

Many people think that RSI hurts only when you're typing. In fact, it can hurt any time—when you're typing, when you're sleeping, when you're carrying groceries, when you pick up your child or take your dog for a walk. And it can hurt when you're not doing anything at all. Sometimes it doesn't hurt much for a while, and then flares up with a vengeance. It doesn't even hurt the same way all the time, or in the same place.

The way RSI comes on makes it easy to ignore. "I'm just getting old," you think, or "Hmm, guess I overdid it at the gym." Or you rub your hands together, wondering why they feel so stiff and cold. "It's stress," you convince yourself. "I'll be okay as soon as I get some rest." You might experience a pain or sensation you've never felt before; not knowing how to categorize it, you just hope it'll go away. Learn to recognize symptoms. All of the following descriptions are from people with various types of RSI. If any of them sound familiar, now is the time to act.

> "I get sore fingertips and tightness across the back of the hand. My neck is stiff and my shoulders are tight, and I get pain under the shoulder blades."

> "My forearm feels bruised inside the muscle, or like it's tight or contracted."

> "It feels like dry ice, that sort of burning—almost a hot then almost a cold."

> "Sometimes it's a really sharp intense pain that goes from my shoulder and neck into my elbows. Other times it's a non-specific pain—I can't really tell where it's coming from. And sometimes it's much worse at night when I'm not doing anything."

> "It's like 500 needles, or else just two or three. Sometimes it feels like they're coming from the outside, like someone actually has a pincushion pressing on the arm. Sometimes it's so faint it's not a problem, but then it goes back up."

> "It feels like there's an electrical storm in my hands, as if someone hooked up electricity to me and is pumping it right through my hands."

> "I started having gripping problems all of a sudden. I'm fumbling for change, trying to count out 47 cents and the coins are just falling out of my hands."

> "Opening anything is hard, especially the heavy doors in office buildings. I have to use my whole left side to open them."

"I'd get sharp pains in my elbow on picking up things that weigh more than a pound or so, including full cups of water."

"My thumb and wrist feel sore, contracted, stiff, tight, weak, heavy, weary. I can't grasp things, can't press with the thumb in simple motions like turning a key in a lock or plugging in an electric cord."

"I might feel okay and then suddenly get an intense stab of pain. I change my position and then maybe I'll be okay. It can come and go that quickly."

"It's an internal throbbing, not a traveling, shooting pain. It has a warm quality to it, and it often feels like something tightening in on itself, or something being stretched."

"Before I developed a ganglionic cyst, I had a sharp band of pain all around my finger. Three fingers would get numb and after a while I'd be typing with just seven fingers."

"The finger pain is a little itching, a little hot, almost like a really bad sunburn, like a scratchiness under the skin. It's unnerving."

"The area feels numb when nothing is touching it, but when you run something over it, it feels more sensitive, even creepy."

"My wrist gets warm and stiff. More often it comes on a couple hours after I did something than when I was actually doing it."

"Sometimes I feel my symptoms late at night when I finally let go. Then I realize I'm really in pain."

"Sometimes I don't feel the pain so much but I just don't want to move my hands. I want to fold my arms into myself, or have some sort of brace to cover my whole body."

"I had sudden, terrible pain. It wasn't gradual at all. One day I didn't have it and one day I did. Then I ignored it. I kept working through it. And it affected my work—I couldn't do a good job. How can you do a good job when you're in pain all day? You can't think properly, you can't do anything."

"I remember waking up with my arm completely numb. It didn't alarm me until I had pain. I just thought I slept on my arm funny, that it had been asleep. But then I thought, how could it feel that way, I was sleeping on my back!"

"My hands seem slow and tight—not flexible, not nimble. Cramped up and cold. It's like there's a clamp around my wrist. It's blocked, like something is supposed to be flowing there but it can't get through."

"It felt like my arm was an alien being, like something was raging around inside of it, like my arm was going to drop off."

"My fingers feel exquisitely sensitive, tender, raw, exposed, sort of creepy-crawly, like I want to jump out of my skin. I just want to scream when I touch something."

tinnus), and be___ of occupational medicine, notes that although these con___ times hereditary) causes, they may contribute to developing RSI.

The injuries described here are the most common for computer users. *Many people suffer from more than one injury at the same time.* Ask your care provider to describe your condition in detail, in terms you understand.

Tendon Injuries

Tendons are fibrous connective tissue that attach muscle to bone, transferring muscle contraction and expansion to body movement. They're strong, but have little blood supply and don't stretch or contract very much. Some tendons, like those in the hands and wrists, move through a sheath that contains lubricating and nourishing synovial fluid. To extend and flex the fingers, tendons glide up to about five centimeters in the sheaths while the sheaths stay in place. Injuries to the tendons themselves are generally termed *tendinitis*, and injuries that involve the tendon sheath are called *tenosynovitis*.

Tendinitis

Tendinitis generally refers to an inflamed or partially torn tissue (see Figure 8-1). Inflamed tendons usually heal in a few weeks with rest—without rest they can become weak and eventually tear. Tendons tear like a rope frays, one fiber at a time. They also heal slowly, fiber by fiber, and are easily re-injured until they are completely healed. Scar tissue develops as fibers tear, heal, and tear again. Scarring increases the risk of reinjury. A tendon may tear in the body of the tendon itself, or where it attaches to the bone or muscle. It may be a matter of several micro-tears on a small scale rather than a single rip. Other connective tissue at the side of the bone where the tendon attaches can become inflamed, too, and the bone can feel tender and sore—this often happens at the elbow.

Tendinitis typically occurs in the flexor and extensor tendons of the fingers, thumb, forearm, elbow, or shoulder. Tendinitis is often characterized by achiness, stiffness, tightness, and burning sensations, or by deep, non-specific pain. It may cause your grip to weaken, so that you suddenly drop things or have trouble holding on to them. Acute tendon injuries may start with a sharp pain that radiates out from the injured spot. As it heals, the pain recedes towards the injured spot, which may remain sensitive or sore for some months. You may feel symp-

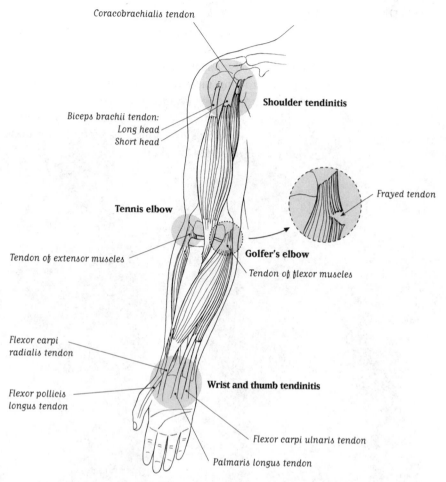

Coracobrachialis tendon

Shoulder tendinitis

Biceps brachii tendon:
Long head
Short head

Frayed tendon

Tennis elbow

Tendon of extensor muscles

Golfer's elbow

Tendon of flexor muscles

Flexor carpi
radialis tendon

Wrist and thumb tendinitis

Flexor pollicis
longus tendon

Flexor carpi ulnaris tendon

Palmaris longus tendon

Figure 8-1. Common sites of tendinitis

toms in both arms, even when only one arm is injured. Examine the following descriptions of common tendon injuries:

- Tennis elbow, or *lateral epicondylitis*, affects the tendons of the finger extensor muscles at the outside of the elbow, and may involve inflammation in the muscles where they attach to the bone.

- Golfer's elbow, or *medial epicondylitis*, affects the tendons of the finger flexor muscles at the inside of the elbow, and may involve inflammation in the muscles where they attach to the bone.

- Shoulder tendinitis, or *rotator cuff tendinitis*, affects the four rotator cuff tendons that stabilize and move the shoulder, help rotate the arms in and out, and move the arms up and down.

up and can make both the sheath and the tendon swell. ̲ ̲ ̲ ̲ ̲ on the tendon, causing the finger or thumb to lock in place. When fluid builds up in one spot, it can form a bump or cyst under the skin.

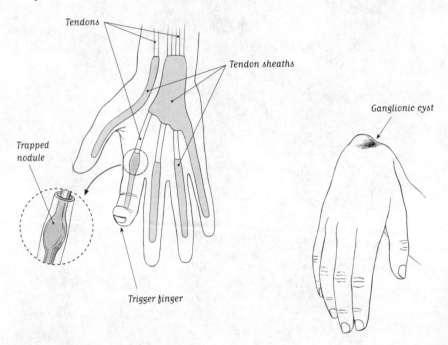

Figure 8-2. Common sites of tenosynovitis

The most notable symptoms of tenosynovitis are jerky, snapping movements and the disturbing sound of grinding or cracking at the tendon. It may be accompanied by tendinitis-type sensations as well. Here are some of the forms tenosynovitis can take:

- *Stenosing tenosynovitis*, or De Quervain's disease, affects the structures used to extend the thumb and move it away from the hand—the extensor tendons in the side of the wrist, and the long abductor and short extensor tendons of the thumb. The tendons that extend the thumb get constricted.

- *Stenosing tenosynovitis crepitans*, or trigger finger, usually affects the flexor tendons of the finger or thumb on the inside of the hand. The finger or thumb might have a jerking movement or lock in place, or have a cracking sound when it moves. You may have to use your other hand to straighten the finger.

- A *ganglionic cyst* is a bump under the skin filled with synovial fluid, usually on the back of the hand, at the wrist or near a joint.

Nerve Injuries

Nerves carry sensory and motor impulses between your body and your brain. The nerves we are most concerned with are the ones that serve the arm and hand—the median, radial, and ulnar nerves (which are part of the *brachial plexus*). These extend out in long branches from the vertebrae in the lower neck, passing through muscles and narrow passageways formed by bones and ligaments on their way down the arm to the hand (see Figure 8-3).

At the neck, this network of nerves plus the brachial artery and veins go through the *thoracic outlet*, the area between the collar bone, the first rib, and the neck muscles. At the inside of the elbow, the ulnar nerve passes through the *cubital tunnel*, a groove in the bone covered by a ligament, and at the little finger side of the wrist it goes through *Guyon's canal*, a small area between two of the carpal bones covered by ligament and muscle. At the outside of the elbow, the radial nerve divides and the deep part passes through the *radial tunnel*, over bone and under muscle. At the wrist, the median nerve, along with some of the tendons that move the fingers, travel through the *carpal tunnel*, formed by the carpal bones at the back of the wrist and a band of ligament at the underside (see Figure 8-4).

These are all prime locations for nerve entrapment. There is little space, so any misalignment can press on a nerve, and if any neighboring tendons or tissues are inflamed, they take up extra space and can press on the nerve. Tight muscles can constrict the nerves, too, especially at the neck.

If a nerve is compressed in more than one place, it's called a *double crush*. Nerves need a certain amount of pressure to cause symptoms. A little pressure in one spot may not be enough to be a problem, but a little here and a little there might put you over the threshold. The symptoms are typically neurological, while the cause may be muscular tightness. Computer users are often tight in several places—especially the neck, shoulders, and forearms—so they're particularly vulnerable to a double crush. According to Rick Mehaffy, DC, a deficiency in vitamin B_6 makes nerves more susceptible.

When a nerve is compressed, you feel the sensations somewhere between the point of compression and your fingertips. Shoulder pain can be referred from a

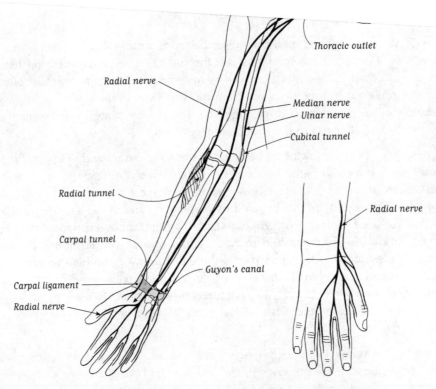

Figure 8-3. The nerves of the upper limb start at the neck

compressed nerve in the neck; pain in the forearm, wrist, or fingers can be referred from the neck or the elbow. That's why when you have hand, wrist, or elbow pain, you have to start looking for causes at the neck and move down.

Nerve compression can be verified with nerve conduction tests. Nerves distribute sensation in characteristic patterns (see Figure 8-5), although the areas can overlap, and are slightly different in different people. For example, if you feel symptoms in your fourth and fifth fingers, a physician would probably look for entrapment of the ulnar nerve. Mehaffy notes that if your symptoms don't follow the general patterns, you may not have nerve compression.

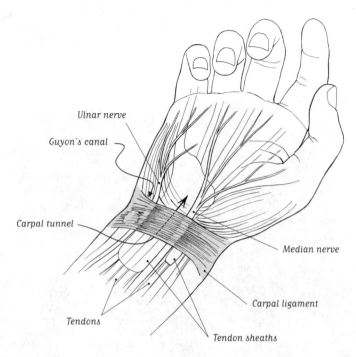

Ulnar nerve

Guyon's canal

Carpal tunnel

Median nerve

Carpal ligament

Tendons

Tendon sheaths

Figure 8-4. The carpal tunnel is one possible location for nerve entrapment

While certain nerve disorders have characteristic symptoms, there are many common symptoms such as numbness, tingling, hypersensitivity, pins-and-needles sensations, loss of muscle strength, and, in severe cases, muscle atrophy and paralysis. Thus, nerve disorders are sometimes misdiagnosed and confused with one another, or with tissue damage.

Cervical Radiculopathy

In this injury, also called *cervical nerve root entrapment*, the root of a nerve becomes compressed where it comes out of the vertebra in the neck, or cervical spine. Depending on which nerve root is compressed, you might feel symptoms from the neck down to the forearm, thumb, or fingers. Symptoms are similar to those of carpal tunnel syndrome.

Thoracic Outlet Syndrome

This injury happens when the nerves and/or blood vessels are compressed in the thoracic outlet. Compression is typically from muscle tightness at the side of the neck, which often stems from poor head posture, and at the front of the chest, from round-shouldered posture. Symptoms are similar to those of carpal tunnel syndrome or ulnar neuropathy, and can be referred to the shoulder, upper arm,

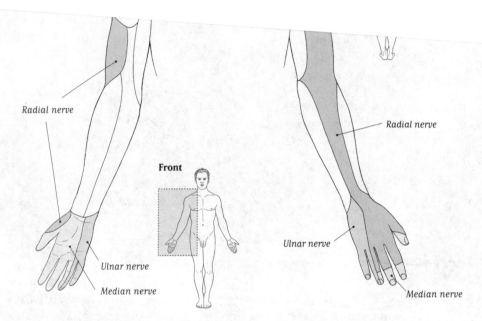

Figure 8-5. The nerves provide sensation to different parts of the hand and arm

forearm, wrist, hand, or fingers. You may also experience swelling, coldness, or purplish discoloration of the hands.

Radial Tunnel Syndrome

This injury refers to radial nerve entrapment, or compression of the radial nerve at the outside of the elbow. You might feel symptoms at the elbow where the nerve is compressed, near the base of the thumb, or somewhere in between. Sometimes this can feel like tennis elbow. You might also have weakness of the wrist.

Cubital Tunnel Syndrome

This injury occurs when the ulnar nerve is entrapped at the inside of the elbow. You might experience symptoms at the elbow or up and down the inside of your arm. It often feels like hitting your "funny bone," with tingling into the ring and little fingers. The ulnar nerve can also be compressed at Guyon's canal in the wrist, but this is less common.

Carpal Tunnel Syndrome

Carpal tunnel syndrome is median nerve entrapment in the carpal tunnel. It can be caused by swelling in the tendon sheath, and, according to Mehaffy, may be preceded by tendinitis. The symptoms of carpal tunnel syndrome are numbness and tingling in the thumb, index, and middle fingers and part of the ring finger, aching in the wrist, and loss of coordination, especially in the thumb. You typically feel the pain from the wrist down. Symptoms are sometimes worse when you're resting, and can wake you from sleep in the night, especially if you sleep with your wrists bent. They're made worse by driving a car, writing, and gripping, and are relieved by shaking your hands or immersing them in cold or warm water. Some women experience carpal tunnel syndrome during pregnancy.

Another disorder called *pronator teres syndrome* is sometimes confused with carpal tunnel syndrome. This also involves compression of the median nerve, not at the wrist but near the elbow by the pronator teres muscle. You feel symptoms mainly in the forearm and not the wrist, and you don't feel them at night. Symptoms get worse with activity, and better with rest.[1]

Muscle Disorders

Myofascial pain is a term for the elusive, diffuse, dull, achy pain, stiffness, or tenderness you can feel deep in your muscles. The fascia (membrane) surrounding the muscles gets tight, adding fibrous tissue and getting thicker, so the muscles can't stretch. Painful nodules or exquisitely tender spots can develop in the muscles or their associated fascia. These sore spots are called *trigger points*. *Fibromyalgia* is a severe, generalized form of myofascial pain associated with chronic fatigue and other systemic symptoms.

Treatment breaks up the nodules and relaxes the fascia, allowing the tissues to stretch back to their normal length. Muscles with trigger points have tight bands or clumps of fibers and are tender to firm touch. When you press a sore spot, the muscle may twitch. The pain often travels out from that spot to distant areas and then recedes (Figure 8-6). The way the pain travels is called a referral pattern, which varies with the muscles, the activity of the trigger point, and the person affected. The site of the trigger point is usually distant from the site of the referred pain. Muscles in the arms refer pain to the elbows, wrists, and hands. Muscles in the neck refer pain to the head, shoulders, upper back, and hand.[2]

Myofascial pain and trigger points can occur in almost any muscle, and often occur in both sides at the same time. They can come on abruptly with a specific movement, or gradually with continual overuse. The pain interferes with sleep patterns, so you wake up feeling stiff and exhausted even when you think you've had enough sleep. You might feel stiff when you get up from sitting in your chair

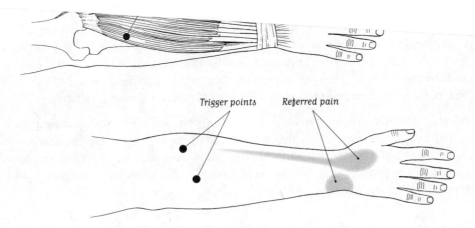

Figure 8-6. Sore muscles may have tender trigger points that refer pain

for a long time. The pain is often made worse by repeated muscle contraction, exposure to cold drafts, cold, damp weather, viral infections, and times of intense stress.

Lowengart finds that many RSI patients suffer from muscle pain and tender trigger points resulting from myofascial pain, and that myofascial pain is sometimes misdiagnosed. "In the neck and shoulder region, myofascial pain contributes to symptoms of tingling and/or pain in the arms and hands, and is occasionally diagnosed as thoracic outlet syndrome or cervical radiculopathy," she explains. "Tender points in the forearms can mimic other conditions such as tennis elbow or tendinitis."[3]

What Brings It On

Forces in the job, in the work environment, in the equipment, and within you come together to make an injury. To understand how you can hurt yourself—and where to concentrate your efforts toward healing—you must take all of these into account. Part I, *The Basics*, addresses many of these factors.

Continuous Muscle Contraction

Constant sitting, typing, gripping, clicking, and dragging keeps your muscles contracted, especially in the neck, shoulders, forearms, and hands. They miss the relaxation cycle that brings in the fresh, oxygenated blood they need to function and stay healthy, and to heal if they are injured. According to Mehaffy, the muscles adapt by shortening themselves with fibrous tissue so they don't have to contract. The tendons then have to stretch more, which they're not designed to do, and the result is soreness, pain, inflammation, and tissue damage.

Repetition and Cumulative Trauma

Repeating the same motions over weeks, months, or years subjects the muscles, tendons, ligaments, and joints to wear and tear. With enough rest, tissues can repair themselves, but if they have to keep working hard when they're not fully recovered, the damage accumulates and they become increasingly tired, weak, and prone to injury.

Poor Posture, Positioning, and Body Mechanics

Doing repetitive motions in awkward, twisted postures and positions—or with tense, jerky movements—significantly increases the trauma. You are asking your body to perform optimally from weak or unstable positions, or from positions of strain. Ill-fitting chairs and furniture or a work area that's not set up to fit you can force you into awkward or unstable postures, or make your movements inefficient. Lack of proper arm support, thrusting your head forward, slumping forward while you sit, and non-neutral hand and arm positions are major problems.

Excessive Force and Muscle Tension

Typing, clicking, or gripping a mouse or pen with excessive force decreases circulation and increases muscle tension and fatigue. Sometimes the equipment requires a lot of force to use, and sometimes out of tenseness, anger, or habit, we use too much force in our movements. We don't just talk about pounding away on the keyboard, we actually *do* it.

Lack of Rest

When you work your body hard and don't get enough rest to recover, tiredness becomes fatigue. You are running on empty. Not enough rest can mean you don't pause often enough while you type or that you're not getting enough sleep, especially during periods of intense work. Fatigue makes you easy prey to any illness, and when you're tired, it's easy to forget about good posture and body mechanics.

likely to be the most ~~~ ~~
contributing factor in RSI.

Pace and Type of Work

Computer work is typically done at a very fast pace, sometimes for several hours
without a break. Dr. Thomas Läubli observes that doing straight computer work
for more than 4 hours a day significantly increases the risk of injury. In some jobs,
computer work goes in phases, with periods of intense work interspersed with
less demanding times. Work surges bring on symptoms in some people, and can
trigger flare-ups in people who are already injured.[4]

Many people feel compelled to work at top speed all the time. This is an excessive demand on the body. Athletes don't ask it of themselves, and neither should
we. To perform optimally, the body needs periods of rest. Jumping right back in
at top speed after you've been sick or injured is especially risky. You need to
build up steam gradually.

Jobs that require only keyboard and mouse work all day are highly problematic.
These jobs often combine highly repetitive work (both in keystrokes and
content), with pressure to work fast. Tying speed to performance rating creates a
stressful environment that fosters injury.

Frequent air travel for business trips can also aggravate symptoms. Carrying a
briefcase, portable computer, and baggage through the airport and then lifting
them into the overhead bins strains the neck and entire upper limb. Vibration,
cold drafts, and cramped postures on the airplane can increase your discomfort.

Direct Pressure on the Nerve

In places where the nerves run close to the skin, it's easy to put pressure directly
on them, compressing them. Resting your elbows or wrists on the sharp edge or
hard surface of a desk, using a stapler, wearing a snug metal watchband or
clothes with tight cuffs, or sleeping on your hands, especially if they're curled or
bent, can all compress the nerves.

Cold

Computer work hurts more and does more damage when your hands are cold.
Excessive cold reduces circulation and decreases the elasticity and flexibility of

your muscles, joints, and tendons. Drafts from air conditioners, cold from cement floors in winter, and cold environments are all contributors. Cold fingers aren't nimble, cold muscles tighten and spasm, and cold, stiff tendons can't glide easily in their sheaths. Dr. Robert Markison, hand surgeon and specialist in both non-surgical and surgical treatment of RSI, noted at the 1993 SIGGRAPH conference that cool limbs are limbs at risk.

Vibration

Vibration jars the tissues, weakening them and triggering pain or other symptoms. You get vibration from using too much force when you type, and from activities outside work, such as driving, riding a bicycle or motorcycle, or using power tools.

Lack of Training

We are not born knowing how to use computer equipment or how to set up our workspace. In general, we don't even think about it. We just sit down and go at it. Though we spend hours and hours of our lifetime with our keyboards, we balk at taking a few days or weeks to learn good typing technique, a new keyboard layout, or keyboard macros. The idea that using a mouse or trackball might require a little bit of instruction seems ridiculous. Arrangement of furniture and equipment is more a function of office space than anything else. As for posture? Well, we sit the way we sit.

Secretaries are trained in touch-typing. Musicians are trained in technique and posture. Assembly workers are trained to use their tools. People who use heavy equipment learn how to operate it. The knowledge that training can prevent injury is just beginning to surface in the world of high-tech. Computer skills classes teach you how computers work, how to program them, and how to use software, but they seldom mention typing technique, posture, or positioning. Computer scientists know how to design and build computer hardware and software, but don't know much about the ergonomics of the products they create.

Few employers provide training for their employees—they assign us a space and we're on our own. Even when we get a computer for home, we don't train ourselves or our children how to use it. Without training, people naturally develop their own habits of keying, clicking, sitting, and moving. Some of these habits are perfectly fine, and some are destructive. All the ergonomic equipment in the world is not going to help someone who doesn't know how to use it. It can even aggravate symptoms if you don't use or adjust it properly.

for the pent-up physical
tense work habits—pounding the keys, gripping the ...
bearing down on the pen and paper when you write—and later in injury.

Your Life Outside Work

You don't stop being susceptible to RSI when you leave work. Instead, you drive, go for a bike ride, play tennis, play a musical instrument, paint, cook, wash the dishes, knit, sew, garden, write, clean house, use your home computer, pick up the baby, fix the car, mow the lawn, hammer some nails, work with power tools. Depending on how you do these things, you may subject yourself to many of the same forces acting on you at work. Stress, lack of sleep, lack of aerobic conditioning, and poor diet make everything worse.

Your Physical Condition

The better shape you're in, the better your circulation and strength, and the more resilient you are to repetitive movements and long hours of typing and clicking. You can still get injured from the wear and tear, but being in good shape reduces your chance of injury. If you do get injured, good health helps you heal faster. Lowengart notes that many RSI sufferers started with poor body strength, especially the younger individuals.

Biochemical Causes and Pre-Existing Conditions

Sometimes symptoms are a result of other medical problems or conditions, such as pregnancy, diabetes, lupus, scleroderma, double-jointedness, wrist, hand, or arm fractures, a tumor in the carpal tunnel, or other anatomical changes. As noted in Chapter 7, *RSI Is Real*, hormonal changes and imbalances may also play a part.

Excess weight can be a problem, since the muscles have to work harder to carry it, especially if it makes you hold your arms out further to the side. Even if you're typing in a neutral position, you still have to hold the extra weight, and that means more strain on the neck and shoulders.

Even long healed injuries can make you more susceptible. If you've had a neck injury or experienced whiplash in an auto accident, you are more susceptible because the parts of the body you rely on for computer work may be the very parts that were weakened in your accident. Habitually grinding your teeth or clenching your jaw can tighten the neck, and aggravate symptoms.

Judy Matsuoka-Sarina, OTR, CHT, notes that former athletes whose bodies are accustomed to frequent movement may have trouble adjusting to constant sitting and can develop complicated injuries.

Why Does It Take So Long to Go Away?

More often than not, RSI takes a long time to heal. This is especially true if you don't discover it early, when it may still be relatively easy to treat. The longer you wait, the more severe and complicated it becomes, and the longer it takes to heal. A very serious injury may never heal completely, and you may have to learn to live with it. If you have a sudden onset of RSI, even early diagnosis and treatment may not guarantee a swift or complete recovery.

RSI primarily affects soft tissue, which by nature can take a long time to heal. It's easy to re-injure soft tissue even if you're careful, as anyone who has sprained an ankle or finger knows. As pain subsides, you may think it's healed and resume the activity that brought it on, when the tissue is really only partially healed and still weak. Soft tissue can recover fully a limited number of times. The more you re-injure it, the longer it takes to heal. With RSI, you can injure and re-injure yourself without being aware of it, or by ignoring seemingly minor discomfort or pain. Working through the pain is a sure way to make the injury worse, and denying the injury sets you up for a long recovery.

Treatment may eventually remove the pain, but to heal and remain pain free, you have to address the causes. Healing requires not just specific medical treatment, therapy, and exercise, but changes in your lifestyle, workstyle, and workplace as well. That's a lot to contend with. Sometimes people simply don't make the changes in their lives that allow for healing. They may be reluctant or unwilling to make the changes, or don't know what changes they need to make. There are so many contributing factors to RSI that it takes time to understand the causes. It also takes time to discover what treatment the injury responds to. What works for one person may not work for another. Usually, people have to try several types of treatment before they find the ones that work.

9

Your Tools Make a Difference

Tool design has long been a factor in workplace safety. Tools that work against the design and function of the body are uncomfortable to use and contribute to injuries. Our keyboards, pointing devices, and software are no exceptions. The design of these tools determines how we position and move our hands, how much force we need to use, and how many keystrokes and mouse movements we need to make.

Tool use is important as well. Improper use of any tool, well-designed or not, is much riskier than using the same tool with good posture, positioning, and technique. Ergonomic design alone doesn't eliminate your risk.

Assess and use your tools with respect.

Keyboards

When you evaluate a keyboard, think about how you have to position your hands and arms to use it, how well it fits your hands, how much force you need to activate the keys, and how your fingers have to move to reach the keys.

Hand Position and Fit

Some keyboard designs let you type with your arms and hands in neutral position, but others don't. Hand sizes vary tremendously, but keyboards don't stretch or shrink to fit. One person's fingers may be uncomfortably cramped, while another's may be straining to reach the keys.

The keyboards we are most familiar with, and until recently had little choice but to use, force our hands out of neutral and into positions that put us most at risk

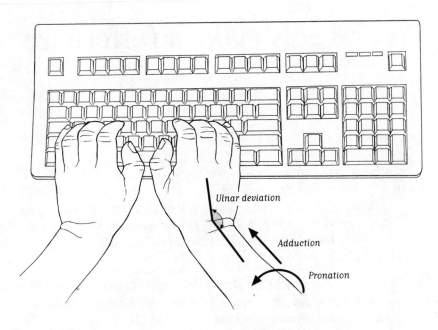

Ulnar deviation

Adduction

Pronation

Figure 9-1. Conventional keyboards encourage stressful hand positions

This design is a direct descendent of the mechanical typewriter, which was designed not for our hands, but to accommodate the physical keying mechanism. While this constraint is now absent and many improvements have been made to increase the safety and comfort of keyboards, the basic shape and layout remain the same. And the technology allows us to type faster than ever before.

Ergonomic keyboard designs attempt to follow the shape and curves of your hands, and promote neutral typing positions. Studies in Germany (from as early as 1926) show that splitting and angling the keyboard reduces muscle tension and fatigue in the hands, arm, shoulder, and neck.[1] Computer keyboards based on these findings have been available in Europe since the 1980s. A design that separates the main keys into two recessed "wells" was developed in England in the 1970s, along with keyboards based on the same principles for use with one hand, a mouthstick, or a headstick. Several innovative designs are now more widely available or are in development.

Figure 9-2 shows the basic design features of some ergonomic keyboards. Some designs may fit certain body types better than others. Evaluate a new keyboard carefully to be sure you're not eliminating one risk factor only to introduce another one. Having a choice of designs means that more people will find a keyboard that fits their hands and lets them type comfortably.

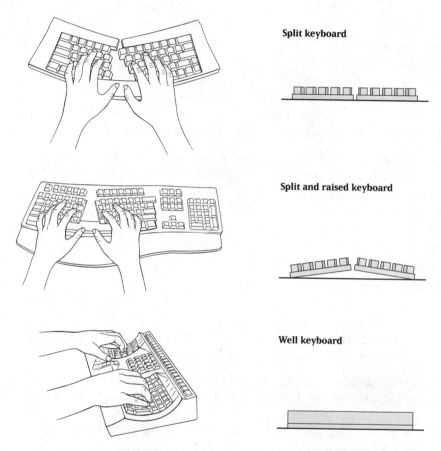

Split keyboard

Split and raised keyboard

Well keyboard

Figure 9-2. Ergonomic keyboard designs encourage neutral hand positions

Key Resistance and Feedback

The harder you have to press the keys, the more strain you put on your fingers. Keys that are not well cushioned, pounding into a hard surface, increase the shock and vibration. If the keys give you little or no tactile and audible feedback, you might not hear or feel when you have activated them, so you are more likely to keep exerting force until the keys bottom out. The physical shock from pounding the keys reverberates up through your hands and arms, even up to

move and which fingers are used most. The familiar *qwerty* layout (named for the first six letters in the top alphabetic row) is another artifact of the mechanical typewriter. Designed to slow typists down so they wouldn't jam the keys, this intentionally awkward layout places some of the most used keys furthest from the home row. Our fingers are still hopping and twisting all over the keyboard to accommodate a mechanism that no longer exists. Computer keyboards also have more keys than a standard typewriter, so there is even more work to do. Our fingers literally travel miles over the keys in a day of typing.

Ergonomic layouts, such as *dvorak*, eliminate this unnecessary obstacle course and significantly shorten the route by putting the letters we use most on the home row and arranging the letters to minimize awkward and excessive movements. Although ergonomic layouts have been available for years and some people find them helpful, they aren't widely used. Perhaps because of reluctance to retrain a workforce already used to the *qwerty* layout, combined with resistance on people's part to learning something new, *qwerty* still persists.

Another problem with conventional layouts is the location of other frequently used keys. The spacebar encourages a stressful straight reach and press by the thumb, which in turn twists the wrists inward, possibly compressing the nerves. Return/Enter, Delete, Backspace, and Shift overwork the little finger, our weakest, making it reach and encouraging a twist in the wrist in the process.

The Control, Command, Option, Alt, and Escape keys, often used for key combination sequences, again call on the little finger, making it travel to the outer reaches of the keyboard and then hold the position while you type the sequence. Function keys are typically spread across the top of the keyboard, forcing you to lift your hands off the home row and reach forward to use them.

Some ergonomic keyboards use *qwerty* or modified *qwerty* layouts to ease the transition to a new design, and provide programmable keys or alternate layouts in hardware or software. Some change the location of function keys to distribute the load more evenly; others do not.

Position of the Numeric Keypad

On many keyboards, the numeric keypad is fixed on the right, forcing you to overuse your right hand and causing you to reach more, especially if you use a mouse on the right side as well. Some keyboards have a separate numeric keypad that you can position where you want.

Pointing Devices—Mice and Trackballs

Mice, trackballs, and other pointing devices control the movement and position of the cursor. For example, in word processing applications, you "point" to where you want the cursor (or insertion point) to be, and click to put it there. Many applications are mouse-intensive—they depend on pointing devices to pull down and navigate through menus, open files, edit text, and create graphics. Pointing devices are relatively new, invented within the last ten years. Some RSI sufferers believe they contribute to injury even more than keyboards.

Rich Pekelney, a pointing device design specialist at Kensington Microware, Ltd., recommends considering size and feel when choosing a pointing device. Gauge how well it supports your hand in its natural resting position, how smoothly and efficiently it controls the cursor, and how much force you need to hold it, click, and drag.

Mouse Operations

Using a mouse is physically demanding. You have to hold the mouse, move it to guide the cursor to precise locations, and then exert force to click the buttons. You need to not only hold up your arm, but to make fine movements with your hands and fingers at the same time, so your muscles are almost continually contracted and blood flow to the tissues in the hand, arm, and shoulder is decreased.

A trackball may take away some of this strain because you don't have to move the entire device to move the cursor. The device is stationary, and you move the ball to control the cursor. However, many trackballs promote a certain degree of wrist extension, and some people find they strain the fingers or thumb. Other pointing devices such as tablets, touchpads, pucks, styluses, and joysticks can also relieve mousestrain, though some of these may be a little harder to control, or work better for graphics or games than text applications. You may want to alternate between various devices to lessen the strain.

While clicking can strain the finger flexor tendons, dragging is potentially the biggest problem. Pete Johnson, researcher at the University of California Ergonomics Lab, has found that moving a mouse while holding down a button increases static pinch forces, and may account for some flexor tendon problems associated with mouse use. He recommends using a click-lock feature that allows you to press a button once to lock it, move the cursor, and press the button again to release it.

Hand Support

The way the body of the device supports your hand is critical to your comfort and safety. A device that doesn't fit you can force you into awkward postures and interfere with precision. A too-long device might put pressure on the back of your palm and be clumsy to use. A too-narrow device makes you curl your fingers in and grasp tightly, and a too-wide one stretches your fingers out into a weak position for moving and clicking. A too-small or too-short device may not be as bad since you can use your fingers to manipulate it with precise movements. A curved surface on a mouse lets the palm help with the motion, so the fingers don't need to grip so much. While some devices accommodate a variety of hand sizes, many fit medium-to-large hands best. A few mice come in small, medium, and large, but these are not readily available and may have to be ordered from the manufacturer.

Handedness is also an issue. Some devices can be used with the right or left hand, but most are right-handed. A few manufacturers make left-handed devices, but you have to order them. This is a big problem for lefties and for right-handed people who want to use the mouse on the left side. When you have both the mouse and numeric keypad on the right side, not only does your right hand have to work more, but you also have to reach. Holding your arm out while your fingers and hands control precise cursor movements and clicks puts an extreme strain on your neck, arm, and shoulder muscles. The problem is worse if the mouse is on a higher level than the keyboard. Pain from this mouse-reach can be felt deep under your shoulder blade, in your neck and shoulders, and all the way down your arm.

Button Design and Action

The placement and design of the buttons affects how you hold your fingers and how they hit the buttons. Some designs lock your fingers into a straightened-out position, which overextends them. If the buttons on a mouse are too far apart, you can't easily alternate which finger(s) you use to press the buttons. Very small buttons force you to press them in the same place, so you can't vary your movement or hand position.

Button action affects the amount of force you need to click. If the buttons are hard to press, you can strain the tendons up to where they attach at the elbow. If the buttons are too light, it's easy to press them accidentally so you might use static muscle force to hold your finger *off* the buttons.

Tracking Action

Tracking action refers to how smoothly the cursor follows the movement of the device. The smoother the action, the better. If it's jumpy, too slow, or too fast, it interferes with precision, and you end up spending a lot of time correcting the cursor position, increasing the workload. Each time you have to correct the cursor position, you may find yourself feeling irritated and tense, and grabbing the mouse harder or rolling the trackball with more force.

Trackball Design

In general, the smaller the trackball, the more potential for problems, though a large one may cause you to overextend your wrist. Small balls can be hard to control, require a lot of repetitive movement, and sometimes don't track well. Depending on the size of your hands, they may cause your fingers to cramp. Small trackballs are most often used when large balls are inappropriate, i.e., with portable computers or in situations where you have limited desk space.

Some keyboards and portables have built-in trackballs—these take up less space and put the trackball and keyboard on the same level, but typically use small balls and have a fixed position and angle.

Some trackballs can be used with footpedals, which can be very helpful. Others are made so the thumb rolls the ball and the fingers click. This may set you up to overuse your thumb, so be careful. If you straighten and stretch the thumb to roll the ball, you strain it more and displace the wrist. It's better either to keep the thumb curved and hold it over the ball, or to use your fingers instead of the thumb to roll the ball.

Software

Software can contribute to overuse if it requires a lot of complex key sequences, excessive keying, or a lot of mouse use—clicking and dragging, scrolling, moving the cursor back and forth across the screen, navigating through hierarchical menus. Software that is difficult or frustrating to use can increase stress and tension.

Good software offers keyboard shortcuts for most or all operations and doesn't rely heavily on embedded menus. It's easy to use, and reduces clicks, drags, keystrokes, and excessive cursor movement.

10

Good Hand Technique Reduces Your Risk

Our hands are second only to our lips in sensitivity and dexterity. In both the sensory and motor cortexes of the brain, the hands, fingers, and thumbs have the largest allotment of space, and the upper limb as a whole takes more space than any other structure. We rely on these supple, complex instruments not only to communicate with our computers, but for countless daily activities. It makes sense to use them well.

Relax Your Hands and Arms

Keeping your hands relaxed and naturally curved maximizes flexibility, makes optimal use of the joints, and puts the least strain on the muscles. To see this for yourself, experiment with how you move your fingers and rest your hands. If you're injured, try the following exercises with extreme caution. If anything hurts, don't do it!

You can practice techniques that encourage relaxation while you work. These efforts don't take much time, but they do require attention until they become automatic. The following techniques are based on principles of movement described by Stephen Tamaribuchi, an RSI consultant who specializes in body mechanics:

- *Rest your hands thumbs up.* Rest both hands during breaks, even for a few seconds at a time. When you're doing a one-handed task, rest the other hand thumb up. When you're sitting and thinking, with your hands poised on the keyboard and mouse, turn your hands over.

- *Keep your fingers and thumbs slightly curved.* Don't straighten and extend them while you work, especially the little finger and thumb. These are the digits most susceptible to overuse, the thumb because of its joint structure,

Figure 10-1. Relaxing your hands and arms.

and the little finger because of its small size and lack of strength. Be extremely careful with your thumbs. Without them, you can't hold on to anything. Keep your fingernails short—long fingernails encourage you to extend your fingers while you type.

- *When you reach, turn and face what you're reaching for.* At least turn in its direction even if you don't face it full on. When turning in a chair, swivel the chair and turn your whole body with it. Don't turn just your upper body. Use your feet to help you turn.

Use Good Typing Technique

Type with the keys you use most directly in front of you, and keep your hands and arms in neutral position. If you use the main keys most, center them in front of you. If you use the numeric keypad most, position it to the right or left, in front of the hand you're using.

If your equipment is set up at an angle to your seat so you can alternate typing with other tasks, such as waiting on customers or doing paperwork, turn your whole body to face the keyboard when you type. Don't type for a long time with your hands out to your sides or with your body twisted.

Type with your wrists raised and floating and in neutral position, as if you were playing the piano (see Figure 10-2). Rest your hands and arms for a few seconds every few minutes by gently shaking them out or resting them thumbs up. You may find it helpful to use a wrist rest as a guide while you're typing, and as a place to rest when you're not.

If you prefer to rest your hands while you type—though this is not generally recommended—use a padded surface or wristrest and keep your wrists in neutral position. Avoid pressing down on your wrists and raising your fingers to type. Again, take a few seconds' rest for every few minutes of typing.

To press a distant key, move your whole hand to position your finger over the key. Don't angle your wrist and stretch your little finger for it. Notice how your wrist goes out of neutral when you extend your little finger or thumb. Keep your thumb curved when you press the space bar, and move it gently. So you don't overuse one thumb, switch thumbs periodically to use the space bar.

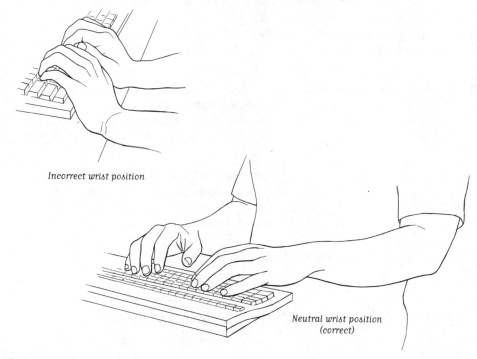

Incorrect wrist position

Neutral wrist position
(correct)

Figure 10-2. Typing with your wrists in neutral position

Use a relaxed touch and don't pound the keys. Use the least amount of force necessary. Your mind might get caught up in the excitement of wailing away on the keyboard, but it doesn't do your fingers and hands any good—the impact causes vibration and cuts off circulation. Develop a smooth rhythm for typing, as if you were playing music.

Try not to look down at the keyboard all the time, since this strains your neck and encourages a head-forward posture. Many keyboards have a small bump on the "d" and "k" keys to help you keep your hands oriented without looking

Stretch Your Hands

With your arms relaxed at your sides, extend your fingers as much as you can. Notice how all the muscles feel, from the fingers up into the arms. Release the stretch, gently shake out your hands, and let them hang naturally without extending or clenching them, relaxing all the muscles of your hands and arms. Notice the natural curves of the fingers and thumbs.

Now wiggle your fingers and thumbs all around, once with your fingers fully extended and once with them relaxed. Notice how the movements are smoother and easier when your muscles are relaxed, and more difficult when they're tense. Notice the hitch in the movement of the thumb joint when the thumb is extended, and how the movement is smooth when the thumb is curved.

Rest your hands in your lap, palms down, noticing any tension you feel in the back of the hands. Now turn your hands over, not completely flat but resting on the little-finger side of the back of the hands. The thumbs are up, and the palms are open, facing your body but not quite vertical. Alternately turn your hands over in your lap, palms down, then thumbs up, feeling how the tension eases when the thumbs are up.

Use Good Mouse and Trackball Technique

Richard Pekelney has noticed that people generally have two main techniques for moving the mouse. They either station their wrist on the table and use just their hand to move it, or they use the whole arm. Many of us use both techniques, or something in between. Whichever one you use, *avoid holding your arm out too far*. This can cause pain under the shoulder blade, in the neck, and all down the arm. Also, don't use a tight grip.

The stationary technique can increase pressure in the wrist and across the back of the hand; the more you press down and the higher you raise your fingers, the greater the pressure. If you use this technique, rest the wrist on a padded surface and don't press down on it. Keep your hand and arm relaxed.

Tamaribuchi considers the whole arm technique less risky. Hold the mouse with the thumb curved, the wrist lifted slightly, and a little pressure on the tips of the ring and little fingers. To move the mouse, move the elbow, not the wrist. Keep the elbow relaxed.

When you click the buttons, keep your fingers (or thumb) slightly curved and relaxed, and your wrist in neutral position. As with keying, use a gentle touch, pressing and not tapping. Experiment with your device and technique to find the least stressful ways of clicking. For example, on some trackballs, you may be able to use the side of your hand instead of your fingers or thumb.

To roll a trackball, use your index and middle fingers, keeping them slightly curved and directly over the ball (see Figure 10-3). Raising your wrists slightly as you move the ball and using your whole arm instead of just the fingers helps reduce muscle tension in the hand. If your trackball requires thumb use, keep the thumb curved and relaxed, or move your hand so your fingers can roll the ball instead. Pete Johnson advises that you may be better off avoiding trackballs designed for thumb use.

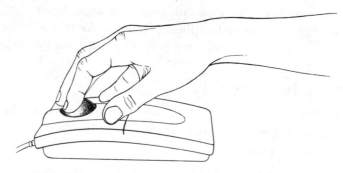

Figure 10-3. Using a trackball

Try using both a mouse and a trackball if your equipment allows it; this lets you take advantage of what each one does best with the least strain. Use the mouse for fine cursor movements, and the trackball for less exacting ones. Switch between them for variety.

If you have difficulty using your hands, use your feet. Some RSI sufferers use a footpedal to click, or roll the trackball with their foot. Footpedals can help eliminate the need to click, hold, and drag all at the same time.

Minimize Clicks and Keystrokes

Take advantage of whatever hardware and software options are available to you for word completion, keyboard shortcuts and macros, and cursor control. Use function keys and easy-to-type key combinations.

Changing direction

time wastes hand and finger movement. Reorganize your comp-
put commonly used files and applications within easy reach. Gary Karp, founder
of Onsight Technology Education Services, advises automating whatever file
management activities you can. For example, using style sheets in a word
processing program can dramatically reduce your keyboard and cursor activity.

Use Just Enough Force

Ruth Lowengart, M.D., recommends reducing the amount of force you use for
typing and other activities. Use an electric stapler or staple fewer things together.
Roll inkstamps instead of pounding them, divide stacks of paper for punching
holes, and hold spring-loaded stamps in a pistol grip with your thumb up.

Grip Firmly but Loosely

Learn to hold things with a relaxed grip, whether it's the mouse, the phone, a
pen, a stylus, a steering wheel, a briefcase, or bicycle handlebars. The tighter the
grip, the greater the pressure.

For writing by hand, use a wide pen or pen grip (a tube that slips over the pen to
widen the grip). Choose pens that glide smoothly across the paper. Keep pencils
sharp and use a soft lead so you don't have to press hard.

Avoid holding paper or other things in a pinch grip between the thumb, index,
and middle fingers. Instead of ripping off the sides of printouts with your fingers,
use a ruler or paper cutter. Keep any binders and folders you work with under
one and a half inches, and be careful when using heavy books.

Judy Matsuoka-Sarina, OTR, CHT, recommends using phones that fit your hand.
Don't overstretch your thumb, and don't cock your wrist back too far, even on a
mobile phone.

Keep Your Hands Warm

Some people have naturally warm hands, but many whose hands run cool find
their hand temperature drops as they type, even when they stretch them
frequently. The colder your hands are, the less blood flows to the tissues.

Keep a hot water bottle or a piece of warm fabric nearby to warm your hands when you take a break. Matsuoka-Sarina advises that putting a heating pad on your neck and upper back can also warm up your hands.

Wear fingerless gloves that cover the wrists, hands, and fingers, leaving the fingertips free to work. To warm the tissues in the forearm and elbow, use gloves that cover the elbow. When you sleep, wear long sleeves to keep your arms warm.

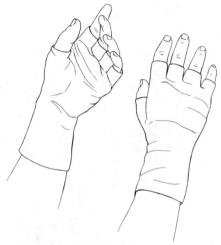

Figure 10-4. Keep your hands warm

Stretch Frequently

Stretch before you start work, just as athletes do before vigorous exercise. Concentrate on your arms, shoulders, and neck, but stretch your whole body, too, for general flexibility (see Chapter 6, *Take Care of Yourself*). Incorporate massage into your routine. Stretch frequently while you work, especially during intensive keyboard and mouse use, and stretch again when you're done.

If you have RSI, don't do any stretch that aggravates your symptoms.

Stretch Your Fingers and Shake Out Your Hands

1. Relax your arms at your sides. Extend your fingers until you feel a stretch. Hold it for a few breaths, and then make a loose fist and relax your fingers. Repeat the sequence a few times.

2. Gently shake out your hands. Keep all the muscles in your hands, arms, and shoulders loose and relaxed—don't snap your wrists or hold your fingers straight and stiff.

Stretch the Forearms (1)

1. Put your hands together in front of your chest in prayer position. Keep the shoulders low and relaxed.

2. Lower your hands until you feel a stretch in the underside of the wrists and forearms. Stretch until you feel it, not until it hurts.

3. If it feels comfortable, press the left hand over the right, bending the right hand back. Press the right hand over the left. Do this a few times. Don't over stretch. Stop and shake out your hands.

Stretch the Forearms (2)

1. Hold your right arm straight out in front of you with your wrist bent back and your fingers pointing up. Keep your shoulder low and relaxed.

2. With your left fingers over the right palm, use your left hand to pull the right hand towards you. Hold the stretch a few breaths.

3. Point the right fingers down, and use the left hand to pull the right hand towards you. Hold the stretch for a few breaths. Stop and shake out your hands.

4. Repeat the stretch for the left arm.

Figure 10-5. Stretch your fingers and forearms

Increase Your Dexterity

Chinese health balls are two balls the same size, usually made of metal, that you hold and rotate in your hand. They strengthen the hands and encourage smooth, efficient movements. Rotate them in one hand five or ten times in both directions, and then switch hands. Keep the wrist in neutral position. Take care not to overdo it. This basic exercise, plus many more designed to promote health and relaxation, are described in Hans Höting's Chinese Health Balls.

Stretch the Shoulder Blades and Upper Back

1. Stand next to the edge of an open door with your left shoulder next to the door and your feet about shoulder-width apart. Brace the door with the side of your left foot if that feels comfortable.

2. Bend your knees, reach across your body, and grab the doorknob with your right hand.

3. Slowly shift weight to the right foot. Bend the right knee more than the left.

4. Leading with the right ribs, turn just your upper body to face the door frame. Let your hand hold you in place.

5. Hang back from the doorknob. Keep your feet and lower body facing straight ahead and your upper body facing towards the door. Sit back with the hips to settle into the stretch.

6. Feel the stretch across the muscles under and around the right shoulder blade. Relax and breathe into that area. Keep sitting back to increase the stretch. Hold the stretch for several breaths or until you've had enough. Repeat the stretch on the other side.

Vary the stretch to loosen the rotator cuff in the shoulder. Instead of turning the body and leading with the ribs, keep your body facing straight ahead and lead with the shoulders, hanging sideways from the doorknob.

Figure 10-6. Increase dexterity and stretch the upper back

forearm into the elbow crease.

Do this three times to cover the center, inside, and outside of the forearm. Push straight down with the heel of the palm to compress rather than stretch the muscles. Avoid leaning into the arm and applying too much pressure. Use the weight of the hand and arm, not of the whole body.

2. Turn the left arm over with the hand on the desk, and repeat the massage on the underside of the forearm.

3. Turn the arm over again to massage the upper arm. Starting at the elbow crease, go up the inner arm, squeezing the muscle between the fingers and heel of the right hand. Massage the shoulder as much as you can. Start again from the elbow and go up the outer arm.

4. Use your fingertips to massage around the elbow crease. Press your fingertips one at a time into the muscles, as if you were walking on them. Start below the crease, moving from the inside out. Walk your fingers across the crease, and then just above it. If you feel a tender spot, rub the spot and the area around it with a gentle, circular motion. End by rubbing the palm in a circular motion over the elbow area.

5. Repeat the sequence for the right arm.

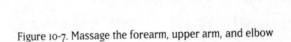

Figure 10-7. Massage the forearm, upper arm, and elbow

CHAPTER

II

Treating the Injury

Medical treatment is essential to your recovery. It relieves pain, reduces inflammation, soothes injured tissues, aligns the joints, and relaxes the muscles so your body can heal. Start the process sooner rather than later. Seek professional help to get an accurate diagnosis and effective care, and take measures on your own to relieve pain.

No matter how effective your medical treatment is, it's not a substitute for changes in the workplace, your work habits, or your daily activities. You need all of these to recover from your injury.

Seek Professional Care

Selecting medical care is a highly personal decision. Choose a treatment that suits you, find a practitioner who is experienced with RSI, and participate in the process—your doctor can't do it alone.

Which Treatment?

"See a doctor" or "get treatment right away" is familiar advice, but the trick is knowing what *kind* of doctor, what *kind* of treatment. Traditional western medicine, traditional eastern medicine, and holistic medicine all have ways of treating RSI. Adjunctive treatments and therapies, such as physical therapy, occupational therapy, biofeedback, massage, and psychological counseling play a part as well. The bottom line is whether the treatment is effective in reducing pain and restoring function.

In the experience of RSI patients, no single method is better than others. People find relief from such diverse treatments as hand therapy, hypnotherapy, and anti-

Choose a treatment you feel comfortable with. If you prefer traditional medicine, start with that. If you rely on holistic medicine, start there, or choose a physician who is open to or utilizes holistic methods. Ultimately, the success of a treatment depends as much on the skill of the practitioner and your own involvement as it does on the treatment itself.

Surgery is not an option to consider lightly. Surgery is not a quick fix for the problem, whether it's to relieve nerve compression or repair injured tendons. Outcomes are mixed. Symptoms may return completely, especially if the person continues behaving exactly as before. Sometimes symptoms persist, but are greatly reduced. Many people still have to limit the use of their hands. For some, the problem goes away entirely and they can return to full activities.

Before you decide on surgery, try preventive measures and other interventions first. In some cases, surgery is necessary and can be helpful. If you get surgery, you *must* make ergonomic and behavioral changes as well or there's a good chance your problem will return. Be sure your surgeon explains the basic procedure, which structures will be affected, the anticipated result, and your chances of full or partial recovery. Don't hesitate to ask questions. It's your body, and you're entitled to answers from your doctor.

Which Practitioner?

Visits to physicians and therapists can be expensive and time consuming, so it's in your best interest to choose carefully. Find care providers who:

- Understand and have experience treating RSI

- Consider all the factors—medical, workplace, and personal

- Conduct a thorough physical exam, looking not just at the painful area but at the whole body, checking for injury from the neck down

- Work with you to find the best ways to treat your injury

- Inspire your trust and confidence

- Believe you

Good rapport and communication are essential. Individuals vary greatly in symptoms and response to treatment, so you need to follow the advice you're given and report your progress, as this determines the treatment's direction.

Choose your primary (treating) physician carefully. Even if the physician doesn't treat you directly, he or she can prescribe or recommend effective therapies, such as occupational therapy, physical therapy, massage therapy, bodywork, acupuncture, or biofeedback. If you have health insurance or if you are in a workers' compensation system, your treating physician is the gateway to all other treatments.

Avoid physicians who:

- View your injury with skepticism

- Take the "wait and see" approach, telling you to do nothing and come back if your symptoms get worse

- Give you a quick diagnosis

- Schedule you for surgery right away

Referrals from other patients can be a good way to choose a physician. Based on the experience of someone's patients, you can decide whether that person sounds like a match. Referral or no, consider talking with the practitioner before you make an appointment. Find out how he or she views RSI, and what you can expect from your visit. The point is not to explain all your symptoms and take a lot of the person's time, but to make sure the type of treatment you will be getting makes sense to you or is a course you want to pursue.

An accurate diagnosis is important for recovery. Doctors have varying backgrounds, skills, and experience, and may interpret signs and symptoms differently. Ruth Lowengart, M.D., notes that a less skilled doctor may think that any pain or numbness in the hand must be carpal tunnel syndrome. A doctor familiar with the relationship of symptoms in the hand to pinched nerves in the neck may more accurately diagnose radicular pain from a pinched nerve. Interpretation of x-rays is also a consideration. Judy Matsuoka-Sarina warns that not all doctors are trained to read x-rays for alignment of the carpal bones in the wrist. Taking x-rays of both wrists for comparison may be helpful, but not all doctors do this. Loosening of ligaments may not appear on x-rays, and doctors may not catch minor misalignments that are considered normal.

Get a second opinion. If you feel comfortable with the diagnosis and treatment you've received, you may not feel this is necessary. If you are the slightest bit uneasy with it, or if you're going the workers' compensation route, getting another diagnosis can be essential, especially for surgery.

Recovery is an evolving process.

Track Your Progress

Record your progress in a journal, on a calendar, or on tape. You don't need a lot of detail, but enough so you remember what you felt when. Include dates and descriptions of medical appointments, phone calls, and conversations regarding your injury. Use body charts to mark painful areas and types of pain—this helps you and your doctor pinpoint symptoms and make an accurate diagnosis (see Figure 11-1). Tracking your symptoms and treatments over time helps you understand how your body responds to what you do. Should you enter the workers' compensation system or apply for disability income, your records will be invaluable.

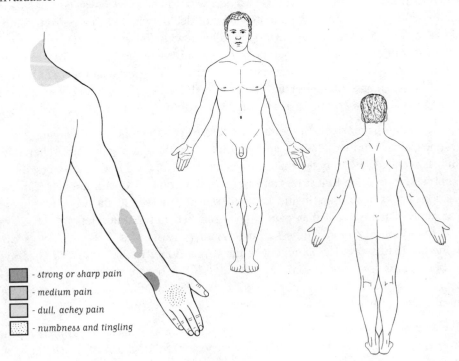

- strong or sharp pain
- medium pain
- dull, achey pain
- numbness and tingling

Figure 11-1. Using a body chart to track your symptoms

Take Care of Yourself

Along with your doctor's care, there's a lot you can do to help yourself heal. Discuss any measures you take with your care provider to make sure you are helping and not hurting yourself.

Use Cold and Heat to Soothe Painful Tissues

Cold reduces swelling and inflammation, and ice relieves pain. Heat increases circulation, flushes out toxins, and aids stretching and flexibility, all of which promote healing and soothe painful muscles. Injuries and individuals vary in response to cold and heat, so you'll have to find what's best for you.

When you apply cold or heat, practice body awareness and relaxation. Feel how the muscles and tendons change with cold or heat. Notice when your hands and arms are tense or relaxed. The more relaxed you are, the more effective the treatment is, and the better the tissues heal.

Applying cold

Using an ice or cold pack at the end of the day or after a long work session can soothe inflamed and swollen tissues. Some people like to apply ice *before* they begin a long work session, before they experience symptoms. A bag of frozen peas is a convenient substitute for a cold pack, and ice made in paper cups is helpful for icing specific sore spots. You can also make a soft ice pack by freezing a mixture of three parts water and one part alcohol in a sealable plastic freezer bag.

Be careful not to apply too much cold for too long, as excessive cold can cause muscle spasms and constrict circulation. If you apply ice, keep it moving over the area for a minute or so at a time. Don't stretch after icing.

Applying heat

Warmth from a heating pad, hot pack, or warm water feels good on tight, achy muscles, and may alleviate numbness and tingling. Moist heat can be deeply penetrating and comforting. Temperatures should be comfortably warm—there's no need to burn yourself. Also, Judy Matsuoka-Sarina, OTR, CHT, warns that too much heat can cause the muscles to dilate and the deeper muscles to shut down. Hot compresses and deep-penetrating salves, such as herbal ointments made from arnica, can soothe pain temporarily.

Contrast baths

Many people find relief from contrast baths—alternately soaking your hands and forearms in basins of cold and comfortably hot water, immersing them completely. Repeat the cycle two or three times, soaking about one minute in cold

Therapeutic massage eases stress and relaxes your ~~~~~~~~~~~~~~~~
to take place. You might notice improvement immediately, or it might take time. A skilled massage therapist can use special techniques such as manual lymph drainage or Swedish lymphatic massage to reduce swelling and soothe injured tendons. Deep tissue, myotherapy, and trigger point massage can help relieve myofascial pain symptoms. Acupressure and shiatsu can also help with specific problems.

You can get therapeutic massage on your own or have it prescribed by your physician. *Choose a well-trained, certified massage therapist who has experience with RSI or other soft tissue injuries.* Be cautious with deep tissue techniques. Listen to your body to determine whether the massage is helping you and whether the technique or pressure applied seems appropriate. If something doesn't feel right, stop it.

Use Medication Only for Immediate Relief

Aspirin, ibuprofen, or anti-inflammatory medications can help reduce swelling over the short term. Use them to relieve pain while you heal, not to continue damaging yourself without pain. Acupuncture may be an effective addition or alternative to medication for reducing inflammation, and myotherapy can help control pain. Arnica ointment or other topical salves may also be helpful.

Your doctor may prescribe nonsteroidal anti-inflammatory drugs (NSAIDs) or corticosteroid injections. Follow the dosage recommendations carefully, and ask about possible side effects. Some of these drugs may adversely affect the stomach and intestines, depress the immune system, or cause headaches, dizziness, and nausea, and may not be appropriate for long-term use. Some physicians recommend blood tests every three or four months to check liver and kidney functions.

Improve Your Nutrition to Strengthen Your Entire System

A balanced diet is the best way to get the nutrients you need. Eat a variety of foods, and use supplements if necessary. Many RSI sufferers recommend quitting or going easy on sugar, caffeine, tobacco, and alcohol as these aggravate symptoms and interfere with healing.

Specific vitamins and minerals may help relieve symptoms. A combination of the antioxidants—vitamins A, C, and E, beta-carotene, and the trace mineral selenium—has been shown to significantly reduce the pain, swelling, and inflammation of arthritis, and may help relieve RSI symptoms.[2] Potassium helps build muscle and is important in cardiovascular and nerve functions. Calcium and magnesium help reduce fatigue, support muscle contraction and relaxation, and relax the nerves.[3]

Vitamin B_6 is sometimes prescribed or recommended by physicians and therapists to help regenerate damaged nerves and ease symptoms of nerve compression injuries. Dr. Elson Haas writes that vitamin B_6 therapy, from 100 to 300 mg daily for 8 to 12 weeks, appears to reduce carpal tunnel syndrome and increase the ability to use the hands in most patients.[4]

If you are already getting enough B_6 in your diet, you may not need to supplement it. Work with your health care provider to determine how much B_6 to take, and how long to take it. The general consensus for the appropriate dose of B_6 is 100 mg per day, either once a day or in two doses of 50 mg. Haas notes that large doses of 2000 mg per day or more can be detrimental and cause more nerve damage.

Vitamins and minerals interact with each other, so changes in the level of one may affect the level of another. Consult a qualified care provider before changing your intake. Some doctors recommend a multi-vitamin or multi-mineral approach, unless laboratory tests show that you have a specific deficiency.

Use Splints Only as Prescribed

Splints help keep your wrist in a neutral position when you work or sleep so you don't cause more damage, and elbow straps can be helpful for treating tennis elbow. Splints and supports can be effective, but they need to be prescribed and monitored carefully to ensure a good fit and appropriate use. *Splints are for treatment only—don't use them without medical supervision, and don't use them for prevention.* This is especially true for hard splints, but be careful with soft splints and support gloves as well.

Splints should allow movement of the fingers and thumb, and not cut off circulation. You can aggravate your symptoms by wearing tight and/or ill-fitting splints, by straining your hands against the splints, or by splinting your wrist at an improper angle. Over-reliance on splints can cause the muscles to weaken and tighten. While many practitioners are skillful at fitting splints, some are not. Many physicians, occupational therapists, and physical therapists feel that a poorly fitting splint causes more harm than no splint at all. Some practitioners even recommend against splinting.

found support gloves to be helpful, not by others. Do not wear tight gloves or bandages since they will cut off circulation and restrict movement!

CHAPTER

12

The Recovery Process

Whether your injury is mild or severe, it will cause you to take stock of your life—a minor injury can affect the smallest details of daily living, and a major one can blow your world apart. It's always there, whatever you do.

Some people, especially those who act early, recover completely. Others regain full or partial use of their hands, though it might take persistence over months or years. Some people have become permanently disabled. Whatever the degree of injury or disability, managing RSI becomes part of your life. Even those who've healed still have to be careful.

The recovery process begins the moment you sit down and say to yourself, "Okay, I'm injured. I'm going to do something about it." There are ups and downs and good cycles and bad cycles. A period of relative calm might be followed by a flare-up. Be patient. You didn't get injured overnight, and it's going to take time to heal. When the ranting and raving is through, you just have to be patient and go through it. You'll discover a lot about yourself as you progress.

The Initial Impact

At this point, you've had your first bout of pain, constant or intermittent, that was strong enough to cut through your defenses and get your attention. You may be off work or have a reduced workload, you've given up anything that might possibly hurt, and you're trying to find a good doctor and a treatment that helps. You're worried about your family, your job, your career, your finances, your future. You hurt, and you're scared. You've got a lot to deal with—your life as you knew it is gone, and you don't know what the new life entails. Mostly you want to be rid of the pain and be able to function again.

This is an emotional time. Fear can terrorize you into action, or ——
to move. Anger consumes the mind and destroys clarity of thought. It generates stress and tension, strains relationships, aggravates your physical symptoms, and increases the pain. Depression wraps you in a fog, dissolving your good spirits and motivation. Despair leaves you feeling helpless and hopeless, and perhaps not even caring if you get better or worse.

These emotions are normal responses to trauma, but when you dwell on them, they take energy away from healing. By developing a desire and commitment to get better, you use their energy to your advantage. Transform fear into kindness toward yourself and motivation for getting better. Use the spark of anger to overcome the dullness and confusion of depression and despair. Believe you can recover. Meditation, relaxation techniques, stress reduction programs, and psychological counseling can help you through this. One sufferer describes his own emotional struggles with RSI:

> For about six weeks, at the depths of my tendinitis, my left forearm and hand 100% disabled, I found that my ego was a real mess. I no longer had the ability to do software work at anywhere near the speed I had only a month before. It gave me a feeling of "career impotence." Even after I had mostly recovered, I still had a semi-conscious fear of taking on a big software merge, or a project like this. After I got the Kinesis keyboard and rediscovered what it was like to type without any pain, this fear was gone, as was the feeling of "impotence" at being unable to type with both hands. In addition to the career/technical ego-fears that severe RSI caused me, it didn't do much for my personal life. I couldn't hug my wife with both arms, or do anything with the left arm/hand. The inability to do most household chores and gardening or cleanup or whatever was a drag. At first I couldn't even go jogging—the impacts from running caused too much tendon pain in my arm! I would suggest finding a psychologist or therapist to discuss these things with, if you keep feeling bummed out.

Getting Your Life Back

As you progress, other challenges emerge and demand attention. Margaret Phillips, manager of Occupational Therapy at San Jose Medical Center in San Jose, California, notes that social changes happen fast for RSI sufferers. People who were once independent now find themselves in need of care. Some experience profound spiritual shifts. People's finances can be devastated—workers' compensation and disability income seldom make up for lost salaries. Relationships with friends, family, and lovers change. Your perception of yourself changes, and your self-esteem can take a beating. Along with all this, you're still dealing with doctors and treatments and insurance carriers. It can all be very frustrating. Examine these personal accounts:

> The latest in my treatment saga is the possibility of a rheumatoid arthritis diagnosis. I felt gypped when I saw all the arthritis brochures at the hospital with photos of people age 50+ while I just celebrated my 23rd birthday this year. I'm clinging to very little these days, and while my usual professional demeanor suffices in the outside world, it's tough to keep a stable mind when I'm at home with my spouse and kitten. I tend to crash when I walk through the door. The system doesn't seem interested in much more than my medical condition and some dollar signs, so I'd really like to locate the resources that can help me become a person again instead of just a patient.

> Driving to and from New Jersey messed up my hand. I had to shift a lot because of all the traffic. My hand was so messed up that I had to drive several miles off the highway to find a full service gas station because I couldn't squeeze the handle to pump it myself. The chiropractor mentioned that I might want to think about getting a car with automatic transmission. I talked to my shrink about it. I just don't want to give up the control, the feeling of really driving. My ego doesn't want to admit that I may have to live with this disability. I resent having to even think about making major accommodations to this alien hand from planet RSI. I don't want to give in to it.

Seek Out Services and Support Groups

Turn to fellow RSI sufferers first—they're the experts. Support groups for RSI sufferers exist or are forming in many locations. Participants invite guest speakers, discuss effective treatments, legal issues, new equipment, tips for working and living, and generally share their experiences. Newsgroups on the Internet and electronic bulletin board services provide similar support online.

Many services are available to disabled people. Some telephone companies provide speaker phones, and some utility companies offer discounts. Organizations for people with disabilities can give you more information.

If you find yourself needing to change careers, you might benefit from career counseling. Vocational rehabilitation programs may or may not be of use—many are not prepared to handle injured computer workers, though they're learning, and you could try asking them to help you devise your own plan. Thousands of dollars in retraining are often available through these programs.

Cultivate Patience and a Positive Attitude

A positive, relaxed state of mind contributes to healing. Use patience and optimism when you approach your manager or human resources representative to ask for equipment, furniture, or job changes that will relieve your symptoms and

you enjoy. Stop chastising yourself for not doing
enough. Be patient with your recovery process. Gary Karp discusses his own recovery efforts:

> Looking back, I see that I overdid my effort at recovery! I surrendered everything, when I could have juggled a bit, gone out more, even played the piano for a couple of minutes without compromising my healing process. Instead, I brought on more loss and depression, which truly interfered. Keep what you can!

Caroline Rose, editor of the *RSI Network* newsletter, recommends setting reasonable goals upon returning to work. Don't make your goal your pre-RSI level of productivity; instead, just aim for improving your productivity from where it is now.

Be Kind to Your Hands

Don't force your hands to do a lot when they hurt. Go at their pace—they'll tell you how much they can do. Try not to get angry with them or do too much too soon. Massage them. Soothe them. Thank them for serving you so well for so long. The better you treat your hands, the more they'll cooperate with you.

Pace Yourself

Whatever you're doing—work, typing, art, music, exercise, housework, shopping, hobbies—pace yourself. Take a lot of short breaks. Rest *before* you get tired. This is tricky, since pain and symptoms often don't set in until you've finished, when it's already too late. Use the breaks to give yourself creative boosts. At first it seems difficult, but it's really just a matter of changing habits and learning your limits, as Carina Chiang explains:

> You can view your job as a type of physical training—you need to pace yourself and your job for better performance, like an athlete, so you don't "overtrain." You need to be proactive. Set a manageable number of tasks to do.

Rose recommends using a software program, like *Lifeguard*, to make sure you aren't doing too much. Be your own monitor. Only you know what your symptoms are, how bad they feel, and when you're pushing too hard. Your boss will never come by and say, "So Janet, I notice you have a burning sensation in your forearm and your hands are feeling stiff. Better go take a break!" Keep yourself from overdoing it, whether "it" is work, exercise, or any activity in which you use your hands and arms. Examine these quotes from a San Francisco RSI support group meeting:

> That's the scariest thing about it, because I don't get the pain when I'm doing something. It's only after I've overdone it when I think, oh no!, I must have done too much typing or lifting or whatever.

> Listen to your body. Do self-hypnosis. I'm a classic type-A, anal retentive, go-getter, obsessive, maniacal person, and I need these techniques to help me learn to relax and stop before I do myself in.

Let Pain Be Your Guide

Pain is your body's way of telling you something's wrong. Pain that lingers often indicates damage and tells you you've overdone it. Discomfort, pain, or soreness after exercise or activities may be acceptable and harmless if it goes away in a day. Learn to distinguish between hurt and harm—a slight twinge doesn't necessarily mean you need to stop immediately. Discuss this with your doctor or therapist.

Learn to Do Daily Activities Differently

Look closely at how you do even the simplest activities to see if you are aggravating your symptoms, and take your injury into consideration. For example, if vibration aggravates your symptoms, then don't ride around on a motorcycle every day of your vacation, or do home improvements with hand-held power tools. Here are a few suggestions for everyday activities:

- Wear padded bicycle gloves for bicycling and driving.
- Put pen grips on pens and toothbrushes.
- During airline travel, wear a neck pillow to support your head.
- Instead of holding and reading a book, use a book stand or prop, or listen to a book on tape.
- Wrap cloth tape around the handles of tools and appliances.
- Use products that minimize twisting, pinching, gripping, and force, such as electric can openers and other appliances.
- Quit shaving.
- Use two hands to lift heavy things.
- Use leverage instead of strength.

Many more tips for making life easier can be found in the *RSI Network* newsletter, Lauren Hebert's *Living with CTD*, Emil Pascarelli and Deborah Quilter's *Repetitive*

assistive technology—computer equipment ~~~ traditional keyboards and pointing devices. Speech recognition systems can keep you working even if you can't type much. Software self-monitoring tools help you pace yourself. Use a tablet instead of a mouse for graphics applications.

New equipment may seem expensive, but it could mean the difference between working and not working. You make the choice. These expenses are often covered by workers' compensation or your insurance carrier.

Exercise

When you are first injured and experiencing severe pain, your first instinct will probably be to stop all activity and simply rest. Rest is necessary to allow the injured tissues to calm down, but rest by itself doesn't heal. Dr. Rene Cailliet explains that in the long run, exercise benefits injured soft tissues. Prolonged inactivity decreases blood supply, encourages weakness and atrophy of muscle tissue, causes bone decalcification, and brings about debility, dependence on drugs, despondency, and depression.[1]

If you do nothing else, walk and stretch to keep up your circulation, strength, and flexibility. When you move, your blood moves, your body heals, and your mood improves. Eventually, you'll work up to more vigorous exercise. One recovering person could eventually go river rafting with no pain, another resumed juggling after reluctantly giving it up, and another built back up to swimming a mile.

As you go through the healing process, the way you exercise will change. When you have acute, severe symptoms, exercise as soon as you can. Begin slowly. Don't push yourself too hard, but don't shy away from increasing your activities, either. A little soreness and pain are okay if they're gone the next day. Discuss appropriate exercise with your care provider.

Avoid exercising in ways that bring on symptoms. If you swim, switch strokes frequently, and use a kickboard sometimes to give your hands and arms a rest. If you bicycle, wear padded gloves. If you walk or jog, wear shock-absorbing shoes. If you do yoga, don't do postures that strain the neck, arms, or wrists.

Stretch for Flexibility and Circulation

Stretching is the foundation for strong, flexible muscles, tendons, ligaments, and joints. It keeps the injured area moving, increases blood flow to it, and maintains its range of motion. Stretch gently, taking care not to overstretch. Even a little bit helps—just opening and closing your hand several times a day can be therapeutic. Stretch not just the injured hand or arm, but your whole body. Try the stretches suggested in Chapter 10, *Good Hand Technique Reduces Your Risk*, and Chapter 6, *Take Care of Yourself*, or do stretching routines that you already know. Check them out with your care provider to make sure they're appropriate for you.

Strengthen the Muscles—Carefully

Strengthening is important, but if you do too much too soon or use too much weight or resistance, you can easily re-injure yourself. To be safe, do general conditioning instead. Elizabeth Klein, OTR, CHT, CWA advises *doing strengthening exercises only when you've had little or no pain for at least two weeks and the injury is well on its way to being healed.* Even then, be careful. If something hurts, stop doing it.

Build up your condition slowly. Exercise to fatigue but not pain. Squeezing a soft foam or rubber ball or stretching a rubber band with your fingers strengthens your hands gently. Tai chi, chi kung, and yoga build strength without the use of weights or resistance. Discuss strengthening exercises with your care provider before you do them.

Re-Learn How to Move

Some RSI sufferers learn to change deeply ingrained habits of moving, sitting, and holding muscle tension that contributed to their injury. Two popular methods for this are the Feldenkrais and Alexander techniques. John Lamp, in a posting to the sorehand Listserv newsgroup in December of 1993, noted that in Australia, physiotherapists who used the Feldenkrais technique during the 1980s had more success with their patients than those who did not. Other types of bodywork are helpful as well, and biofeedback can be useful for understanding the effects of specific movements. Tai chi, chi kung, and yoga can also improve your body mechanics.

Coming Out of the Tunnel

Over time, you'll probably find that you can do more and hurt less. You might still have pain, and you might have flare-ups, but you'll be able to put them in perspective and know what to do when they happen. You might pick up where you left off, or try a completely different path. Maybe you have a new career,

managed muscle

uses an ergonomic keyboard, wears fingerless gloves, tries not to
and now works without pain most of the time.

- A former vice president of a small company is now recovering from bilateral
  tendinitis and nerve compression injuries and has started his own consulting
  business. His positive outlook, commitment to healing, use of an ergonomic
  keyboard, software monitoring tools, and speech recognition system all help
  make it possible.

- A former technical writer is now editor-in-chief of a corporate magazine. She
  still has symptoms of tendinitis in her hands and shoulder, but has learned
  how to pace herself, manage her injury, and participate at least occasionally
  in favorite hobbies, like playing the flute.

- A former switchboard operator, still partly disabled from tendinitis and related
  upper body weakness, finished her bachelor's degree and went on to grad-
  uate school while continuing her medical treatment. She gets help from her
  school's disabled students' center, tape-records lectures, and modifies her
  study techniques and daily routines to include good use of her hands and
  arms.

Coming out of the tunnel has as much to do with your state of mind and heart as
it does with your physical recovery. You'll know you're there when you look
back on your ordeal with peace of mind and appreciation of your new life,
knowing how bad it was and how far you've come.

Legal Concerns

If you are disabled by RSI from your work, you have legal rights to certain health
care benefits and disability payments. In the U.S., the primary source is the
worker's compensation system, a government program administered by states and
supported in part by insurance premiums paid by employers. You may also be
eligible for Social Security payments.

Standing up for your rights is often a complicated and frustrating process.
Although this is a pressing issue and there are many questions, a full discussion is
beyond the scope of this book. This section offers a few general suggestions for
journeying into a workers' compensation system, and summarizes your rights

under the Americans with Disabilities Act (ADA), relatively new legislation that has already helped many RSI sufferers.

Government systems for compensating workers injured on the job vary from country to country and state to state. For more detailed coverage of the legal issues in the U.S., see *Repetitive Strain Injury*, by Emil Pascarelli and Deborah Quilter, and *Your Rights in the Workplace*, by Dan Lacey. For a list of agencies worldwide, including a description of what each one does, check the International Labor Organization's *International Directory of Occupational Safety and Health Institutions, Occupational Safety and Health Series, #66.*

Workers' Compensation

When the conversation among RSI sufferers turns to workers' compensation, it often spirals downward into a confusion of details and tales of frustration. The system is set up to handle clear-cut injuries and one-time trauma, not conditions like RSI that are ambiguous, difficult to diagnose, and lengthy to treat. It knows how to handle a hand that's cut off, not a hand that's still there but no longer functions.

Some agencies are helpful and cooperative, while others take an adversarial stance from the outset. As the number of disability claims for RSI grows worldwide, agencies may change the way they handle RSI. It's in your own best interest to understand the laws—and interpretation of the laws—regarding RSI and disability compensation.

Know where you're going

Find out about your particular workers' compensation system *before you get involved in it*. Equipped with knowledge, you are much more likely to have a positive experience, and more able to watch out for yourself. Find out which agencies you need to go through, and find out *from them* what their requirements and regulations are, and what you are entitled to. If the first person you talk to doesn't seem to know what's going on, or if you're still confused, keep talking to more people until you feel you have a good understanding of what you need to do.

Choose your treating physician *before* you file a claim. Otherwise, your employer's insurance agency assigns one, and you may not be able to switch easily, even though you have the right to do so.

Ask directions

Put aside any desire to go unassisted. Those RSI sufferers who've gone ahead of you are experienced, and you can avoid a lot of problems by learning from their mistakes and triumphs. There's no need to struggle alone—if you're applying for

Think twice about hiring an attorney

The system is complex, and some people have found that hiring a workers' compensation attorney from the beginning can save a lot of trouble. A good attorney can make sure you start out with all the right forms, a crucial step. If you disagree with your treatment, or if you're not being treated fairly, you may need an attorney. Attorneys are listed by specialty in the telephone book under workers' compensation, personal injury, and social security.

An attorney can also be an obstacle. Once you're represented, you're not allowed to talk directly with your insurance adjuster, and your lawyer may not have the time or incentive to do so. The presence of a lawyer may escalate an adversarial relationship. Collins Flannery, an experienced RSI sufferer, suggests that if you're articulate and willing to do the research, you'll probably be your own best advocate.

Keep a journal

Watch out for yourself. In a system that goes by specifics, you're better off keeping track of them for yourself. Keep a log of medical symptoms and treatment. Log all phone calls regarding treatment, insurance, and legal matters. Record all out-of-pocket expenses. Don't assume the system will act in your best interest. It may, or it may not. Events won't always proceed by logic. Keeping good records helps stack the odds in your favor and helps the system help you, like it's supposed to do.

Don't give up

There are often difficulties along the way. In some cases, your employer, doctor, or insurance company may suspect you of "secondary gain"—of using the system to get out of an unpleasant job, or to get money for doing nothing. While it's true that some people do try to take advantage of the situation, for the majority this is simply not the case. Be prepared for suspicion, but also be aware that you cannot legally be fired for filing a claim.

Many claims, no matter how valid they are, are refused the first time. Keep filling out the forms and filing the claims—your efforts will pay off in the long run. Deep frustration with an unwieldy system is not uncommon. If you hit this stage, make good use of your support network. Many people have been through this and can offer invaluable assistance.

Share your experience

Contribute in whatever way you can to the groups and networks that helped you, or pass along the knowledge you've gained. Help smooth the way for those who follow.

The Americans with Disabilities Act

If you have become disabled by RSI, you may be protected from job discrimination by the Americans with Disabilities Act (ADA) or similar legislation. Agencies and organizations devoted to assisting people with disabilities can help you find out about your legal rights and the services available to you. In the words of the ADA, you are protected if:

- You have an impairment that substantially limits a major life activity, including performing manual tasks; *and*

- You are qualified to perform the essential functions of the job with or without reasonable accommodation.[2]

Essential functions are the fundamental duties of the job. Reasonable accommodation is any change or adjustment to a job or work environment that permits you to do the job, including providing or modifying equipment or devices, job restructuring, and part-time or modified work schedules.

Changes such as these can be inexpensive and easy to make, and can make the difference between your being able to work or not. Talk to your health care provider for suggestions. The Job Accommodation Network (JAN) can also give you suggestions for making changes. For more information about the ADA, contact the Equal Employment Opportunity Commission (EEOC) or the Disability Rights Education and Defense Fund, Inc. (DREDF). Addresses and phone numbers are listed in Appendix B, *Resources*.

Eyestrain

If you don't learn anything else about eyestrain, be aware that:

- Computer work places great demands on your eyes. It requires your eyes to focus at an unchanging distance on a reflective surface, reading imperceptibly flickering text. The air near your computer is dry and filled with dust particles. Computer work often "hypnotizes" you—leaving you staring without moving or blinking.

- You can give your eyes (and your stress level) a real break if you remember to move, blink, yawn, and look into the distance several times an hour.

- Your office may be too brightly-lit for working comfortably at a reflective computer screen. Position your equipment to avoid bright spots in your vision from lights, sunlight, or reflections. Turn lights off or down to the level of light that you need. Shade or screen bright light from windows.

- Computers alone do not cause eyestrain. You can often make changes and do exercises to improve your visual comfort. Get regular vision checkups from an eye doctor who knows about your work situation.

13

Eyestrain Is Common

Computer jobs have all the visual demands of traditional office work, plus new demands from the computer technology. The more hours you work, the more likely you are to strain your eyes. If you already wear glasses, you're even more at risk. Eyestrain is pervasive—almost seventy-five percent of computer users experience it.[1]

Many of us seem to have a great tolerance for eyestrain. It's more irritating than debilitating, so we just rub our eyes, plunk in a few eyedrops, and keep going. But there's a lot more to eyestrain than sore eyes. Visual comfort affects productivity, physical comfort, susceptibility to RSI, and mental health and well-being.

When you relieve eyestrain, you also relieve stress and relax your body. There's a lot to figure out at first, but the solutions are straightforward and easy to implement. Once you start making changes, the benefits come quickly. When your eyes feel good, you feel good too.

Symptoms Can Be Mild or Severe

Eyestrain can be mild or severe, occasional or constant. It might come on early in the day and build slowly until you just don't want to look at the screen anymore, or it might hit you only after a project is completed. Symptoms might go away after an hour or two of rest, or persist into the evening with some residual tension the next morning. If you start out day after day with your eyes already a little tired, your symptoms may get progressively worse.

Sore Eyes

The obvious symptoms of eyestrain are sore, tired, red, dry, watery, itchy, burning, gritty, or otherwise uncomfortable eyes. The muscles around the eyes

When your mind, your eyes, and the muscles that support them are overworked, your vision starts to slide, too. Your vision gets blurry, or you have trouble changing focus, or everything looks jittery. Instead of moving smoothly, your eyes get stuck and jump in fits and starts. The world may appear flat and colors dull. You may sometimes see double or have trouble keeping both eyes focused on the same spot. Your visual field narrows, and you perceive less and less in your peripheral vision.

Computer work tends to make existing eyestrain or vision problems worse, or bring out problems that aren't noticeable in the less exacting visual tasks of daily life. This is especially true of *presbyopia* (difficulty focusing close up). Some people may already have it, but aren't bothered by it until they start doing the demanding close work of computing.

Headaches, Mental Fatigue, and Lowered Productivity

Sore eyes and muscle tension often lead to headaches and general mental fatigue. Concentration and mental clarity decline, accuracy drops, and you become less productive and less interested in your work.

Eyestrain May Be Related to Other Problems

Eyestrain has repercussions beyond the eyes, and influences posture, muscle tension, and levels of stress. The influence is reciprocal. Poor posture, tight muscles, and high stress can all increase eyestrain.

Stress

Forcing your eyes to keep working even when they hurt, or exposing them to glare, drafts, and air pollution can trigger the stress response and increase tension throughout your body. In the view of Chinese medicine, stress weakens the liver and kidneys, organs that strongly influence the health of the eyes and the musculoskeletal system. Imbalances in these organs interfere with your vision and increase your susceptibility to RSI and other ailments. Stress and eyestrain feed on each other—they can be both cause and effect.

Stiff Neck, Tight Shoulders, and Poor Posture

Many people who have eyestrain also have a stiff neck and tight shoulders, usually from poor posture and awkward head positions. When your eyes hurt or you're straining to see—whether it's because of the positioning of the equipment, blurry characters on the screen, or the prescription of your eyeglasses—you move your head forward or back to see better, which takes you out of neutral posture.

Lighting has a strong effect—if something is too bright, you squeeze your eyelids shut and turn your face away from it. You tilt your head and hunch your shoulders to see around a reflection on the screen. You may unconsciously tighten your muscles when you work all day under harsh, glaring lights. Poor posture and muscle tension reduce blood circulation to the eyes and brain, depriving them of the oxygen and nutrients they need. This increases eyestrain, which again encourages awkward head positions. It's a vicious cycle.

RSI

Although the relationship between eyestrain and RSI has not been studied, eyestrain may well be associated with RSI. Injuries often originate in the neck, possibly from hunched, tight shoulders and poor posture. If you can't see the screen well using good posture, you'll compromise your posture in order to see properly. The poor posture you fall into and the resulting muscle tension in the neck and shoulders could be contributing to RSI. Relieving eyestrain could restore neutral head posture, ease the tension in your body, and therefore help you prevent or recover from RSI.

What About Eye Disease?

There is little evidence that computer work causes serious eye disease, including glaucoma, cataracts, and retinal detachment. Most studies have found that eyestrain and visual distress from computer work are reversible and usually go away with rest. Many users have, however, experienced deteriorating vision that does not go away. The most common complaint is progressive myopia—increasing nearsightedness over months or years of computer work. Long-time contact lens wearers sometimes reach a point where they can't wear their lenses comfortably for computer work. Some eyeglass wearers start having trouble getting a prescription that really works for them.

Though the prevailing opinion among researchers and optometrists is that the computer itself is not the cause, these problems could stem from the visual demands of computing, combined with poor ergonomics and a person's way of seeing. Some people are concerned that radiation from computer screens may cause eye disease. This connection has not been established, and many researchers believe that computer radiation does not harm the eyes.

Video games are a bigger problem, and have ~~~~~~~~~~
tible people. Tolerance levels vary—some people can play them for one or two hours without problems, while others can play only for a short time or not at all. The Nintendo Company issues warnings with their products, advising people with a known epileptic condition to consult a physician before they play the game.

Computer Work Affects the Entire Visual System

Vision is a product not just of the eyes, but of the muscles, eyes, brain, and mind working together. The various eye muscles direct the eyes where we want to look, control the amount of light coming in, and change the curvature of the lens to focus the light rays in the eyes. The light receptor cells in the retina convert the light to nerve impulses and send them, via the optic nerve, to the visual centers in the back of the brain. The brain creates the visual images, and the mind perceives, interprets, and responds to what we see. (See Figures 13-1 and 13-2.)

Using a computer causes us to use our visual system in an imbalanced way. The eyes are confined to detailed, close point work, and typically move more than twice as fast as they do for traditional office work.[2] Such fast, exacting movements and constant close focusing tire the muscles, narrow the visual field, and make no use of far point and peripheral vision skills.

Computer work encourages staring and discourages blinking. These habits make your eyes dry and sore, and can also make you feel detached and spaced out. Using eyeglasses that are the wrong prescription intensifies the strain and can give you headaches.

The whole computer environment is hard on the eyes as well. Office lighting often overloads them with glare, flicker, and extremes of bright and dark. The brain processes these harsh images, while the mind tries to ignore them. The screen may be another source of glare, reflections, and flicker, and can make close work more difficult if the characters are blurry or hard to read. Office air may expose the eyes to dryness, dust, and pollutants.

The Eye Muscles Work Hard

Computing requires fast, coordinated eye movements for focusing, reading, fixating, and following moving images. Your eyes are busy with these tasks the

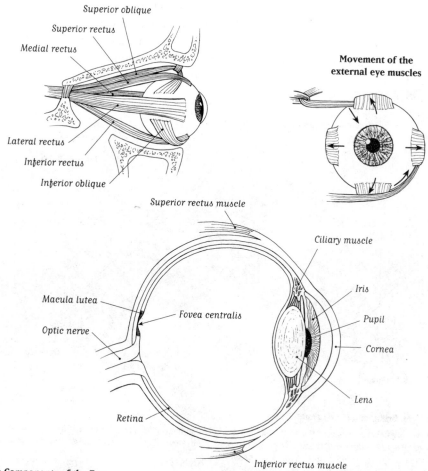

Superior oblique
Superior rectus
Medial rectus
Lateral rectus
Inferior rectus
Inferior oblique

Movement of the external eye muscles

Superior rectus muscle
Ciliary muscle
Iris
Macula lutea
Fovea centralis
Pupil
Optic nerve
Cornea
Lens
Retina
Inferior rectus muscle

The Components of the Eye

The **cornea** is the clear, transparent outer coating of the eye. It has a role in refracting light rays. The **lens** refracts incoming light rays to focus them on the retina.

The **ciliary** muscle holds the lens in place and changes its curvature for focusing.

The **iris** is the colored part of the eye surrounding the **pupil**, the black opening that lets light in. The muscles of the iris control the aperture of the pupil. The pupil contracts with more light and for focusing on a near object, and expands with less light and for focusing in the distance.

The **retina** is the light-sensitive lining of the inside of the eyeball. It contains 137 million photoreceptor cells called rods and cones.

Rods detect movement, form, and very low levels of light. **Cones** detect detail and color. Most of the rods are spread out across the retina, with a few cones interspersed.

The **macula lutea** is a small area of the retina that contains mainly cones and only a few rods. The **fovea centralis** is a tiny pit within the macula, filled with densely packed cones.

The **external eye muscles** move the eyes up, down, inward, outward, diagonally, and around.

Figure 13-1. Musculature and components of the eye

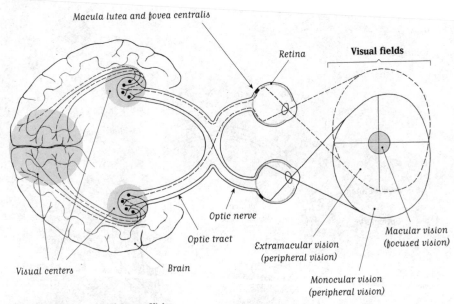

Macula lutea and fovea centralis

Retina

Visual fields

Optic nerve

Optic tract

Brain

Visual centers

Extramacular vision
(peripheral vision)

Macular vision
(focused vision)

Monocular vision
(peripheral vision)

The Eyes, Brain, and Mind Create Vision

The eyes are light receptors for the brain. They convert incoming light rays to nerve impulses and send them via the optic nerve to the visual centers in the back of the brain. The brain creates the visual images, and the mind perceives, interprets, and responds emotionally to what we see.

Visual fields. The visual fields of the right and left eyes overlap. In the center is the area of greatest clarity, color, and detail. Away from the center, we detect movement and form. We rely on images from all areas of the visual field to get a complete picture.

Focused vision. Light from the center of the visual field—from the exact part of the object we are looking at—is directed to the fovea centralis and macula lutea, activating the cones. The fovea is the point of our clearest vision, where we detect the smallest of details.

The macula gives clear vision just around the fovea. We use macular vision for reading and similar tasks.

Peripheral vision. Light from the rest of the visual field is distributed across the retina, activating the rods. When there's not enough light to activate the cones, we rely on rod vision, seeing in black and white and picking up movement and form. When we look directly at a speck of dim light in the dark, it disappears-its light rays are directed to the fovea, but there isn't enough light to activate the cones, so we don't see it.

Reflections on the screen can interfere with accommodation. Your eyes tend to focus on the reflections, so there's a constant struggle to maintain focus on the screen image instead of the reflection, or to see around the reflection. This can also be annoying, distracting, and stressful.

Figure 13-2. The visual system

Seeing clearly close up

When you look at a computer screen, you are continually focusing on words and images within a few feet of your eyes. You need good *visual acuity* to see them clearly, and good *accommodation skills* to change focus between near and far. The iris muscles change the pupil size to let in the light from the object, and the ciliary muscle adjusts the curvature of the lens so the light rays bend and converge on the retina. The muscles relax for focusing in the distance, and contract for focusing close up. The closer the object, the more effort required. The longer you maintain close focus, the greater the strain.

During a long session of computer work, the ciliary muscle gets tired and the near point (the closest distance the eyes can focus) moves further away. Your eyes want to relax and focus in the distance, so you need even more effort to keep your eyes focused, and your eyes get even more tired. Some people respond to the strain by overfocusing, as if the screen were closer than it is, and draw the muscles in even tighter.[3] After a session, the ciliary muscle may need several minutes to relax and return the lens to its normal position, making distant objects temporarily blurry.[4]

Changing focus up close

For some tasks, you need to continually change focus from screen to hardcopy, from screen to screen, or from window to window on the screen. Some people also look back and forth between the keyboard and screen, especially if they use function keys often or don't touch type. This is constant shifting between various near points, often without a relaxing glance into the distance.

Changing focus this way keeps the eye muscles moving, but in strained positions. Over time, it becomes more difficult to change focus between near and far. Instead of being quick and smooth, movements of accommodation are jerky and slow. Look from this page to a point across the room and back. How are your eye movements? We need to change focus periodically to keep the eye muscles limber, but we need to change from near to *far*, not near to near. Close focusing can also be difficult if the lens becomes stiff, as it often does with age.

Reflections on the screen can interfere with accommodation. Your eyes tend to focus on the reflections, so there's a constant struggle to maintain focus on the screen image instead of the reflection, or to see around the reflection. This can also be annoying, distracting, and stressful.

Reading and scanning text

Much computer work involves reading and scanning text. Reading requires thousands of *saccadic movements*, tiny jumps from word to word, and a sharp return to the beginning of the next line. Reading on a screen is more difficult than

mouse-intensive text ~~~~~

moving the pointing device, we fix our eyes on the exact spot where ...

insertion point to be. We rely on *vergence movements* to hold both eyes simultaneously on a single point. These minute adjustments line up the eyes so their
gaze meets at the same spot. To see something near, the eyes turn inward. To see
something far, they look ahead.

When the eyes are aligned, the brain can fuse the separate images sent by each
eye, creating a single image and giving us depth and distance perception. If these
movements are not balanced, we see double. Maintaining vergence for prolonged
close work takes muscular effort. For people whose eyes tend naturally to look
inward (esophoria) or outward (exophoria), the close work of computing tires the
muscles even more.[5]

Following moving images

Often the eyes have to follow moving images and scrolling text. For smooth
tracking movements, the muscles must be flexible and agile. Tracking is more
demanding up close, for long periods of time without rest.

Glare and Bad Lighting Overload the Retina

In a computer environment, we are exposed simultaneously to light from the
computer screen and some combination of overhead lights, lamps, and windows.
Shiny surfaces expose us to bright reflected light as well. The screen itself may
reflect glare and objects from around the room. Your workspace might have
extreme contrasts between light and dark, as from bright white walls, a black
desk, and dark carpet.

Extreme changes in light strain the *adaptive process* of the eyes, distorting the
signals the brain uses to discern shape and form—contrast, shading, and changing
levels of brightness. We experience glare when the eyes attempt to adapt to the
brightest of lights. The retina, like film, gets overexposed and the images we see
are washed out and unclear. Flickering light repeatedly overexposes the retina.

Alternately looking between bright spots and dark spots, such as from white
paper to a dark computer screen and back, can keep the eyes in a state of
perpetual "adaptive catch-up"—the eyes take longer to adapt to darkness than to
brightness, so they never get a chance to fully adapt to either. You end up

looking at the dark area with your eyes adapted for the bright one, and look back at the bright one just as your eyes start adapting to the dark one. It can go on like this all day.

Occasionally people who use dark monochrome screens with green letters see a pink or red after-image after a long work session (the McCullough effect). This happens when the cone cells that detect green are temporarily overloaded, and goes away when you rest your eyes.

Flicker Tires the Eyes and the Brain

The eyes are an extension of the brain—whatever the eyes notice, the brain processes, whether you're aware of it or not. The eyes register not only minute and continual changes in brightness, contrast, and color, but the slightest movements of light as well—if the screen or lights flicker, the eyes notice. At the same time, the muscles around the eyes and face get tight from squinting against bright light. You may train your mind to tune out undesirable visual stimulation, but your brain still has to deal with it. Many people attribute their migraine headaches, irritation, and loss of concentration to glare and flicker.

Flicker is extremely tiring. You may not see it when you are looking directly at the screen or the lights, but you notice it on the edge of your vision when you turn your eyes away. If you do much data entry or work where you mainly look at paper documents, you could be picking up a lot of flicker. Flicker might come from fluorescent lights, a single screen, or two screens right next to each other (closer than two feet). Old or defective fluorescent lights and older monitors with low refresh rates are the biggest offenders. Flicker may also show up as a strobe effect on people or objects moving through the room.

Even imperceptible flicker can increase tension on the biological level, since the brain recognizes it when the mind does not. This may be one reason why it's so hard for us to tear ourselves away from the screen to take a break. When the screen flickers, however slightly, the brain receives the information as movement and is drawn to it.

We Neglect Our Peripheral Vision

The anatomy of our eyes gives us focused (central) vision for seeing color and sharp detail, and peripheral vision for detecting movement and low levels of light. By joining the specific and ambiguous images of focused and peripheral vision, we get a complete picture—movement, form, color, detail, dimension. These ways of seeing correspond to how we understand the world.

Focused vision is associated with our conscious mental processes of reasoning and logic. We look directly at something and see it clearly, detail by detail. Periph-

rarely required. As we put more and more ~~........~~
one task at hand, we get more stressed and tired and our peripheral awareness
shrinks. This narrowing of the visual field a measurable indicator of fatigue. With
it can come a corresponding mental narrowness and a sense of diminished possibilities. We may even get in the habit of using focused vision (and logic) for all
situations, even when peripheral vision (and intuition) would serve us better.

It's Easy to Develop Bad Vision Habits

Working at a computer doesn't automatically give you bad vision habits, but it
certainly encourages them. They creep in and take root without your even
knowing they're there. The eyes are drawn to the screen as it radiates light,
catching you with barely perceptible flicker. We're all susceptible—have you ever
noticed where people's eyes go first when they enter a room with a powered-on
computer screen?

As you work away and your concentration grows, your eyes become fixed on the
screen, your body rooted in the chair, your hands attached to the keyboard. All
your attention goes into the screen and you stay there for hours, staring at it, not
moving your eyes away for even a fraction of a second, afraid you'll lose your
train of thought. You become tense, and forget to blink and breathe deeply. Your
shoulders hunch up to your ears, your head gravitates toward the screen, and
neutral posture goes out the window. The longer you stay there, the harder it
becomes to break away, the deeper the tension goes. It takes a conscious effort to
pull some of your attention back to your eyes and body.

Solutions Involve the Environment, the Equipment, and You

To prevent or relieve eyestrain, you need to address the major causes:

- The way you use and take care of your eyes

- The visual comfort of the screen and software

- Air quality, color, and visual variety in the office environment

- Lighting conditions

You may have to experiment for a while before you come up with a solution that works. It's an ongoing process of modifying habits and making changes to your equipment and work environment.

C H A P T E R

14

Take Care of Your Eyes

Though we all rely on our eyes all the time, we rarely consider that the *way* we use them influences how they feel and how well they see. We have a way of seeing, just as we have a way of walking or talking, and our visual system thrives or declines because of it. Working on a computer makes it easy to develop ways of using our eyes that ignore their need for relaxed movement, lubrication, oxygen, and nutrients. These habits become so ingrained that we're hardly even aware of what we're doing.

Taking care of your eyes is easy. All you have to do is:

- Make sure your posture is good.

- Pay attention to how your eyes feel.

- Learn a few good vision habits and some ways to relieve sore eyes.

- Get your eyes examined.

- Make sure you've got the right prescription lenses for your work.

- Keep your glasses or contact lenses clean.

- Use assistive technology if it helps you.

When you use your eyes well, you augment the positive effects of any other changes you make to reduce eyestrain. You don't have to spend a lot of money on equipment and you don't have to ask your boss for special permission. You can just do it.

cutting off their vital supply of oxygen. Slumping your shoulders and upper body intensifies the effect. Moving your head when it's out of neutral posture puts an additional strain on your neck, eyes, and shoulders.

It's easy to fall into these postures if your screen is too high or too far away, if the characters are too small to read easily, or if you are trying to see the screen through the bottom part of conventional bifocals. You may twist your head sideways and down to read papers flat on your desk, or bend your head down to see a screen that's too low or to look at the keyboard or function keys as you type.

To keep your eyes and body comfortable, you *must* arrange your equipment so you can see the screen and documents comfortably *and* maintain neutral posture—especially neutral head posture. The positions of the monitor, documents, additional screens (if you have any), and the keyboard all determine where you put your eyes, and in turn, how you hold your head, neck, and body. All of this is described in Chapter 2, *Get Comfortable*, and Chapter 3, *Customize Your Work Area*.

Use Your Eyes Well

How do your eyes feel right now? Are they rested? Relaxed? Moist? Dry? Irritated? Sore? Start noticing how your eyes feel throughout the day, what they respond to. *As soon as you notice strain, stop and take care of your eyes.* Better yet, take care of them *before* they hurt. As with RSI, it's easy to ignore the initial signs and keep working; like most pains and strains, the more you work through them, the worse they get. While the result may not be as drastic as with RSI, it can still make your eyes extremely uncomfortable, and can interfere with your visual pleasures outside work as well, such as watching movies, reading, or doing any hobby that requires close, detailed work.

How do you use your eyes? Do you fixate on one spot and stare? Do you hardly ever blink? Do you squint and strain to see? Do you hold your breath or breathe shallowly when you work? These are all habits that cause eyestrain. Changing them isn't difficult, but it does require conscious effort at first. The basic activities and exercises described here give you the foundation for reducing eyestrain if you already have it, and preventing it if you don't. From there, you can go on to enhance your vision and really enjoy your visual sense.

You may find that your vision actually improves when you change the way you use your eyes. If you notice that your eyeglasses or contact lenses are too strong, or if they start giving you headaches, have your optometrist check your prescription and change it if necessary.

Learn Good Vision Habits for Ongoing Comfort

One of the easiest ways to keep your eyes comfortable is to practice good vision habits—yawning, blinking, breathing, seeing without staring, and relaxing to see. Yawning oxygenates the blood and lubricates your eyes. Blinking cleanses and moistens them. Full breathing relaxes you. Seeing without staring and relaxing to see get your eyes moving and help you break the tense, forward-leaning stare encouraged by computer work. They help keep your eyes in shape, just as regular stretching and exercise keep your body in shape.

You can practice these habits any time. For example, breathe and blink before you answer the phone. Take off your glasses and look around the room while you talk, tracing objects and looking near and far. Stand up or lean back comfortably in your chair as you talk. Breathe, blink, and maybe yawn a few times after you hang up. After a while, you may find yourself doing these vision habits automatically.

Take frequent, short vision breaks throughout the day. If you like, use a software self-monitoring tool to help you remember. Karl G. Nyman, M.D., recommends walking away from your desk for a few minutes every fifteen minutes to give your eyes a rest from reading. Even a ten-second break to blink, breathe, yawn, or look around is helpful.

Keep your screen and eyeglasses clean. Your eyes don't need the added hindrance of looking through fingerprints, smudges, and dust.

Give Sore Eyes Immediate Relief

Palming and *self-massage* can relieve tense, tired, burning eyes right away. Do them when you notice fatigue setting in, or to recover after a long session. As a preventive measure, do them *before* your eyes start hurting or any time you feel like it—throughout the day, after work, when you wake up in the morning, or before you sleep at night. Short, frequent palming can be very helpful. Figure 14-1 describes palming and some basic self-massage techniques for your head, face, and neck. *Never rub or press against your eyes when palming or doing massage.*

Compresses and *eyewashes* soothe, cleanse, and moisten the eyes. To make a compress, dip a cloth either in water or in a weak herbal infusion (e.g., of eyebright, pot marigold, cornflowers, or strawberry leaves), wring it out, and apply it to your eyes, eyelids closed. Compresses can be hot, warm, or cool,

Palming

Sit comfortably with your elbows supported on your desk, or lie down with a pillow under your elbows. Rub your hands together to warm them. Place your palms gently over your eyes, eyelids closed, fingers resting on your forehead. The palms should fit over the eye sockets only—do not touch your eyelids or press against your eyes. Relax into the darkness and warmth of your palms and breathe. Imagine a pleasant scene or just relax. Keep your hands and arms relaxed.

Acupressure massage

Some of these points may be sore or tender at first or if your eyes are very tired. Be firm but gentle, and ease up if it's painful.

1. *With your thumbs, massage the hollows just above the inside corners of your eyes, below where your eyebrows begin. Use small circular motions.*

2. *Use the thumb and index finger of one hand to massage the points on each side of the bridge of your nose, next to the corners of your eyes.*

3. *With your index fingers, massage the points on your cheekbones about an inch or so below the center of each eye where there is an indentation. Put your thumbs on your chin to brace your hands.*

4. *Use the knuckles of your index fingers to massage the points along the bony ridge of the eye socket. Start above the eye by stroking your finger across the eyebrow from the inside corner out. Then stroke the ridge below the eye from the inside corner out.*

5. *Squeeze and knead your eyebrows with your thumbs and index fingers. Go back and forth across your eyebrows, inside to out and back in again.*

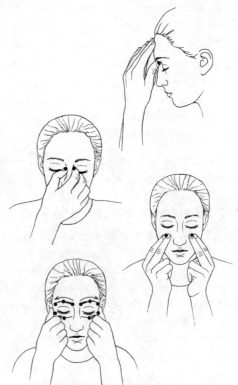

Figure 14-1. Give sore eyes immediate relief

Head, face, and neck massage

Using a circular motion with your fingertips, gently massage your whole face—forehead, temples, scalp, eye sockets, bridge of the nose, nose, cheeks, hinge of the jaw, jaw bone, above and below the lips. Massage the base of the skull, down your neck, and across your shoulders.

Tap your fingers gently all over your head, including the face, around the eye sockets, and the base of the skull. Continue the finger pats down to your neck and shoulders.

Head and face relaxation

Put your elbows on the desk and rest your head in your hands. Put the heels of the palms just underneath the cheekbones, not directly on top of them. (This is different from palming.)

Relax your cheekbones into the heels of your palms, close your eyes and breathe. Rest here for a while, or continue to deepen the relaxation.

Put your attention on your forehead, feeling the muscles relax. Let the relaxation soak down to your eye muscles, loosening them. Feel your eyes held gently in place by the muscles with no excess pressure. Feel the force of gravity on them as they settle into perfect spheres. Let the relaxation move down the face to the jaw, loosening and unclenching the jaw muscles. Feel the jaw hanging, suspended only from its hinge. Feel the neck and shoulder muscles loosen and relax.

Figure 14-1. Give sore eyes immediate relief (Continued)

whichever feels better. Alternate between warm and cool or steaming and cold. For eyewashes, use an eyecup to bathe your eyes with an over-the-counter preparation or weak rosewater infusion.[1]

Many people use *eyedrops* throughout the day to relieve strained, red, dry eyes, or to keep contact lenses lubricated. Eyedrops can help, though some have chemicals that can cause allergic reactions, and some people find them to be habit-forming. You may be able to eliminate or reduce your need for eyedrops through yawning, blinking, palming, and self-massage.

You can also use an *eye pillow* to cover your eyes, block out the light, and give your eyes a complete rest. Eye pillows are usually made of silk or cotton and filled with lightweight husks or pellets.

Sunning is also a good way to relax tired eyes. Sunning is always done with the eyelids closed.

Enhance Your Visual Abilities

By practicing specific visual skills, such as shifting focus from near to far and opening your vision, you can go beyond reducing eyestrain and actually enhance your vision, not just for computer work, but for all your other activities as well. You can learn more in vision training programs or in any of the several books available on vision improvement.

Enjoy Your Visual Sense

Vision is not just eyesight, but a *sense*—almost three-quarters of all our sensory experience comes through our eyes. The perceptions of movement, form, color, and space belong to vision. They augment our mental processes of imagination, attention, intuition, and memory, and are deeply connected with our awareness of beauty, energy, and aliveness in the world.

As your eyes start feeling better and your vision improves, you may notice that the world looks different, more vibrant, full of life, colorful, and three-dimensional. Some people find that their powers of memory and attention become stronger, and the ability to visualize images and colors and space improves.[2] Try to explore and enjoy these qualities of vision.

Enhancing Your Visual Abilities

Shifting focus from near to far. Focusing on objects at various distances improves your skills of focusing and accommodation. As you practice shifting focus, *keep breathing and blinking.*

Toss a ball, following its movement with your eyes and head as it goes up and down. Bounce it off a wall or play catch with a friend, following the ball as it comes towards you and goes away.

Choose something interesting to look at in the distance. Imagine holding a loose rope in front of you that extends between your hand and the distant point. Follow the rope out slowly, smoothly, and continuously from your hand to the distance and back. For variety, choose a few points along the rope to stop and blink and breathe, or imagine the rope winding its way out, and follow its curves into the distance and back. Close your eyes and do the same exercise with your imagination.

Sunning. Always done with the eyelids closed, sunning increases your tolerance to light and improves your adaptive abilities. It's also very relaxing. If the sun is too bright, use a bright incandescent bulb, keeping your face at least one foot away. Never use a halogen bulb or a sunlamp for sunning.

Keeping your eyelids closed, turn your face towards the sun or lamp and move your head slowly from side to side, up and down, in diagonals, in circles. Feel the light warming your eyes, loosening your muscles. Breathe.

Take Care of Your General Health

Your eyes are intimately connected to your internal organs, your psychological state, and your emotions. Yoga teaches us that the kidneys, liver, stomach, and intestines all regulate body processes that affect ocular health and vision.[3] Your health and mental states are reflected in the color and appearance of the eyeball, cornea, and iris; the size of the pupil; the speed and agility of eye movements;

Open your vision

We see best where we put our attention. By learning to shift your attention between focused and peripheral vision, you expand both your vision and your awareness.

Get two pencils of the same bright color and hold them together in front of you. Notice their color, shape, texture, and any other details about them. Slowly move them apart, keeping your attention on the pencil in your left hand. Notice that the image of the left pencil stays clear and detailed, while the image of the right pencil becomes softer and more ambiguous.

Keep your focus on the left pencil and shift just your attention to the right pencil. Notice how you perceive it. Its color is less bright and its form less sharp, but you are aware of it. Breathe calmly and blink. Notice whether your eyes want to change focus to the right pencil. Move the right pencil around—up, down, above the left pencil and below it. Be aware of where it leaves and enters your field of vision. Put the right pencil down and move your attention around your entire visual field, expanding your awareness of the surrounding space and objects within it—even behind you. Stop to palm and rest your eyes.

Try a similar exercise with your hands. Hold them together in front of you, and then slowly move them out to your sides. Keep your focus in front of you, and notice how far out you can see the images of your hands.

When you're walking or riding in a car, fix your gaze on a point just above the horizon. Shift your attention and let the landscape enter your mind through your peripheral awareness. Blink and breathe.

and the look of the eye—whether it is clear, dull, bright, glassy, alert. Vision fluctuates with the state of your eyes, mind, and body. When you eat well, stay in shape, reduce stress, and work reasonable hours, your body feels better, your mind is clearer, your eyes stay healthier, and your vision improves.

Vision Training

You can strengthen and develop these ways of using your eyes through vision training—educational programs designed to enhance your visual skills, teach you good vision habits and hygiene, and reintroduce you to your visual sense. At the very least, you learn how to reduce eyestrain and make your eyes feel more comfortable. Training can often prevent or reverse vision problems. Through it, many people have improved their eyesight and reduced their dependence on glasses. Some have actually regained their acuity and no longer need corrective lenses.

Various methods are available—most include some or all of the suggestions presented in this book and explore them much further. Traditional vision training (or vision therapy) is taught by behavioral optometrists, who use it in conjunction with their usual optometric methods. Syntonic optometrists may include light therapy in treatment. Natural vision improvement programs take a holistic approach to healing and improving eyesight.

Get Your Eyes Examined

Working on a computer is a special occupational use of your eyes, and for many people this means specially prescribed eyeglasses. It's a good idea to get your eyes checked periodically if you do a lot of computer work, especially if you already wear glasses. Even if you don't wear glasses, consider the visit preventative. A yearly exam helps you detect emergent problems so you can take care of them right away. You may even be able to regain your clear vision through ergonomics and changing your vision habits—glasses may not become necessary at all, or you may only need them when your eyes are very tired. If you are just starting to work with computers, get an eye exam early on, and pay attention to how your eyes are doing.

Optometrists and ophthalmologists examine your eyes to determine their physical health, their visual abilities, and which lenses are appropriate, if any. Given information about your job requirements and working conditions, they can prescribe lenses that let you see clearly and comfortably at all the right distances. Behavioral optometrists can also help you with vision training to help you relieve eyestrain. Choose an eye doctor who is familiar with the visual demands of computers.

What Information Should You Bring to the Appointment?

Your eye doctor can help you best if you supply the following information:

- The distance between your eyes and the screen for all the postures you use (reclined, upright, or forward)

- The distance between your eyes and the keyboard

- The distance between your eyes and your hardcopy

- How much of your job involves looking at the screen, the hardcopy, and into the distance

- The number of hours you spend working on the computer

- What your physical work environment is like—lighting, air quality, positioning of the equipment, posture

- The qualities of your screen—does it flicker? Is it clear and easy to read? Does any aspect of it seem to bother your eyes?

- Your symptoms—what are they? When do they start? What brings them on? How long do they last? Do they go away in the evenings and on weekends? What seems to help them?

What Should the Eye Exam Include?

The eye exam should check your ocular health and the visual skills you use for computing, including:

- *Visual acuity*—how clearly you see up close and in the distance

- *Focusing abilities*—how well your eyes accommodate

- *Vergence skills*—how well your eyes work together

- *Peripheral vision*—how wide your visual field is

Many eye doctors do consider your working environment when testing your vision and prescribing lenses. Even so, most eye exams cannot recreate your exact working environment. Your visual acuity on the eye chart won't necessarily be the same as it is at work, especially if your screen has poor resolution and blurry characters. Visual acuity is better with good lighting, good contrast, and dark symbols on a light background.[4]

Vision fluctuates with changing conditions—you may start out seeing just fine at the beginning of the day, and be in a blur by evening. You may see well in bright daylight, but not indoors under artificial light. Your vision may deteriorate with stress, and improve with relaxation. Also, acuity and speed of accommodation both tend to decline with age.

Use the Right Glasses for the Task

Because computers make special demands on your eyes, conventional eyeglasses are not always appropriate for computer work. They may even cause eyestrain and poor posture if they are too strong or too weak for reading the screen. Bifocals designed for reading are not right for computing—they make you hold your head backwards in a fixed position to see through the bottom portion of the lens, which is often the wrong prescription for the screen. This gives you both eyestrain and a stiff neck.

Specially designed monofocal, bifocal, trifocal, and variable focus lenses are available for computer work, and many people find them much more comfortable. Some contact lens users wear glasses over their contacts for computer work. Decide with your eye doctor which computer glasses are best for you. The choice

Vision Habits for Ongoing Comfort

Yawning. A few good yawns will relax your jaw and face, put more oxygen in your blood, and get your eyes watering. Yawning helps lubricate and cleanse dry eyes and dry contact lenses. If you can't get any yawns going, fake a few and real ones will come. Gently massage the hinge of the jaw with your fingertips, moving them in small circles. Slowly open your mouth a few times as wide as it will go. Stretch your arms up, open your chest, take a deep breath in, and yawn. Blink, breathe, and yawn again and again.

Blinking. Blinking once every three to five seconds cleanses and lubricates your eyes. Start with three long, complete blinks. Close your eyelids gently—don't squeeze them shut. Keep them closed long enough to feel your eyes relax. Open them briefly and close them again. After three long blinks, start blinking normally. Make sure you close your eyelids completely every time you blink.

Breathing. Any full breathing exercise described in Chapter 5, *Breathe* helps your eyes. For extra benefit, imagine breathing through your eyes, feeling the eyeballs move in and out with each breath.

Seeing without staring. Practice moving your eyes and head to see. Staring is a sedentary, constrained posture for your eyes. When you stare, your eyes and your head are locked into one position, and your neck muscles stiffen up. To loosen things up, get your eyes moving. Unglue them from the screen and look around, and let your head move, too. When your eyes lead, your head follows naturally. When you look at something that isn't directly in front of you, turn your head and your eyes to see it, just like you would turn in your chair to reach for something. When you move your head, make sure it is aligned over your spine.

Move your eyes and head to visually trace the outlines of shapes and objects in the room—doorways, windows, furniture, the plant on your desk, the edge of your screen, or anything you see, close to you and further away. Follow moving objects with your gaze—birds or cars or animations or the cursor on the screen. Exaggerate the movements at first to get the idea, and then make them more subtle.

Relaxing to see. Straining your eyes and head forward to see encourages staring, and discourages breathing and blinking. Soften your focus. Let your eyes relax back into your head and let the images come to you. When you lie down on your back, imagine your eyes floating, perfectly round, towards the back of your head.

depends on your distance from the screen, your visual acuity, and how much of your job you spend looking close up, at the screen, and in the distance. Use your computer glasses just for computer work, and switch to your regular glasses the rest of the time.

Whatever type of computer eyeglasses you use, they should have these qualities:

- The prescription should be based on the distance between your eyes and your work (screen, papers, and/or keyboard).

- The design of multiple focus lenses should let you see your work clearly without causing you to hold your head in an awkward posture.

Computer Glasses for Nearsightedness (Myopia)

Nearsighted people can see clearly up close, but have blur in the distance. In *myopia*, the eyeball is elongated. This causes the lens to bend the light rays too much, so they converge in front of the retina and the image is blurred. If you are very nearsighted, your glasses may be overcorrecting you for computer work. Glasses with weaker monofocal lenses ease the strain by giving you clear vision just for the screen and your papers.

If you need to see clearly in the distance while you work, and if switching glasses is inconvenient, bifocals might be helpful. The top third of the lens would be stronger for distance viewing, with the middle and bottom portions weaker for screen viewing. If you are only mildly myopic and can see the screen comfortably without glasses, then work without them. Use your regular glasses when you need to see clearly beyond the screen.

Computer Glasses for Farsightedness (Hyperopia and Presbyopia)

Farsighted people see clearly in the distance, but have blur close up. In *hyperopia*, the shape of the eyeball is too flat, so the lens can't bend the light rays enough and the image comes into focus behind the retina. In *presbyopia*, the lens becomes stiff with age or lack of oxygen and nutrients, and doesn't bend easily to refract the light. Some nearsighted people also become presbyopic and need glasses for both distance and close viewing. Because computer work requires so much close-range viewing, it can be very frustrating and tiring for farsights.

If you don't need to see clearly past the screen, monofocal or bifocal computer glasses would probably work for you. Otherwise, trifocals or varifocals might help. In varifocal lenses, also called progressive addition lenses, the focusing power changes gradually, usually from distance focus on top to progressively closer focus at the bottom. Varifocals may have some distortion in the lower portion of the lens, and may not always be appropriate. If you can see clearly in the distance without glasses, consider monofocal lenses just for computer work, or bifocals with the prescription only in the part of the lens you use for viewing the screen.

Computer Glasses for Astigmatism

In *astigmatism*, the cornea is warped and bends the light rays unevenly, creating blurred, distorted images. Near- and farsightedness are often compounded by astigmatism, so correction for astigmatism is added to the lens prescription.

Sunglasses and Tinted Lenses

Don't use sunglasses for computer work. They may lessen the glare from over-head lights, but they also reduce the brightness and contrast you need on the screen. You're much better off reducing glare through other means, such as re-arranging your work area, or shading overly bright lights or windows (see Chapter 16, *Work in the Right Light*).

Wearing tinted eyeglasses may have the same effect as wearing sunglasses, though to a lesser degree. Some eye doctors recommend them, others don't. Color tints change the balance of the light rays entering your eyes, and could have subtle emotional or physical effects that we don't fully understand. If you want tinted lenses, discuss your options with your eye doctor. Neutral gray is a conservative choice since it reduces the light intensity in the most balanced way.

A Note on Wearing Glasses

All eyeglasses, however well-prescribed, are an *aid* to vision, not a substitute for it. They are wonderful devices that help you see clearly what would otherwise be a blur, but they have their drawbacks, too. Wearing glasses can inhibit eye, head, and body movements, consciously or unconsciously. Many people stop moving to see through a specific part of the lens (especially with bifocals and trifocals), or to be sure the glasses stay put on their face.

Glasses can be annoying if you continually see reflections in the lenses or pick up the image of the frame in your peripheral vision. Antireflective lenses are extremely helpful and worth the extra cost.

Having glasses resting on your nose and ears all the time can be physically irri-tating and uncomfortable, especially if the frames don't fit you well. If they have become crooked or too loose or too tight, go to your optician to get them adjusted.

Take off your glasses frequently, even for a moment or two, to rest your eyes and let them see on their own. Let your eyes roam. Note what you *can* see instead of what you can't see—light, color, and texture may come alive for you. Do some of the eye exercises described in this book. At first this may be uncomfortable if your eyes are unaccustomed to moving and seeing without glasses. This isn't surprising—the body might complain at first, too, when you start exercising after being sedentary for a while. In the long run, your eyes will be more relaxed and comfortable with or without your glasses.

Dirty, scratched lenses interfere with your vision. Get in the habit of cleaning your glasses when you first start working in the morning, and again in the afternoon. Keep a soft cloth and lens cleaner by your desk so it's easy to remember. If your lenses have a lot of scratches, polish or replace them.

Hints for Contact Lens Wearers

The comfort of contact lenses varies. Some people have no complaints, others use a lot of lubricating eye drops, and others have to take their contacts out and use glasses for computer work. The biggest problems with contact lenses are dryness, redness, and reduced blinking, which can leave your eyes with a gritty feeling. When you don't blink enough, the eyes are continually exposed to dust or airborne particles and don't have enough lubrication to wash them away. The lenses may also become dirty or cloudy sooner than usual.

Contact lenses can deprive the eyes of oxygen, causing redness and soreness. Rigid gas-permeable contacts let in the most oxygen. Soft lenses (regular, extended wear, or disposable), with their high water content, let in more than regular hard lenses, but not as much as gas-permeables. Soft lenses are initially more comfortable to wear, but gas-permeables may be better over the long haul. Consult with your eye doctor to see which lenses are appropriate for you.

Increase the Comfort of Your Lenses

Clean your contacts frequently. (Wash your hands first).

Clean your lens case every week or so.

Put your contacts in before you apply lotion or makeup, and remove your lenses before you wash them off.

Go without your contacts for at least an hour or so every day. Take them out at night, even if you use extended wear lenses.

Practice frequent blinking, yawning, breathing, and palming.

Make Use of Assistive Technology

If your vision is such that eyeglasses and contact lenses cannot give you enough correction to easily do computer work, don't despair. *You do not have to give up computing because of severe eyestrain or vision impairments.* Software products are now available that enlarge the entire screen image, or use voice output to read off what's on the screen (some systems require additional hardware for audio). If you are using print enlargement, you may wish to use a large screen, such as a 21- or 27-inch monitor, so you can display an entire page of text in large print. Under the Americans with Disabilities Act (ADA), your employer may be required to provide assistive technology as reasonable accommodation for you to do your job (see Chapter 12, *The Recovery Process*).

CHAPTER

15

Create a Visually Comfortable Environment

Your visual environment includes everything you look at—your screen, your software, your office surroundings. It also includes the quality of the air that touches your eyes, which affects their comfort and your general health. Office lighting is a major environmental factor, and is described in Chapter 16, *Work in the Right Light*.

Use a Screen with Good Visual Qualities

The screen is your visual connection to the computer. You look at it almost all the time you're working, so you want to be sure it isn't hurting your eyes. Screen technology is always changing and improving, and various text-only terminals, graphics monitors, and flat panel displays are now in the workplace. The qualities you need for visual comfort are the same for all of them. If your screen has the following qualities, you're in good shape:

- Lack of flicker and a fast refresh rate

- Sharp, clear graphics

- Good contrast

- Easy to read text

- Pleasing, comfortable colors

- Plenty of work space and fast response time

- Lack of glare

Whether you use your computer intermittently or work long sessions with your eyes glued to the screen, these qualities can make all the difference between comfortable viewing and eyestrain.

The Screen Must Not Flicker

The picture you see on your screen is constantly in motion, even when you're not typing. Every fraction of a second, the image is redrawn so that it doesn't fade out. The speed at which it's redrawn is the screen's *refresh rate*, given in Hertz (cycles per second). The faster the refresh rate, the less flicker there is, and the less likely you are to experience eyestrain, headaches, stress, and irritation from your screen.

People's sensitivity to screen flicker varies. You might think a screen is flickering, but someone else might not. Maybe you only see the flicker when you look away from the screen. Sometimes flicker is more visible on large, bright parts of the screen, as in Windows applications.

What Makes a Screen Flicker?

Video display terminals (VDT). In displays that use a cathode ray tube (CRT), images are created and redrawn when an electron beam lights up the phosphors on the inside of the screen. The electron beam sweeps across the back of the screen, lighting up the phosphor coating pixel by pixel. Color monitors use three electron beams that converge on each pixel to create colors. Color screens and screens with light backgrounds need higher refresh rates.

The electron beam scans each horizontal line from top to bottom. A screen that uses non-interlaced scanning has less flicker because the beam scans every line on every pass. On screens that use interlaced scanning, the beam sweeps alternate lines on each pass. This technique is sometimes used to make a slow refresh rate seem faster, but it can make the image jitter and may not eliminate flicker. For a screen to be flicker-free, the refresh rate must be at least 76 Hz and use non-interlaced scanning.

Flat panel displays. Flat panel displays don't flicker like VDTs do. To create the screen image, they use electrodes instead of an electron beam, and various substances instead of phosphor (either liquid crystals, zinc sulphide, or neon gas, depending on the technology). When voltage is applied to the electrode, the substance lights up each pixel.

Other causes of flicker. A CRT screen might flicker if it's near fluorescent lights or building wiring. Two screens side by side may flicker, depending on the interaction of their refresh rates. Fluctuations in a screen's power source or problems with the refresh mechanism can cause the images to jitter or drift. These problems can be helped by using surge protectors and performing proper screen maintenance.

We notice flicker anywhere between 50 and 80 Hz. A refresh rate of about 92 Hz would probably be considered flicker-free by even the most sensitive people. Rolf Ilg, Dipl.-Ing., notes that we may be better off with refresh rates of 100 to 120 Hz, due to our unconscious perception of flicker. Old screens typically have refresh rates of 50 to 60 Hz, and some have even more noticeable flicker when they get hot or if they have not been maintained. The more common rate now is 76 Hz, while some screens have refresh rates of over 100.

Images Must Be Sharp and Clear

The eyes like strong, sharp edges to focus on. When we look at a blurred line, the eyes compensate by adjusting their own focus. If your screen has blurry characters and lines, your eyes will constantly be working to bring them into focus— an impossible task. Because screen images are made up of tiny dots, called *pixels*, and not solid, continuous lines, the edges of text and graphic objects are never totally sharp, though some screens come close. Curves and diagonal lines show the dots the most. Characters and lines are clearest when the screen can group many pixels close together—high *resolution* and high *pixel density*.[1]

The Screen Should Have Good Contrast

Good contrast enhances both visual comfort and comprehension. Follow these suggestions for best contrast and readability:[2]

- *Use a screen with a light color background and outer casing.* In most offices, this ensures a smooth visual transition between the area you are working on, the edge of the screen, the frame around the screen, and the surrounding area. This avoids extremes as you go from the most contrast in the center of your visual field to less contrast further out.

  Try not to cover the edge of the monitor with notes to yourself, and don't use a border with fancy designs and bright colors. Keep that area clear to avoid visual distractions so close to your eyes and work. Add the variety further away.

- *Use black text on a paper-white background.* This is important for jobs that require a lot of screen work and high legibility. Many people find dark text on a light-color background comfortable to work with.

  If you have a dark screen, you are more likely to have problems with extreme contrast and reflections, especially if the general office environment is bright and you look back and forth a lot between the screen and white paper documents. For good contrast with dark screens, you need a generally darker environment—reduced lighting and dark surrounding colors.

- *Adjust the brightness and contrast controls.* The screen should have separate controls so you can adjust each one for yourself (within the manufacturer's guidelines).

Producing a Clear Screen Image

Resolution, pixel density, and screen size. Resolution refers to the number of pixels per line—a screen with 1152 882 pixels has 1152 pixels per horizontal line, and 882 per vertical line. Pixel density is the number of dots per inch (dpi). The denser the pixels, the less space between them, and the more solid the image. Screen size affects pixel density—a 19" screen with a resolution of 1152 882 has a pixel density of 82 dpi, while a 21" screen with the same resolution has a pixel density of 74 dpi. The characters seem less sharp on the larger screen because the pixels are more spread out.

Focusing mechanism. VDTs should have a dynamic focusing mechanism so the electron beam can focus sharply on all parts of the screen (center and edges). If the beam focuses well only on the center, characters on the edges look blurry. If the focusing mechanism isn't working properly, the entire screen may be out of focus.

Phosphor quality. Fine-grained phosphors create well-defined, clear lines, while course-grained phosphors create fuzzy ones.[a] Long-persistence phosphors continue to glow for a while after being struck by the electron beam, and may leave ghost images when you scroll and the screen is updated. This is most common on older monochrome screens with green phosphor and a dark background. Ghost images can be annoying and interfere with the legibility of the newly displayed characters.

---

a. *Screen Facts.* Stockholm: TCO (The Swedish Confederation for Professional Employees), 1991. 4.

Text Should Be Easy to Read

Whether you work primarily with words or with graphics, any text you read on the screen should be clearly legible. This depends mainly on the shape, size and distinctness of the characters. Check to see whether the text in your programs and on your system follows these guidelines:

- *Character shapes should be simple, distinct, and well-proportioned.* The strokes that make up the characters should be strong and clear. Decorative, cursive, and stylized fonts are pretty, but make text-intensive work visually stressful.

  Mixed case text is easier to read than all upper case, since the varying shape of the letters gives the words distinct, recognizable shapes.

Characters are formed within a dot matrix of pixels. The more pixels, the clearer the character. A dot matrix of 7 x 9 pixels is usually sufficient, but you need 11 x 14 for good quality character shaping.

Characters should be slightly higher than they are wide for good proportion. For distinctness, they should have true ascenders and descenders (the parts of the letters that extend above and below the letter, like the lines in the letters "b" and "p"). On some older screens, the descenders don't go below the line, so the letters are harder to read.

- *The characters should be big enough for you to see comfortably at arm's length from the screen.* The Swedish Confederation of Professional Employees (TCO) recommends characters between 3.5 to 4.5 millimeters in height.[3] The space between characters must be at least as much as the width of the character strokes, but you might want to use different sizes, depending on your visual ability and on how far you are sitting from the screen. Small characters need better contrast. Don't use tiny letters for your working text.

- *Text should be spaced evenly and distinctly.* Characters shouldn't run into their neighbors, and the tops and bottoms of lines should not merge with each other. Words are hard to read when the letters are too close together, and begin to lose their shape and distinctiveness when they are too far apart.

The ability to zoom and change character sizes and styles on your screen is a great advantage—it gives you flexibility to change postures and work closer to or further from the screen without compromising your vision, or to zoom in for detailed work and zoom out for an overview. Experiment with your system and software to see what they let you do. Some options are provided in hardware (either in the screen, the computer, or a graphics card), and some in either the system or the application software.

The Screen Should be Big Enough and Fast Enough

Whether you work with text or graphics, the screen should be big enough to accommodate your work. For intensive work that requires high legibility, the TCO recommends that your screen should measure at least 14 inches diagonally.

For text-based applications, such as desktop publishing, the screen should hold at least one full page of text. A screen that displays two full pages helps reduce scrolling and paging through the document, and gives you a good, overall view (though larger screens take up more of your visual field).

For graphics applications, the screen should display the entire graphic image you are working on. The screen should also be fast enough to redisplay the text and graphics rapidly and without lingering images. Larger screens need more processing power to achieve a fast response time. In general, flat panel displays are slower and smaller than regular screens.

The Screen Should Have a Good Anti-Glare Treatment

Effective glare protection neutralizes glare and reflections without compromising the brightness and clarity of the screen image—it doesn't darken the screen too much and it doesn't make the characters blurry. If your screen has good glare protection, you will probably not need to use an additional glare filter, and you will be less constrained in how you arrange your office.

With good anti-glare treatment, brightness from a troublesome lamp or overhead fixture may barely show up on the screen. Various methods are in use—some screens are etched or roughened, while others are coated the way camera lenses are. Some screens are made of special non-reflective materials. Anti-glare treatments are getting better all the time.

Screen Colors Should Be Pleasing and Comfortable

In general, monochrome screens are visually more comfortable than color screens, though it depends on other qualities, too. A flicker-free, high-resolution color monitor will probably be more comfortable than a flickering, low-resolution monochrome screen.

Everyone has a different perception of which screen colors are the most comfortable to work with. However, there are some general guidelines that can help you use colors in ways that are most restful for your eyes.

Use a mid-range color for text on a monochrome screen

On monochrome screens with dark backgrounds, green, amber, or white characters seem brighter, clearer, and more comfortable than blue or red ones. On color screens, overlaying blue and red creates a three-dimensional effect, which may be good in certain applications but annoying and visually stressful in others. We perceive these effects because of the way our eyes process color.

Colors are light rays of different wavelengths—blues are the shortest and reds the longest. The eyes refract each wavelength differently, so each color comes into focus at a slightly different depth. Blue light is refracted the most, and comes into focus in front of the retina. Green, yellow, and orange light is focused pretty much on the retina, and red light behind it. The mid-range colors appear sharpest, while blue and red appear slightly out of focus. Blue gives a nearsighted effect and red a farsighted one.

Use balanced colors on color screens

Color screens give you hundreds of choices. Use these suggestions to help you find colors that give you the most visual comfort.[4]

- *Use pastels and avoid bright, saturated colors.* For long-term viewing, deep, bright colors become visually stressful, while pastels are much more relaxing. Avoid dark colors for window backgrounds, although they are acceptable for the screen background.

- Use blues and greens for background, and yellows and reds for foreground.

- *Use only three major colors and the shades within them.* Too many colors on the screen can be visually overwhelming and detract from the work at hand.

Use Software That's Easy on Your Eyes

Software visually organizes the interchange of information between you and your computer. Usually, we only think about what the software does, and rarely consider how it *presents* information. Visually ergonomic software is both easy to look at and easy to follow. The layout, menu design, and use of color all affect the software's readability and ease of use. These qualities affect our visual comfort and levels of stress and irritation, which in turn affect our work and health.

Software ergonomics applies to application software as well as to the computer's *graphical user interface*—the general design that both system and application software use.

- *The screen layout should be well organized, consistent, and easy to use.* The screen should be uncluttered, and menus and windows should be readily accessible. The active area of the screen should be distinct. The icons, layout, and ways to use the software should reflect the way people think, and be consistent throughout the program.

- *Items on the screen should be easy to see.* Text, icons, and menu items should be big enough to see and recognize easily from arm's distance. Items you click on should not be so small that they require precision eye and mouse movements, since these strain both the eyes and the hands.

- *Menu items should be easy to access and select.* Menus should be organized according to the task, not according to the technical capacity of the computer or software. They should be easy to pull down, read, and scan, so that selecting items doesn't require a lot of concentration and precision.

- *Colors should enhance meaning and readability.* Use of color should be consistent throughout the program. If color-coding is used to convey information, it should be accompanied by other signals as well, such as text or icons, so the meaning isn't lost on monochrome displays or for people who have color-perception defects. In general, use of color should follow the recommendations earlier in this chapter to ensure good contrast and readability.

- *The program should let you zoom and/or change the character size.* This lets you adjust your working area to accommodate your own visual abilities and preferences.

- *Text should be easy to read*, as described earlier in this chapter.

Improve Your Office Environment

You spend a lot of time in your office, sometimes more than you spend at home. Make it be a place you like, a place where you feel good. Bring in things you like to look at, do what you can to make the air you breathe clean and fresh, and use color well.

Add Visual Variety

Our eyes like to engage the world and examine shapes and objects. Offices don't always have enough visual variety to keep our eyes relaxed and energized. Even if your screen is visually entertaining, full of color and graphics and animations, you still need to surround yourself with completely different things to look at, and stacks of papers don't count. Bring in things that are pretty or fun to see—plants, flowers, figures, sculptures, photos, pictures, toys, anything that stimulates your visual sense.

Create at least one area where you can easily look into the distance, preferably out a window but at least into open space. Just notice what you see and let your eyes go where they please—they've spent enough time trained on the computer screen. Bring in a picture of a landscape, one with a horizon and a big view so you get the feeling of looking off into the distance. Even a postcard with a view can give you that effect. Using a mirror lets you look further, too—your eyes register the distance from you to the mirror to the object reflected in the mirror. Aquariums can be a visual treat—follow the fish with your eyes and enjoy their colors and forms. Watching the movement of the fish, water, and plants can be very relaxing.

Reduce Dust and Dryness

Your eyes are exposed directly to the air and all the tiny specks floating in it. Dust and airborne particles that get into our eyes can cause soreness, redness, irritation, and conjunctivitis, and may be responsible for skin rashes and dermatitis. When you breathe these particles in, any pollutants they are carrying get distributed throughout your body and affect your general health.

Dust and particles are drawn to your monitor by its static electric fields, and that's where they concentrate—right by your face, eyes, and nose. They accumulate on the screen where they interfere with vision, and pile up on the desk where they are easily swept back into the air. Don't let dust build up. Clean your desk, screen, and computer frequently, and consider using an air filter. Ionizers filter the air and increase the count of negative ions, which are depleted by static electric fields.

Dry air makes the eyes dry, too, and increases the effect of static electric fields, so they attract more dust. Dry, unblinking eyes are more susceptible to irritation because they don't have the lubrication to wash the particles away. You can add moisture and oxygen to your office air with aquariums or plants growing in damp soil or peat moss. Humidifiers can help, though they need to be cleaned frequently to prevent a build-up of bacteria and fungus.

Improve the Air Quality

Indoor air pollution exposes us to toxic gases and particles that harm the internal organs and irritate the eyes, nose, throat, and skin. Photocopiers, printers, paints, inks, adhesives, fire retardants, plastics, rubber, cleaning agents, and even some paper towels and tissues release hazardous chemicals into the air. Computer equipment and furniture give off tiny particles of plastics and sheet metal as they age. Cigarette smoke adds harmful gases and particles. In sick building syndrome—a concern in sealed office buildings—malfunctioning ventilation systems trap the pollutants and expose people to high concentrations of synthetic chemicals and gases, carbon dioxide, and disease-causing micro-organisms.

Encourage your employer to reduce pollution at the source by following a strict maintenance program for your building's ventilation system, changing printer filters regularly, keeping photocopiers and printers in separate, well-ventilated rooms, and using products that do not contain hazardous chemicals.

You can detoxify the air yourself simply by keeping a lot of plants in your office. NASA studies have found that certain houseplants can remove from the air significant amounts of benzene, formaldehyde, and trichloroethylene (TCE), three common indoor pollutants.[5]

Add Color

We all have personal color preferences, based on our own taste and experience. We also have a general response to color as a species. Color affects us biologically and psychologically, and this shows up in our health, behavior, and emotions. Blues, indigos, and violets are calming, rejuvenating, and restorative. They promote relaxation, lessen anxiety, and soften hostility. Reds, oranges, and yellows are vitalizing and energizing, and increase excitement and tension.[6] In

Plants That Help Clean the Air

Mother-in-law's tongue (sansevieria laurentii): formaldehyde, benzene, trichloroethylene

English ivy (hedera helix): F, B, TCE

Gerbera daisy (gerbera jamesonii): B, TCE

Pot mum (chrysanthemum morifolium): B

Peace lily (spathiphyllum "Mauna Loa"): B, TCE

Bamboo palm (chamaedorea seifritzii): F, B, TCE

Janet Craig (dracaena deremensis "Janet Craig"): F, B, TCE

Marginata (dracaenea marginata): F, B, TCE

Warneckei (dracaenea deremensis "Warneckei"): B, TCE

Banana (musa oriana): F

Heart leaf philodendron (philodendron oxycardium): F

Elephant ear philodendron (philodendron domesticum): F

Green spider plant (chlorophytum elatum): F

offices, we do best with pastel colors on the walls and colors of similar brightness in the rest of the room. Saturated colors on large areas are distracting and cause eyestrain. Black and white or strong colors together create too much contrast.[7]

In the end, color choice comes down to preference and aesthetics, within the constraints of ergonomics and the character of the environment you want to create. Blues and greens give distance, making rooms seem larger, cooler, and more restful. Reds and oranges bring closeness, warmth, and excitement. Browns are close and cozy. Most employers aren't likely to rush out and redecorate the office in your favorite color scheme, but you can bring in pictures, wall hangings, and all kinds of things in colors you enjoy.

CHAPTER

16

Work in the Right Light

Lighting has a profound effect on your eyes, your general health, and your productivity. Good lighting means comfortable eyes, better health, a stronger sense of well-being, and the ability to do your job well and comfortably at the same time. For your employer, it means a healthier workforce, less risk of injury, reduced medical costs, and higher productivity. It could even mean lower energy costs. The principles of ergonomic lighting are straightforward, and the payback in comfort from implementing them is almost immediate.

Lighting needs to be adjusted according to the job you are doing, the office layout, your visual skills, your general sensitivity to light, and your personal preference. Finding the right combination takes both examination and experimentation. No matter what your situation, start by eliminating glare, reflections, and flicker. Just doing this could solve many of your problems. Once those are under control, find the right illumination levels for your work, and consider upgrading the quality of the lights. Here's what to aim for:

- A workspace free of glare, reflections, and flicker

- Adjustable levels of brightness

- Good task lighting

- A balanced mix of daylight and artificial light

- Pleasant light color and temperature

- Lights that emit low levels of electromagnetic radiation

- Energy-efficient lighting

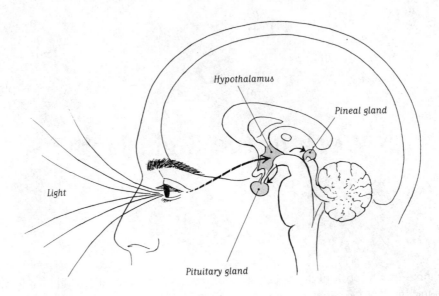

Light and Health

The **hypothalamus**. This area of the brain uses light (in part) to coordinate the activities of the sympathetic and parasympathetic nervous systems. It regulates certain aspects of our metabolism, including body temperature, water balance, metabolism of sugar and fat, and hormone secretion. The hypothalamus also controls hormonal secretions of the pituitary and pineal glands, thus influencing both the endocrine system and our biological cycles.

The **pituitary gland**. This small gland located at the base of the brain is part of the endocrine system. Its hormonal secretions are determined by information sent from the hypothalamus, and regulate growth,

reproduction, several metabolic activities, and many other bodily functions.

The **pineal gland**. This tiny, pinecone-shaped gland located in the very center of the brain keeps our biological functions in sync with our environment, primarily through its secretion of melatonin and other hormones. The pineal gland responds not only to light energy it receives via the hypothalamus, but also to magnetic fields. Thus the pineal is doubly significant—through it, our health and biological cycles are affected both by the light we receive and by our exposure to electromagnetic fields. For more on the pineal gland and electromagnetic radiation, see Chapter 19, The Radiation Question.

Figure 16-1. Light and health

Light Affects Your Eyes and Your Health

When you work on a computer, you are dealing with light. You look directly at the computer screen, a light source, and you are surrounded by light in the office from overhead fixtures, lamps, and windows, and sometimes by the flashing light from photocopiers. Poor lighting affects the entire visual system, causing eyestrain, deteriorating vision, and related problems. Office lighting alone is responsible for much of the eyestrain we experience.

The light that enters our eyes affects more than the visual system. It also influences the nervous system through the hypothalamus, the part of the brain that coordinates and regulates our biological functions and rhythms, including our response to stress. Thus, the quality and quantity of the light we receive affects our general health

We know intuitively and experientially that the light we receive affects us physically, emotionally, and psychologically. Various forms of phototherapy (light therapy) have been employed through the ages, from the use of color for healing by the ancient Greeks, Romans, and Egyptians, to the use of high mountain light in Swiss alpine spas in the early 1900s to cure tuberculosis, to the current use of special banks of bright lights to treat seasonal affective disorder.

Modern science is just beginning to explore the connection between sunlight, artificial light, and health. Results are contradictory and controversial, but interest in the topic is growing, and, with time, more conclusive results may reveal the specific qualities of light necessary for our health and well-being. In his book *Light, Medicine of the Future*, Jacob Liberman provides an in-depth, thoughtful examination of light as an essential medicine and food for the body.

So what does all this mean? Most of us work indoors under artificial light, usually fluorescent. Many of us are in windowless offices or cubicles and get little natural light. These lighting conditions may be affecting you more than you realize. For example, we know that fluorescent lights are a factor in headaches, eyestrain, fatigue, and stress.[1] These aspects of fluorescent lights are discussed later in this chapter.

Control Glare and Reflections

According to ergonomist Etienne Grandjean, avoiding glare inside a room is one of the most important ergonomic considerations in office design. Glare and troublesome reflections overload the adaptive process of the eyes, and in doing so cause headaches, eyestrain, and visual fatigue. The optimal solutions are re-positioning the equipment and moving or adjusting the lights. This isn't always possible, so we often need to use other measures, like covering windows, using a screen hood or glare filter, or wearing a visor. Don't wear sunglasses to reduce glare. Figure 16-2 shows how to set up your work area to eliminate glare and reflections.

Check for Glare

Any bright light that we see directly or that we detect with our peripheral vision can produce glare. The biggest offenders are typically overhead fluorescent lights and unshaded windows that get bright sunlight. Lights or windows in front of you are directly in your field of vision; those behind you can be reflected on the

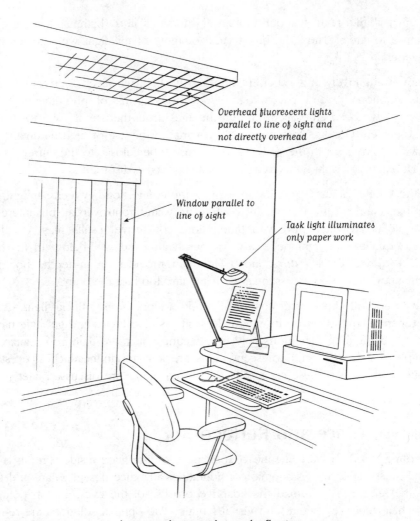

Overhead fluorescent lights
parallel to line of sight and
not directly overhead

Window parallel to
line of sight

Task light illuminates
only paper work

Figure 16-2. Setting up your work area to eliminate glare and reflections

screen; lights right overhead wash out the screen image. Lamps and shiny surfaces can also appear in your peripheral vision, or be reflected on the screen.

Vertical, curved computer screens are excellent reflectors—they can reflect objects and light from all over the room. The greater the curve and the shinier the screen, the more reflections you have to deal with. Flat screens and flat panel displays reflect the least Glare and reflections can also appear on other surfaces in the room—picture frames, glass partitions, windows, shiny desktops, and so on. You need to eliminate glare in these places as well.

To find the sources of glare and reflections, try these simple exercises. Check your workspace before and after you've made changes to see the difference.

- *Glare.* Turn on all the lights you usually use when you work. Sit at your computer and look at the screen. Keep your eyes on the screen, but put your *attention* further out in your peripheral vision. Check all directions, moving *just your attention* around your field of vision, up, down, to the sides. Note all the lights and bright objects you can actually perceive. Note where you sense uncomfortable brightness. These are your sources of glare.

- *Reflections.* Turn the screen off, sit in front of it as you would to work, and note what shows up. Your image will be there, too, and will be brighter if you are wearing light-colored clothing. Try checking for reflections with the screen on, too. Dark screen backgrounds reflect more than light backgrounds. Sometimes the reflection is diminished in the light of the screen. Holding a hand mirror over different areas of the screen (with its back side next to the screen) shows you even more clearly what's reflected..

Lighting and Flat Panel Displays

Flat panel displays, such as those used with laptop and portable computers, typically have fewer problems with reflections and ambient light than regular computer screens (video displays). They have a flat, non-reflective surface, which adds flexibility to the positioning of furniture and equipment, and some are more tolerant of brighter ambient light than regular screens.

There are many types of flat panel displays. Some are better than others, depending on the technology. Active matrix LCDs (liquid crystal displays) are the most versatile, followed by passive matrix LCDs with backlight. Active matrix LCDs are still readable when placed at upright angles (like regular screens) and have excellent color rendition and contrast, even in sunshine.

Other flat panels are more sensitive to ambient light or light shining right on them. Passive matrix LCDs without backlight can't be used in dim light because they depend on the ambient light to illuminate their light background. Plasma displays and electroluminescent displays (ELDs) lose contrast when too much light hits the screen.[a] Also, many flat panels can't be seen at too great an angle, and some don't have very good contrast.

---

a. *Screen Facts,* TCO. 27-31.

Keep Overhead Fixtures Parallel with Your Line of Sight

Arrange your work area so overhead fixtures are not directly above you, but on either side, parallel with your line of sight to the screen. This usually takes the overhead lights out of your field of vision and out of "reflectance range" of your screen. If you can't do this, try turning off or removing the offending light, supplementing it with well-placed lamps, if necessary. You might also try wearing a visor to shade your eyes, or using a screen hood or glare filter to shade the screen.

Overhead fixtures should direct the light mainly downward, and shouldn't let it spread out to the sides. The more the light spreads, the more possibility for glare and reflections. Parabolic (curved), louvered fixtures direct light effectively, while straight louvers or baffles are less helpful. Don't use flat plastic panels or any other type of fixtures that spread out the light. Bare bulbs are unquestionably not for use with computers.

Indirect lighting is an alternative to overhead fixtures. Indirect lights shine on the ceiling or walls, which reflect the light into the room. This eliminates direct glare from the fixtures themselves, but can cause problems if the light spreads out and brightens the ceiling and walls too much.

Keep Windows Parallel with Your Line of Sight

Sit with windows to your sides, so that they are parallel with your line of sight and not reflected in the screen. Window coverings can be very helpful, especially if you can't move your equipment. Mini-blinds and louvered, transparent, mesh blinds give you the most flexibility. You can still see through them when they're closed, so you eliminate the brightness but maintain the view and all its opportunity for relaxing and refreshing your vision. It seems a shame to be seated near a window only to have it covered up. Mesh blinds can help mitigate "light wars" in open or shared offices, where some people want the windows covered and others don't. Outdoor awnings can also eliminate glare. If you're in a woodsy or shaded location, the light from the windows may not be bright enough to cause problems.

Move Bright Lamps and Shiny Objects

If you can, move bright lamps and objects to a place where they won't bother you, and won't be reflected. Cover shiny objects if you have to. Make sure you don't see any bare light bulbs. Sometimes just changing the tilt or angle of the monitor even slightly can eliminate some reflections, but be careful to keep it comfortable for reading and for maintaining neutral head posture.

What About Screen Hoods and Glare Filters?

Screen hoods and glare filters are options to consider when you can't reduce glare and reflections through repositioning your equipment and adjusting the lighting. A hood shades the screen the way a visor shades your face. You can make a screen hood from file folders or cardboard and tape it to the monitor, or buy a ready-made one. Experiment by holding up a file folder or two to see which part of the screen needs to be shaded, and how far the hood needs to extend. You may only need to shade part of the screen. If the hood comes out more than about four to six inches, it may interfere with seeing your work, or just make you feel closed in. Try it and find out what works for you.

Glare filters are usually the first solution that comes to mind. They're often recommended in catalogs and brochures as the optimal way to prevent eyestrain. They can be very helpful and in some cases are indispensable, but they aren't always necessary or appropriate. Some screens already come with an anti-glare treatment. You can often reduce glare and reflections by rearranging the furniture, equipment, or lights. This is by far a better solution.

Many glare filters reduce contrast, clarity, and readability, so if you do decide you need one, get a good one, for example, approved by the American Optometric Association. Several filter types are available, and products are being improved all the time. Some are also designed to reduce static electricity and shield low frequency electric fields.

Even the highest quality filter adds another layer for the eyes to look through. We already have to look through the computer's glass screen to focus on the characters, and people who wear glasses must look through their lenses as well. Reading on the computer is slower than reading on paper at the same resolution, and that dust and fingerprints on the screen interfere with focusing on the characters. Smudged and dusty filters and eyeglasses are a hindrance, too.

Balance the Lighting Levels

Lighting for computer work is often a compromise. It must be low enough so the screen is easy to read, and bright enough for reading paper documents and for meeting with customers, clients, or co-workers. Bank tellers, customer service representatives, software engineers, writers, graphics designers, and administrative assistants may have vastly different lighting needs. Everyone is different, and brings to the job their own visual abilities, sensitivities, and preferences. Even people doing exactly the same tasks are likely to adjust their light levels differently, given the chance.

Dimmer Is Usually Better than Brighter

In general, computer work needs less light than paperwork. People typically need and prefer lower levels of overall light—about half the brightness levels commonly used in many offices. Dimmer ambient light enhances the readability of the screen and creates less extreme contrast in the room, making computer work more comfortable. It also creates less glare and fewer reflections.

But dim lights are not appropriate for all tasks. Papers are harder to read in dim light, so people who frequently refer to hardcopy typically need brighter light, especially for documents that aren't printed clearly. Off-screen tasks that involve high legibility, acuity, precise color perception, and attention to detail require more light. People tend to need more light as they get older, and some people feel depressed in dim light. Some businesses feel a dim office puts off customers and are reluctant to lower the lights.

Finding the right levels of light requires compromise, especially when people share offices or work in cubicles. Adjustability in lighting is the key—what's necessary is a combination of variable ambient light and supplemental task lighting. People will be more productive, more comfortable, and more satisfied with their jobs when they can adjust the light to suit themselves and their work.

Get in the habit of adjusting the lighting if you need to when you switch tasks. Don't work too long in poor light. Karl Nyman, M.D., recommends the following guidelines:

- The screen should be slightly brighter (have higher luminance) than the surroundings.

- Whatever you are reading, whether it's hardcopy or the screen, should be slightly brighter than the ambient light.

- The ambient light should be bright enough to stimulate your daily rhythms.

The screen's background color is a factor in the general lighting environment as well. In a bright office, use a lighter background and colors that don't wash out or cause extreme contrast in bright light. In less light, use a darker background.

Some flat panel displays are more sensitive to ambient light than regular screens, while others are not. Adjust the lighting so you can easily see the display.

Make Sure the Ambient Light is Evenly Distributed

Good ambient lighting distributes light evenly to all parts of the room. In most offices, ambient light is provided by overhead fluorescent tubes. Unfortunately, fluorescents can't be dimmed, so to change the light levels you have to either leave a particular bank of lights turned off, remove a tube here and there, or cover them up with cardboard or dark plastic. *Check with your facilities department before randomly removing fluorescent tubes.* Phase-shifted fluorescents work in pairs to reduce flicker—while one tube is on, the other is off, so they balance each other. Removing one of such a pair increases flicker.

Some people like to supplement or replace the overhead lights with incandescent lamps or indirect lighting. Using more low-powered lights instead of a few high-powered ones provides more uniform illumination.

Get a good mix of artificial light and daylight. No artificial light matches natural daylight exactly, and we need exposure to the full spectrum of natural light. Full spectrum lights, described later in the chapter, are the closest match, and may be a good choice for offices that get little or no natural light. Work with daylight as much as possible. As the brightness of the outside light changes with the time of day, turn the artificial lights on or off as needed.

Use Task Lights Carefully

Task lights are small lamps designed to illuminate just the papers you are looking at without shining on the screen. Good task lighting should provide enough light to show the print on the page, but not so much as to cause reflections, glare, or extreme contrast with the screen and the ambient light.

A good task light has these qualities:

- It's adjustable so you can direct the light where you need it.

- It has an asymmetric reflector that concentrates the light on your paper work without spilling light onto the screen.

- The bulb isn't visible to you or your officemates—especially halogen bulbs.

- The light isn't in your line of sight or reflected on the screen.

- The light isn't excessively bright. It should be no more than about three times brighter than the screen, or five times brighter than the ambient light. Use a light meter if you want an accurate measurement.

Many people like halogen task lights because they provide a bright, white light that is concentrated in one direction. Conventional desk lamps cast light in all directions equally, including your computer screen, and are more likely to create glare and reflections or to wash out the screen image.

Avoid Extremes of Bright and Dark

As you look around your office, most of what you see should have similar *luminances*—that is, the objects in your field of view should give off about the same amount of light. An office with bright walls, dark furniture, light-colored equipment, and very dark carpet is hard on your eyes. There should be no extremely bright or extremely dark areas, or objects contrasting with each other close to your line of sight. Moderate contrast is acceptable further out in your visual field. Dimming the lights in your office might help, since very bright lights create more shadows and more contrast, especially in offices with cubicles or open floor plans.

If you work with paper documents and the computer at the same time, try to achieve similar levels of *illumination* for both—that is, they should both have about the same amount of light falling on them. The document should be at most three times brighter than the screen. This is much easier to achieve if you have good quality task lighting for your papers and a light-colored or paper-white background on your screen. Contrast on the screen itself is different from contrast in your office, and is described in Chapter 15, *Create a Visually Comfortable Environment*.

Flashing light from photocopiers or other machines strains your eyes, too. If you work near a photocopier, ask to have it moved. Otherwise, be sure everyone closes its cover completely when they use it. (Photocopiers should be located in a separate room, due to their negative impact on noise and air quality.)

What Types of Lights Are Good to Use?

Lighting technology offers us three main types of light to work by—incandescent, halogen, and fluorescent. Each has its own properties and best uses (see Table 16-1). By combining them wisely, you can create a lighting environment that is cost effective, comfortable, and suits your needs. Some of the choices in lighting may not be yours to make. You can suggest them to your employer, however, and you can probably make minor changes yourself.

To get the best of current technology, use:

- Improved incandescents and/or full-spectrum incandescents

- Halogen bulbs in a lamp with a plastic shield

- Electronically ballasted, full-spectrum or tri-phosphor fluorescent lights

Incandescent

The incandescent bulb is the old standby, the icon that everyone recognizes as light. Its warm, red-yellow light is created by heating a tungsten filament. A large part of the energy it consumes produces heat, which can be annoying to some people, and a very small portion produces light. These bulbs generally have a warm (though imbalanced) color and don't cost much, but they use a lot of energy, last only about 1,000 hours, and lose about 25% of their light output before they burn out.

Improved incandescents have stronger filaments (or special gases in the bulb) that don't increase energy efficiency, but do increase longevity to about 3,000 hours. Full spectrum incandescent bulbs are also available. These are sometimes called *neodymium* bulbs.

Incandescents can be a good supplement to fluorescent lighting, because of their warmth and lack of flicker. However, it is expensive to use incandescents alone for ambient lighting. A 75-watt frosted full-spectrum flood lamp in a clamp-on fixture can make a reasonable, inexpensive task light if you can't afford something better. Regular-shaped bulbs aren't as effective, as they spill light in too many directions.

Table 16-1. Summary of Light Choices[a]

	Benefits	Drawbacks	Recommendations
Incandescent	No flicker. Regular bulbs are inexpensive. Improved incandescent bulbs cost more, but last longer (3,000 hours).	Poorly balanced color. Expensive due to lack of energy efficiency. Regular bulbs burn out quickly (after about 1,000 hours).	Use improved incandescent or full spectrum bulbs.
Halogen	Emits steady, bright white light. More energy efficient than incandescent. Light is easily directed for task lighting. Longer life than regular incandescent bulbs (about 2500 hours).	Bulb gets hot and is easily damaged. Its brightness may cause a hot spot of glare. UV emissions may be harmful.	Halogen task lights should have a plastic shield to protect the bulb and absorb UV emissions.
Fluorescent	Energy efficient. Long life (10,000 hours). Advances in technology have improved color quality, bulb design, and ballasting.	Standard fluorescent tubes have problems with flicker, hum, color quality, and electromagnetic emissions.	Use electronically ballasted triphosphor or full spectrum fluorescents for best color, least flicker, and lowest electromagnetic emissions. Compact fluorescent bulbs offer more flexibility in lighting design and furniture placement.

a. *Alternative Energy Sourcebook*, 7th edition. Edited by John Schaeffer. Ukiah: Real Goods Trading Corporation, 1993. 31-37.

Halogen

Also called tungsten-halogen or quartz halogen, these bulbs have a tungsten filament enclosed in a quartz-glass envelope filled with halogen gas. The filament is heated to higher temperatures, and uses less energy per watt to produce a brighter, whiter light than incandescents. Halogen bulbs last up to 2,500 hours, and lose less than 10% of their light output over their lifetime.

Halogen is a popular choice for task lights. The color quality is good and the light can be easily directed to illuminate a specific spot. The light is very bright, but this can become a drawback if it causes glare. If you're concerned about ultraviolet emissions from halogen bulbs, use a task light that has a plastic shield over the bulb. The shield also keeps you from accidentally touching the bulb, which gets very hot and is easily damaged.

Fluorescent Tubes

Long, fluorescent tubes have been the mainstay of office lighting for years. They use less energy, put out a lot of light, and have a long life—about 10,000 hours. Fluorescents use a phosphor coating instead of filaments to produce light, and a ballast to regulate the incoming current and voltage. When electricity passes through the tube, the gas inside gives off ultraviolet rays, which react with the phosphors and cause them to glow.

Fluorescents are not everyone's favorite. Some people may always prefer the warmth of incandescents over the coolness of fluorescents. Their flicker and poor color quality have not increased their popularity. Their length and shape limit design possibilities, locking us into long, inflexible banks of overhead lights that can cause glare and constrain our furniture arrangement. There is also concern about the health effects of ultraviolet and electromagnetic radiation emissions from fluorescent lights, as well as hazardous chemical leakage from old fixtures and tubes.

New developments in phosphor blends, ballasts, and bulb design are improving the quality and safety of fluorescent lights. Electronically ballasted, full-spectrum or tri-phosphor lights currently offer you the best in fluorescent lighting. These have the best color rendition, the least flicker, and the lowest electromagnetic emissions.

Color quality

The color of the phosphor determines the color quality of the light. The "cool white" and "warm white" fluorescents we are most familiar with use phosphors that render color poorly, taking the brilliance out of a colorful environment and giving people an unflattering pallor. Photographers know this well, and use special filters to correct the color imbalances of these lights. New phosphors, such as *tri-stimulus phosphors*, are more expensive but provide better color rendition and produce 15% more visible light.

Flicker

The ballast determines the frequency of the light, which determines how much the light flickers. The ballast pulses the lights on and off—the current travels through the light, activating and de-activating the phosphors, producing flicker. The higher (faster) the frequency, the less perceptible the flicker. Until recently, all ballasts used core-coil electromagnetic technology. Now solid-state electronic ballasts are also available. Most ballasts run on alternating current, though some electronic ballasts run on direct current.

Core-coil magnetic ballasts typically run at frequencies of 60 Hz, pulsing the lights on and off 120 times every second. Though at this frequency flicker is considered invisible, many people still find it troublesome. Some magnetic ballasts also hum slightly, which can be annoying. *Electronic ballasts* pulse the lights at 20,000 Hz or more, putting the flicker way out of perceptible range. These ballasts cost more and last 10,000 hours, compared to 50,000 hours for magnetic ballasts, but they have several advantages—they are more efficient, weigh less, don't hum, and don't flicker on startup or when they're running.

Electromagnetic emissions

Some studies in the early 1980s found that people exposed to fluorescent lights at work have a higher risk of skin cancer (malignant melanoma) than those who are exposed regularly to sunlight, though these results were not confirmed by later research. Other studies found that fluorescent office lights may cause mutations in cultures of animal cells. Some people believe these effects are due to the emissions of ultraviolet rays, and the U.S. Food and Drug Administration recommends the use of UV-absorbing shields or diffusers. However, studies about the effects of ultraviolet emissions from fluorescent lights are contradictory and inconclusive. More study is warranted.

Complicating matters are emissions of low frequency electromagnetic fields. Magnetic ballasts generate 60 Hz fields, similar to those produced by computer monitors, and in fact are a greater source of these fields than monitors. These emissions are implicated in skin problems, hypersensitivity to electromagnetic fields, cancer, and other cellular changes (see Part V, *The Potential Risks of Electromagnetic Fields*). The effects of the higher frequencies of electronic ballasts are unknown. Some fluorescent lights are grounded and shielded to prevent emissions of x-rays and radio waves.

Some people who are sensitive to electromagnetic fields may not be able to use fluorescent lights of any sort, and may need to use only shielded incandescent and halogen lights (see Chapter 20, *Health Risks We Wonder About*).

Hazardous substances

Fluorescent lights contain *mercury*, a known toxic substance, and may give off mercury vapor, which is harmful to health and distorts the light color.[2] Magnetic ballasts contain traces of *radioactive materials*, similar to the amounts found in smoke alarms, some watches, and other appliances. Magnetic ballasts made before 1982 may contain highly toxic PCBs (polychlorinated biphenyls). PCBs were banned in the U.S. in 1977, but transformers containing PCBs were allowed in office buildings until 1982.[3] Electronic ballasts don't contain these substances.

Compact Fluorescents

These new bulbs make fluorescent lighting more versatile, convenient, and efficient, and open new possibilities in lighting design. They come in several shapes and sizes, usually a rounded capsule or small interconnected tubes. The ballast, electronic or magnetic, is incorporated into a base that screws into a conventional light bulb socket. They last 10,000 hours and are extremely efficient. Wattages and equivalencies vary, but a typical compact fluorescent uses only 15 watts to produce as much light as a 60 watt incandescent bulb.

Compact fluorescent bulbs are not cheap and can't be used with dimmers. Some are too big or too wide at the base to fit easily into existing fixtures and lamps. The technology is evolving, and as compact fluorescents catch on, the bulbs themselves may become smaller, and more fixtures suited to them will become available. It's also possible to adapt existing lamps and fixtures to fit them. Whether compact fluorescents are safer than tubes is unknown, and people who are uncomfortable with fluorescent tubes are likely to be uncomfortable with compact fluorescents as well. However, they do reduce some of the problems with standard fluorescent lighting.

What Is Full-Spectrum Lighting?

The term *full spectrum* describes artificial light, fluorescent or incandescent, that closely duplicates natural sunlight. Full-spectrum lighting provides good color rendition and a comfortable, natural-feeling light to work under. Some full-spectrum fluorescent lights also contain an ultraviolet portion.

Not all full-spectrum lights have the same quality of light. If you're shopping for full-spectrum lights, compare the light from various bulbs or tubes and choose the one that feels most natural—though you may be so used to standard fluorescent or incandescent lights that full-spectrum light seems strange at first.

If you want to get technical, check the light's color and temperature ratings to see how it compares to sunlight. This information is not always printed on the packaging, so you may have to ask the dealer or call the manufacturer.

Color-Rendering Index and Color Temperature Ratings

A light's *rating* on the color rendering index (CRI) indicates how well it renders color as compared to sunlight. A CRI rating over 80 is considered reasonable, and a CRI over 90 is considered full spectrum. Sunlight rates 100.

A light's *color temperature* is its absolute temperature measured in degrees Kelvin. Temperature correlates to color. 1,500°K appears orange-red, and 9,000°K appears blue. Lower temperatures appear warmer, and higher ones cooler.

Sunlight and full spectrum lights have peak temperatures of about 5,500°K, in the blue-green range. Technically, a full spectrum light has a CRI of 90 or above and a color temperature between about 5,000 and 7,500 degrees Kelvin.

Standard incandescents have a high CRI but a low color temperature, so they are not full spectrum—their light peaks in the yellow-red range. Triphosphor fluorescents have a CRI of 80+ and peak in the blue-green-red range. Cool white fluorescents have a CRI of about 65 and peak in the yellow-red range.

Full-Spectrum Lighting with Ultraviolet

Ultraviolet light is often considered part of the full spectrum of natural sunlight. It has three distinct wavelengths, each with its own effects. The longest waves, called near-UV, or UVA, are next to violet in the visible spectrum. These waves stimulate the immune system and are responsible for our tanning response. Mid-UV, or UVB, is necessary for the synthesis of vitamin D, calcium, and other nutrients. Far-UV, or UVC, is germicidal, and can kill bacteria and viruses.

Some full-spectrum fluorescent lights include low levels of near- and mid-UV light similar in proportion to the naturally occurring UV of daylight. However, the UV portion burns out relatively quickly, and you can't tell when it's gone. Many fixtures absorb UV, so if you want it, you'll need UV-transmitting fixtures. To solve these technical difficulties, one company has created a full-spectrum light system that combines an ultraviolet tube with visible spectrum tubes in a special fixture. The UV tube can be replaced when it burns out.

Why Add Ultraviolet Light?

Exposure to ultraviolet rays is a highly controversial issue. Overexposure to mid- and far-UV is clearly harmful, and is known to cause burns, skin cancer, and cataracts. We're now commonly advised to block all exposure to all UV. However, reasonable exposure to mid- and near-UV is beneficial and necessary for good health. Many studies have demonstrated the health benefits of ultraviolet light, from assisting in weight loss to improving the efficiency of the heart, lowering blood pressure, and reducing cholesterol levels.[4]

Until recently, the earth's atmosphere filtered out much mid-UV and all but tiny amounts of far-UV. With the depletion of the UV-absorbing ozone layer, we now receive greater doses of all ranges of ultraviolet light from the sun than ever before. This could result in serious health problems for all living beings. However, there is also the possibility that, by blocking out ultraviolet rays every chance we get, many of us don't get enough of it—we avoid the dangers but deprive ourselves of the benefits.

Are There Health Benefits?

Proponents of full-spectrum lighting believe that these lights can provide balanced colors and healthy doses of ultraviolet light, and thereby help reverse the ill-effects of working indoors under artificial light. Decades of observation and pioneering research in photobiology by Dr. John Ott and other scientists have shown that the health of people, animals, and plants improves under full-spectrum fluorescent lights, and deteriorates under standard warm and cool white fluorescents.

Among numerous other biological effects, cool white fluorescent lights increase agitation, fatigue, and concentration loss, and increase levels of the stress hormones ACTH and cortisol. None of these effects were present under full-spectrum lights. In schools and offices, performance is better with full-spectrum lighting, and absences due to illness are fewer.[5]

Balanced, safe doses of ultraviolet may be important for people who work indoors and get little natural light. Plastic and glass absorb ultraviolet light, so it's blocked by windows, eyeglasses, and contact lenses (unless these are made of UV-transmitting materials). If you spend a lot of time indoors or in motor vehicles, and only get a few minutes of sunlight each day, your main source of ultraviolet may be the fluorescent lights you work under. The quality of that light may make a big difference in your health.

Plan for Energy-Efficient Lighting

A *single* compact fluorescent lamp replacing, say, 75 watts of incandescent lighting with 14-18 watts (but yielding the same light and lasting about 13 times as long) will, over its life, keep out of the air a *ton* of carbon dioxide (a major cause of global warming), twenty pounds of sulfur oxides (which cause acid rain), and various other nasty things.

—AMORY LOVINS, from the foreword to the *Alternative Energy Sourcebook*

Installing energy-efficient lighting systems makes economic sense. Lowered lighting costs—from both conservation and use of efficient lights—improves a company's financial health, potentially freeing up funds to spend on jobs and creating a healthier, ergonomic workplace.

Diana Roose, in *Facts on Fluorescents*, notes that electric lighting accounts for about 25% of the total electricity used in the United States. More than half is wasted by inefficient technology and design, according to the US Environmental Protection Agency. Energy consumption for lighting can be the single largest energy expense in many office buildings today.

Energy efficiency also makes environmental sense. Reduced energy consumption means less energy production, less pollution, and less environmental damage at every stage of energy use, from procurement and transport of raw materials to emissions from power plants. These are not tangential issues—a better workplace and a cleaner environment mean better health, which benefits everyone.

Consider this mix to create an energy-efficient lighting system:

- For ambient light, use daylight and electronically ballasted, full-spectrum or tri-phosphor fluorescent lights.

- For task lights, use halogen bulbs. Full-spectrum incandescent bulbs are a possibility if the fixture doesn't spill too much light. Small compact fluorescents may work, too, depending on your brightness and color rendition needs.

- For supplemental ambient light, if you need it, use compact fluorescents, full-spectrum incandescent bulbs, or improved incandescents. Combine them. Use compact fluorescents for hallways or lights that you leave on all the time, and full spectrum or improved incandescents for your work area.

- Use the lowest wattage bulbs that still give you enough light.

- Use lights that are grounded and shielded and have low electromagnetic emissions.

PART

IV

Stress

If you learn only a few things about stress, realize that:

- Psychological stress comes from our own internal response to outside conditions and perceived threats. Sometimes you can change outside conditions and sometimes you can only change your response.

- Some stress is entirely physical; it comes from noise, pollution, electromagnetic fields, and so on. Reduce your exposure to environmental stresses as much as possible.

- Stress is not just a minor irritant. Chronic stress robs you of physical health, productivity, creativity, and joy.

- To break the cycle of chronic stress, you have to put aside stressful thoughts and replace them with other thoughts. The simple, time-tested way to break the cycle is by focusing on your breath. Once you have the tools to break the stress cycle, you can regain calm and perspective any time you need it.

CHAPTER

17

Are You Stressed?

Stress is your body's response to a challenge, whether it's a threat to your life or the pressure to get a new product out fast. It can be exciting, even thrilling. Your body gives you bursts of energy to work at high speed, alert, efficient. But how long can you maintain it?

To get the charge, you need reserves, built up through rest, relaxation, and less demanding times. When your work or your workstyle offer no respite, excitement becomes anxiety and your body rebels. Even those who thrive on stress have their limits. First you feel stressed, and eventually you feel burned out. The charge is gone and you don't even want to think about getting it back.

Stress is a factor in almost every ailment related to computer work. The strength of its influence varies with the situation and each person's response, but it's always something to be reckoned with.

The Signs of Stress

Though everyone manifests stress in different ways, these signs are definite clues that your stress levels are running high:

- *Irregular breathing.* You hold your breath, breathe only to your chest, breathe shallowly, or gasp for air.

- *Irritability.* You're easily angered and plagued by constant anxiety, impatience, and intolerance.

- *Humorlessness.* Everything becomes very serious, and you don't let yourself loosen up and see things in a broader perspective.

- *Increased muscle tension throughout the body.* Every muscle feels tight, stiff, and sore.

Many other signs of stress appear in your body, your emotions, and your behavior. Scan the lists of symptoms in this chapter. Do you recognize yourself anywhere?

Physical Signs of Stress

Irregular or shallow breathing

Muscle tension, soreness, and pain

Stiff joints

Frequent tension or migraine headaches

Tight jaw, grinding your teeth (bruxism)

Eyestrain and vision problems

Fatigue, exhaustion, loss of energy

Upset stomach, nausea, vomiting

Indigestion, diarrhea, constipation

Frequent infections or colds

Sporadic rapid heartbeat

Drastic changes in appetite or weight

Allergies, skin rashes, hives

Premenstrual tension or missed menstrual cycles

The Physiological Stress Response

Stress contributes to so many ailments because it affects virtually all of our organs and biological functions, via the nervous system. In *Freedom from Stress*, Phil Nuernberger describes stress as an imbalance in the interplay of the sympathetic and parasympathetic nervous systems. The sympathetic system activates and arouses the internal organs, while the parasympathetic inhibits them and slows them down. When we are at rest, both systems act on the organs in a balanced way, maintaining equilibrium. When we are under stress, one system or the other dominates to meet the challenge.

In the well-known *fight-or-flight* response, the sympathetic system dominates, sending out hormones that provide us with extra energy, alertness, and strength for physical action. But this is not the only way our body responds to stress. In

Emotional Signs of Stress

Boredom, lethargy, dissatisfaction

Anxiety, fear, panic

Irritability, anger, hostility

Sadness, depression, hopelessness

Irritability

Emotional instability

Difficulty expressing emotion, or having "no feelings" in an emotional situation

Difficulty being present with others, especially when they are emotional

Feeling overwhelmed or pressed; can't stop to see the big picture

Feeling like you're going to explode

Behavioral Signs of Stress

Loss of concentration

Procrastination, difficulty getting organized, can't get motivated

Difficulty making decisions

Trouble sleeping—difficulty falling asleep, insomnia, oversleeping, waking up feeling groggy

Social isolation

Going back to work at night or on weekends, bringing a lot of work home

Difficulty doing nothing, can't sit still and relax

Unwillingness to laugh at yourself, taking yourself too seriously

Reliance on tobacco, alcohol, or drugs

Decreased enjoyment of sex

what Nuernberger calls the *possum* response, the parasympathetic dominates—when confronted with a threat, the body shuts down. Instead of gearing up for physical action, we freeze, as if rolling over and playing dead.

These responses in themselves aren't necessarily harmful—we feel stressed only when arousal and activity aren't balanced with relaxation, or when inhibition and relaxation aren't balanced with activity. A prolonged fight-or-flight response eventually burns up reserves and leads to exhaustion. A prolonged possum response doesn't use the reserves at all, but suppresses bodily functions and leads to lethargy and depression. Both states can lead to discomfort and disease. If you already have a health problem, chronic stress makes it linger or get worse.

Medical Conditions Related to Chronic Stress

Gastrointestinal diseases, digestive diseases

Infections

Cardiovascular disease

Allergic and hypersensitivity diseases

High blood pressure

Inflammatory diseases of the skin and eyes

Rheumatic and rheumatoid arthritis

Metabolic diseases

Repetitive strain injury (RSI)

Kidney diseases

Temporomandibular joint syndrome (TMJ syndrome)

Immune system diseases

Problem pregnancies, eclampsia

Nervous and mental diseases

Ulcers

Cancer

In office work, the triggering of the fight-or-flight response is a major source of stress. This response prepares us to overcome a sudden physical threat, yet many of our office threats are mental or emotional—they aren't resolved with a burst of physical action. Even a ringing phone or a jammed printer might set you off. You may *imagine* doing something physically rash, but you just stay at your desk, tense and twitching, with the stress hormones coursing through you without any immediate release. Tension builds over time and stays with you.

The Consequences of Too Much Stress

Chronic stress wears down our physical and mental health, and costs businesses billions of dollars in absenteeism, poor performance, and health care. Insurance claims for stress-related health problems have increased steadily over the years. In 1992, the Northwestern National Life Insurance Company examined the effects of workplace stress on American workers and its cost to employers. Here's what they found:[1]

- *4 in 10 workers say their job is very or extremely stressful.* Many feel pressure to prove themselves to their employer because of the poor economy, and many say they don't have enough time to get things done. Almost one third think they will burn out in the next year.

- *One in two workers say job stress reduces their productivity.* Almost 40% frequently think about quitting their jobs. Poor performance can affect customer relations and even drive customers away.

- *Workers reporting high stress are three times as likely as workers reporting low stress to suffer from frequent stress-related conditions.* Almost two-thirds of highly stressed workers experience exhaustion and tight neck or shoulder muscles, and around half experience headaches, insomnia, anxiety, and anger.

- *At highest risk of job burnout are low-income workers, especially those with college degrees, and single women with children.* Workers with low incomes and low control over their work are more likely to burn out than those with higher incomes and more control. The most likely to burn out are sales, administrative, technical, and service workers.

- *Employees who have a supportive supervisor report a significantly lower rate of burnout.* Supervisors and managers reduce stress when they delegate control to employees and minimize overtime requirements.

- *Many stress-related illnesses are turning into long-term disabilities.* Long-term disability can typically cost an employer more than $73,000 when a worker is not rehabilitated and returned to work.[2] The financial consequences of high turnover, frequent stress-related illness, and lower productivity can be devastating for employers.

Working women are more likely than men to experience the adverse effects of stress.[3] This is not because women are inherently less able to cope with stress, but because they typically live and work in stressful environments. Women predominate in the most stressful jobs, are generally paid less than men for the same work, and often have more family and household responsibilities. A 1989 survey found that stress and computer-related ailments are the most serious health hazards facing working women.[4]

Stress at Work

Computer work is often part of demanding, fast-paced jobs in high-pressure work-places. Whether that work is stressful depends primarily on *how* the computer is integrated into the job. Using a computer can give you autonomy, enhance your skills, and increase your enjoyment of work, or it can take away control, decrease your skills and opportunities, dehumanize your work, and make your job unpleasant.

Researchers the world over have found that computer workers in stressful jobs have higher rates of general muscle tension and pain, RSI symptoms, eyestrain, headaches, skin rashes, and menstrual problems. People whose jobs combine long hours of straight computer work, high demand, low control, unsupportive supervisors, and certain types of electronic performance monitoring are definitely at risk. Many researchers believe that the influence of stress on injury is as impor-tant as the office environment, furniture, equipment, and physical demands of computer work. [5]

Jobs with Low Control Are Problematic

In some jobs, such as straight data entry or word processing, lack of control over your work and schedule significantly increases stress. You may not be allowed to pace yourself, take breaks when you need them, organize your own work, or even discuss a problem with your peers. You may feel like you can't even take a few seconds to stand up, stretch your legs, shake out your hands, or look away from the screen. If you deal with customers over the phone, you may not be able to provide the best quality service, because you're evaluated not on how well you handle the calls, but on how fast you handle them, leaving both you and the customer dissatisfied.

Overemphasizing speed and quantity gets in the way of quality, and makes little use of your experience, judgment, and decision-making skills—the elements that make a job engaging, interesting, and challenging. If your job is something like this, you're probably under a lot of stress:

- Lack of control over scheduling, break times, and how the work is done

- Lack of diverse or engaging tasks

- Long hours of straight computer work (more than four hours per day)

- Fast pace and heavy workload

- Electronic monitoring to measure performance and/or push productivity

- Lack of opportunities to interact with your co-workers

- Little opportunity to advance your career

Jobs with High Control Are Stressful in Different Ways

Some jobs have a high degree of autonomy, such as research and development, writing, managing, and consulting. In these types of jobs, you can often control your hours, your activities, and the way you work. This means you are also responsible for pacing yourself and taking breaks. Sometimes taking care of yourself on the job gets pushed aside by your own internal pressure to do a good job and get a lot done. You may even end up working 50 or 60 hours a week, almost voluntarily sacrificing exercise and social activities in the process. Many people put more pressure on themselves than their boss does.

Your job may involve so many varied activities and extra responsibilities, like training new people or serving on committees, that you come in early and stay late so that you can work without interruptions. Just keeping up on email and newsgroups can take up huge chunks of time. Deadlines increase the pressure to work long hours and take work home—with beepers, portable telephones, and a home computer or laptop, you're never completely separated from your job.

Amidst these pressures, you may know that something is wrong, but you're so caught up in the current task that there's no time to step back and assess the situation. If you think of your job as having these qualities, you may be more stressed than you realize:

- Complex tasks and extra responsibilities

- Unrealistic deadlines .

- Long hours in general, including sessions of intense computer work

- Information overload

- Support for overworking

Electronic Performance Monitoring Can Be a Hindrance

While workers in the computer industry itself typically have a lot of autonomy and aren't usually subject to electronic monitoring, millions of people who use the computer systems they make are monitored in ways high-tech workers would likely find invasive and demeaning. Airline reservation agents, data entry workers, telecommunications operators, and customer service representatives are commonly monitored not only to "ensure quality service" but also to evaluate their performance and keep productivity levels high.

At its worst, monitoring takes away autonomy, reduces your skill level, and leaves you feeling exposed and unmotivated. It takes the pleasure out of work and makes it a high-stress experience. Monitoring shifts the focus of a job from quality to quantity—it tracks the number of keystrokes you make, how long you spend on a phone call, when you take breaks, and how long you are away from your computer.

Some systems collect information irrelevant to job performance. Supervisors may have access to your personal phone calls and electronic files, with or without your knowledge or permission. Many unions and trade associations believe this violates your privacy, and question how much employers need to know about you in order to evaluate your performance.

Electronic surveillance, constant or random, announced or secret, can increase fear and tension, and lead to mistrust between workers and bosses at all levels. It encourages people to think up ways to beat the system instead of ways to do their job better. Instead of increasing productivity, monitoring may actually reduce it over the long term. It certainly increases stress.

Experience and research show that monitored workers suffer more from both psychological and physical stress symptoms—high tension, boredom, anger, anxiety, depression, fatigue, headaches, muscular aches and pains, and symptoms of RSI.[6] Just how deeply monitoring and automation can affect people's lives and careers is revealed in Barbara Garson's engrossing book, *The Electronic Sweatshop*.

Monitoring at its best measures the performance of teams, not individuals. It is never unannounced, and never used to set production quotas or track unnecessary information. Effective monitoring allows you control over when you are monitored, what is being measured, and what are reasonable goals. It lets you access and verify the information gathered.[7] In general, people *want* to do a good job and perform well. Done well, monitoring may help them do that.

The Corporate Environment Can Increase Pressure

Corporations are never static. They shrink, grow, reorganize, and change character under the influence of new or changing management styles. The way changes are implemented seriously affects the concentration and stress levels of everyone involved.

There's potential for stress in many types of change in the corporate climate, whether they're perceived as positive or negative. With downsizing and reorganizations, it's questionable whether the short-term savings are offset by the costs of the stress they create. Corporate culture and the attitudes of supervisors and managers also make a big difference in your experience of corporate stress.

- *Downsizing (and fear of downsizing).* When corporations reduce staff to cut expenses, there is not always a corresponding reduction in the amount of work to be done, and the remaining workers are expected to put in the extra hours to do it. Some take on supervisory or management roles without getting a raise or even a new job description. Fear keeps people from protesting—they don't want to be the next to lose their job. These conditions may lead to injury and burnout.

- *Rapid expansion.* In fast-growing companies, there is constant change in both the physical workplace and the organizational structure. People are crowded into existing offices, conference rooms are converted to offices, cubicles are installed in hallways. Layers of management are added and new groups are formed. New ways of doing things evolve. Corporate politics become more complicated. Concentrating on the job, or even finding out what exactly your job is, can be difficult within a rapidly changing structure.

- *Frequent "reorgs."* Stress sets in from the first rumors of a corporate reorganization. Who will go to what group? Who will be let go? Who will report to whom? Will I have to move my office? Will my project still exist? Will I have a new manager? The uncertainty of reorgs—especially when they happen every 6 to 12 months—breeds anxiety, dissatisfaction, cynicism, and lots of stress.

- *High-pressure corporate culture.* In this atmosphere, pressure can come from both management and peers to work fast, work hard, take on more than you can possibly manage, and deliver in record time. Vacations can get put off indefinitely. Unless you look stressed and work overtime, people think you don't have enough to do. High stress may even become symbolic of importance—the more stressed you are, the more important you must be.

- *Unsupportive management.* Mistrust or unsupportive relationships between workers and managers, or between levels of management, add tension and discord to your workplace. If your immediate supervisor doesn't support your efforts, you are more likely to burn out and have stress-related problems. Also, if your boss or other people in your group are stressed, their stress can increase stress levels in your entire group.

The Physical Environment Plays a Part

Stressors in the physical environment can weaken the body and exacerbate emotional stress. Some of the main physical stressors to watch out for are these:

- *The office layout.* Office plans that crowd people in can make you feel nervous, closed in, and unable to concentrate—mental energy you could be using for your work is spent tuning out your environment. On the other hand, layouts that separate you from your colleagues inhibit social contact and can make you feel isolated and detached. You lose interactions that generate ideas and make your job meaningful. While some people prefer seclusion and others like to be in the middle of the action, everyone needs a balance of privacy and social interaction to work comfortably and efficiently.

- *Noise.* Noise makes doing concentrated work more difficult and frustrating. Having to tune out other people's conversations, ringing phones, noise from nearby construction sites, or the constant hum of machines can be distracting, disruptive, and irritating. Even music can be stressful if you are forced to listen all day to music you don't like. If you work at home, you may be stressed by noise in your neighborhood. Continual exposure to noise decreases blood circulation to the limbs, causes a sustained rise in blood pressure, and raises the levels of stress hormones in the blood.[8]

  If you are sensitive to noise you may be conscious of its presence. Even if you don't perceive it consciously, your body is continually responding to it. Have you ever breathed a sigh of relief when you powered down the computer and noticed how quiet it was without the steady hum? Chances are you were operating with a slight level of stress all day long and didn't realize it until you turned the computer off.

- *Other factors.* Air quality and chemical pollutants, electromagnetic radiation, uncomfortable furniture and equipment, and poor lighting can all contribute to stress.

What Can You Do About It?

If you work for a company, you may not be able to redesign your job, change the social structure, or remodel your office, but you can learn to recognize what's causing stress, make changes where you can, and encourage your employer to make changes where you don't personally have control.

If you work at home, managing stress is all up to you. You create your own job, your own corporate culture. You have lots of control over your physical environment. What kind of atmosphere are you creating for yourself?

If you're a student and use computers a lot, see which qualities in this chapter characterize your situation. What is expected of you as a student or teaching assistant? What responsibilities do you have in your department? What kind of atmosphere does your school have? What are your physical conditions for computer work? In some ways, studying can be a high demand, high control job, in a high-pressure environment.

If you are dissatisfied with your job, or feel you can't do enough to make it less stressful, then maybe it's time for a change. Think it through carefully—putting yourself in the same type of job in a similar work environment probably won't give you the relief you're seeking.

Whatever your situation, implement the changes recommended in Part I, *The Basics*, and practice the suggestions in the next chapter. These help you control your own personal response to stress. Act when you can, even if it's a small action. For example, if you're bothered by noise, see if you can work at home or work different hours. Try to resolve stressful situations on your own or within your group first. If you need more help, talk to your manager about job demands or conditions that you think get in the way of productivity. Help them solve the problem. You may have more control over your situation than you realize.

What Can Your Employer Do About It?

Reducing stress takes a cooperative effort. This book concentrates on what you can do personally to reduce stress, but to get at the root of the problem, changes have to occur in the workplace as well. *Corporate involvement is crucial.* Employers need to address sources of stress in their organizations, and high-tech companies need to create products that do the job and are easy to use. Individual efforts can only go so far when stressful jobs and working conditions remain unchanged.

Some companies offer stress reduction programs, exercise programs, and counseling through employee assistance programs. These measures can be very effective *when combined with other efforts to create a low stress work environment.* Employers must become aware of and change jobs, organizational processes, and elements of corporate culture that contribute to stress among all employees.

By eliminating dangerously high levels of stress, businesses can significantly reduce the risk of *all* computer-related ailments and injury, improve the health and morale of their workforce, increase profitability through higher productivity, and create tremendous savings each year in health care and workers' compensation costs. There is much to gain.

CHAPTER

18

Breaking the Internal Cycle

We frequently perceive stress as something imposed on us from outside. Although we do have to contend with stressful surroundings and events, they are only part of the problem. We are quite capable of perpetuating and even escalating stressful states through our habits of thought, behavior, exercise, and diet. By breaking the cycle of emotional stress within ourselves, we can fare much better in highly stressful environments.

There are many excellent books and programs about reducing stress. The approaches vary, but most contain these elements:

- Calming the mind through relaxation techniques or meditation

- Breathing

- Exercise and movement

- Diet

- Rest and relaxation

The suggestions in this chapter and in Part I, *The Basics*, give you the fundamentals for reducing stress. If you want to go further, ask your health care providers for their recommendations, check the listings under "Stress Management" in your telephone directory, or look for books on stress reduction at your local library or bookstore. *Full Catastrophe Living* by Jon Kabat-Zinn, and *Freedom from Stress* by Phil Nuernberger are particularly helpful.

Stress Begins in the Mind

When the mind perceives a challenge, real or imagined, the brain discharges stress hormones into the blood (epinephrine or adrenaline, adrenocorticoids and others). The challenge can be a threat to your physical well-being, your sense of self, or something you feel emotionally attached to.

If your mind dwells on that threat, reliving it, getting angry, feeling afraid, thinking about what you should have done or should have said, then you maintain the mental and physical agitation long past the moment when the threat actually occurred. Anticipating a threat and worrying about it tirelessly can have the same effect. In this state, you are more likely to respond with irritation and anger, or to feel overwhelmed and unable to function when other demands keep coming in and you're pressed for time.

The mind will think anything, any time. It can be calm in a stressful environment, or agitated in a calm one. It worries about your upcoming review in the middle of the night when you can't do anything about it. It constructs elaborate scenarios of future or past events, and then reacts to them in the present with anger or worry, as if they were real. You might be going along just fine, when something triggers a memory and your mind launches into a diatribe about an event that happened months ago. Suddenly your muscles tense up, your stomach is churning, and your concentration is gone.

Because thoughts alone can create or perpetuate stress, one of the first steps in reducing stress is learning to recognize thought patterns that agitate your mind. And one of the easiest ways to calm the mind when it's agitated is to shift your attention away from your inner dialog and onto your breath. There are several methods for dealing with stressful emotions and calming the mind. Many books on psychology and meditation offer guidance in these areas.

Thought Patterns Can Perpetuate Stress

Thoughts coming from anger, hopelessness, boredom, anxiety, and fear all have a way of dominating the mind. Like invasive plants, they multiply and crowd out other thoughts. Often, we just let these thoughts grow, and even encourage them. When you are angry, and you keep feeding that emotion, every thought you have becomes an angry one, until you are consumed by anger. In this state, you are unavailable to yourself and others. You lose perspective and your ability to think clearly about the situation.

Along with thoughts that come up spontaneously, we have habitual ways of talking to ourselves. For many of us, this inner dialog is often critical, judgmental, and absolutely without humor. This starts you on a downward spiral of negative thinking that can easily leave you feeling overwhelmed by your work or situation, and with a narrow view of life's possibilities.

Simply by becoming aware of your thought patterns, you begin to break the cycle. Watching the process rather than the content of your thoughts disentangles you from their drama. The moment you realize what your mind is doing, you can choose to bring your attention back to your body, focus on your breathing, and start to calm down. When the mind is calm, you have the mental spaciousness to change patterns of negative thinking.

Breathe to Calm the Mind

Paying attention to your breath calms you when you're anxious, and concentrates your mind when it's running all over the place. In *Full Catastrophe Living*, Jon Kabat-Zinn describes the advantages of what he calls "mindful breathing":

> When we are mindful of our breathing, it helps us to calm the body and the mind. Then we are able to be aware of our thoughts and feelings with a greater degree of calmness and with a more discerning eye. We are able to see things more clearly and with a larger perspective, all because we are a little more awake, a little more aware. And with this awareness comes a feeling of having more room to move, of having more options, of being free to choose effective and appropriate responses in stressful situations rather than losing our equilibrium and sense of self as a result of feeling overwhelmed, thrown off balance by our own knee-jerk reactions.

You can watch your breath any time, any place, but it's helpful to set aside a few minutes a day to practice. Then, when stressful situations and thoughts come up, shifting your attention to your breath is easier and more natural. Learning good breathing patterns, as described in Chapter 5, *Breathe*, is also fundamental to reducing stress and promoting better health.

To practice paying attention to your breath:

- Sit comfortably, or lie down. Focus on the inbreath and the outbreath. Choose a point to be aware of—the nose, where the breath goes in and out, or the belly as it goes up and down with the breath. You may want to count your breaths. Just keep your attention on your breathing. When your mind wanders, as it inevitably will, just note that it was wandering and then go back to watching the breath. Be patient—your breath is always there, and your mind can always return to it.

- As your mind slows down, notice the types of thoughts that arise. Instead of getting into their story line, notice their effects in your body. When you're angry, where do you feel it? What happens to your breathing? What happens in your body when you're bored, anxious, afraid? Keep breathing.

- Notice how you talk to yourself. Are you critical and judgmental, or supportive and accepting? When negative thoughts come up, counter them with positive thoughts and humor. Remind yourself of your good qualities.

- Notice how you breathe. You may be breathing irregularly, or only to your chest, or holding your breath. Just focusing your mind on the breath often helps regulate and deepen your breathing. If you like, breathe to the belly as described in Chapter 5.

Awareness of the breath is one of the most common techniques for calming the mind. You might also want to experiment with other techniques. Figure 18-1 shows a few exercises from *Educational Kinesiology*, a series of movements designed to stimulate balanced use of both hemispheres of the brain.[1]

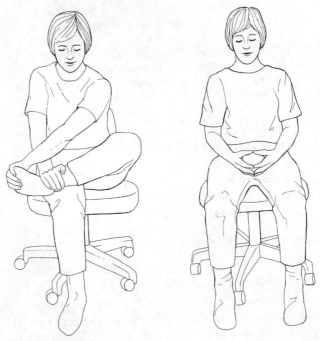

Cook's hook-ups help relieve stress, sadness, confusion, or anger:

a. *Sit down and cross your left ankle over your right knee. Hold your left ankle with your right hand. Hold the ball of your left foot with your right hand. Close your eyes, put your tongue on the roof of your mouth, and breathe deeply. Do this for about a minute, or until you're ready to stop. If you like, do the same movement on the other side.*

b. *Uncross your legs, put your feet on the floor, and hold your fingertips together. Continue to breathe with your eyes closed for another minute or until you feel finished.*

Figure 18-1. Educational kinesiology movements to calm the mind

Exercise with Awareness

We store stress in our muscles and joints. Over time, they become stiff and sore, leaving us susceptible to RSI and other injuries. To release the tension, we need a combination of vigorous exercise to get the blood moving, and slow, sustained stretching to lengthen and relax tight muscles. Whatever your exercise routine, you will get the most benefit from it by paying attention to what your body is doing, and coordinating your breath with your movements.[2]

You can do any sport, exercise, or movement with awareness, whether it's stretching, walking, running, weight training, swimming, bicycling, dancing, or splitting wood. The more you keep your mind focused on your activity, the more it will reduce stress. Pay attention to different parts of your body or to the feeling of the movements, and breathe evenly. *Don't hold your breath.*

When you walk, for example, notice the sensations in each foot as you step. Try inhaling for two steps and exhaling for three. For stretching, go slowly, paying attention to the movements and sensations of the muscles. Breathe evenly and fully as you relax into the stretch and hold it. When you swim, note the feeling of your arms pulling through the water, and breathe rhythmically, inhaling for one stroke and exhaling for two.

Some systems of exercise have awareness practice built in. Yoga, tai chi, chi kung, and martial arts in general are great stress reducers. Because their movements are designed to coordinate mind, body, and breath, you get exercise, mind training, and breathing practice all at the same time. They stretch, strengthen, and relax the muscles, improve circulation, and sharpen your concentration.

Relax and Recharge Your Senses

We all know we need to relax, but often there's the fear that if we do, we'll completely lose our momentum. If you've been pushing yourself hard for a long time, you may need some time to recover once you ease the pressure. It doesn't have to be all or nothing, totally stressed or totally gone. If you relax a little bit every day, some days more than others, you won't get to the point of collapse.

Many of us have lived with chronic stress for so long that we don't know how to relax anymore, or even what it feels like to be relaxed. Relaxing does *not* mean being catatonic, flopped out on the sofa staring blankly at the walls or the TV. When you are relaxed, you feel awake, alert, and rested. You feel limber, active, energetic, creative, and open-minded.

You also start feeling things again, both pleasure and pain. This is natural. Stress numbs pain, which allows you to keep going, but it also numbs the mind and the senses. When your foot has been asleep, it tingles uncomfortably when it wakes up, but this is not a reason to keep it asleep.

Here are some suggestions for breaking the cycle of chronic stress:

- *Recharge your senses.* Get out in nature and notice the sights, smells, and sounds. Feel the sun on your skin, watch the wind move the trees, absorb the blue of the sky or the grey of the clouds. Go to a concert or listen to your favorite music and let the sound penetrate. Soak in a hot bath, hot tub, or mineral spring. Breathe in the fragrance of fresh flowers or herbs.

  Put a few drops of essential oils in a diffuser to release their aroma into the air. The essential oils of geranium, lavender, rosemary, and tea tree stimulate the immune system and help mitigate stress; cypress, lemon, orange, bergamot, pine, bois de rose, cedarwood, grapefruit, pettigraine, patchouli, and sandalwood may enhance the effectiveness of negative ions and improve the office environment.[3] (Check with your officemates before using any kind of scent in the office.)

- *Whatever you do, put your full attention on it and keep breathing.* Try eating an apple this way. Notice its color and smoothness as you hold it in your hand, the sound as you take a bite, its flavor, texture, smell. Even the smallest action can stimulate all your senses.

- *Get a massage or bodywork.* Therapeutic touch relaxes sore muscles and releases tension stored deep in your body. Regular massage helps keep your stress level down.

- *Do something completely different.* Step out of your routine, do something out of character, out of the ordinary. When you do the same thing every day, the mind can become stiff and closed to new ideas. Something as simple as taking a different route to work or wearing clothes that aren't your style can loosen up your mind.

- *Lighten up.* Laughter and a good sense of humor make even the most stressful situations more bearable.

Replenish your Reserves

Human beings are quite resilient—the body repairs itself and the mind refreshes itself relatively easily as long as you give them what they need. To stay healthy and alert, we need food, water, light, and sleep.

Feeling stressed and eating well don't often go together. Instead, you either forget about food or feel too tired to shop or cook, so you eat junk food or just have a cup of coffee or go out to eat (again!). If you eat in a hurry, you might gulp your food down, hardly noticing what you're eating or how it tastes. Instead of feeling nourished, you feel worse, have even less energy to make the effort to eat well, and fall into the junk food cycle again and again.

- *Eat fresh, whole, organically grown foods.* Rely less on processed foods that contain a lot of chemicals, sugar, salt, and fat. Consider taking multi-vitamin supplements if you're not sure you're getting all the nutrients you need.

- *Slow down just a little and enjoy your meals.* Chew your food thoroughly, and swallow liquids slowly. Notice the flavors and textures of the food.

- *Use caffeine judiciously or not at all.* Black tea has less caffeine than coffee, may give you the charge you are looking for, and is easier on your system. Herbal teas with ginseng and ginger are energizing, and a mix of juice and sparkling water is refreshing. Avoid soft drinks that contain caffeine, sugar, and chemical additives.

- *Stay well hydrated.* Drink pure or filtered water so you don't ingest chlorine or other chemicals. Sip water throughout the day rather than drinking it in a few big gulps a few times a day. Keep a glass of water or a water bottle at your desk to make sure you always have some handy. Use your empty glass or bottle as a cue to take a break—get up and go fill it again from your favorite source.

- *Get outdoors, even for a few minutes a day.* Natural light is a nutrient. If you don't get enough of it, you can feel depressed and sluggish. If you're concerned about getting too much sun, avoid exposure at midday.

- *Get enough sleep.* Stress can make you toss and turn all night, or have intense dreams where you recreate the craziness of the day. Or you might sleep soundly for a few hours and wake in the middle of the night. When your sleep is disturbed, you wake up groggy and still stressed from the day before, and your resilience gradually dwindles slightly.

Don't Work Too Much

In almost any computer job, it's easy to fall into the habit of overworking. Your company may require overtime or long hours, and your choice may be overwork or no work at all. Your job demands may be so great that you work long days and weekends. You may internalize the pressure and work more to prove your worth or do an outstanding job. Maybe you have to work two jobs to get by financially. Overworking has become socially acceptable—if you miss out on something because of work, your friends and family are disappointed, but they understand. What can they do? You had to work. It's okay.

Suggestions for Getting a Good Night's Sleep[a]

First, calm your mind. Stop concentrated mental activity about an hour before bed. Have a cup of chamomile tea or hot milk with honey, stretch, take a hot bath, listen to some quiet music, or just sit and relax.

Get into bed and settle in to a comfortable position on your back. Breathe smoothly, evenly, and deeply to your abdomen. Let the outbreath be longer than the inbreath.

Visualize a relaxing scene or just enjoy the darkness. Imagine soothing music or pleasant sounds, or just notice the sounds around you.

Let go of the tension in your head, around your eyes, forehead, neck, shoulders, back, belly, legs, feet, toes. Continue soft, easy breathing.

Luxuriate in the feeling of relaxation. Let any remaining tension slip away. Continue noticing the breath, keeping its rhythm slow and steady, the outbreath longer than the inbreath.

Start counting your breath. Count 8 full breaths, in and out while lying on your back. Turn to your right side and count 16 breaths. Turn to your left side and count 32 breaths.

a. Sleep suggestions based loosely on Nurenberger, *Freedom from Stress*, 197.

Overworking uses up your reserves—you don't have enough recovery time, so you get fatigued and are more likely to get sick or injured. The more tired you get, the less productive you are, and your return for your hours declines. Overworking takes up time you might spend exercising, socializing, and generally having a life outside of work. You may even get so used to working that you don't know what to do with yourself when you *do* take time off, or you're too tired to enjoy yourself. You start to get a sense of limited possibilities. If everyone in your group is overworking, you'll tend to have more trouble communicating with each other and resolving conflicts.

As much as you can, resist pressure to work to exhaustion. Give yourself at least one full day a week off. Take your vacations, even if you just stay home. Cut back your hours and make the hours that you do work more productive. If you must work a second job, choose one that's very different from your first job. If overwork is a serious problem at your company, discuss the situation with your boss to see what you can do about it.

Balance Computer Time and Social Time

A lot of us work on computers all day, and then spend more time on a computer at home. There's a lot of fascinating stuff there—a whole other world of information, bulletin boards, newsgroups, email, games, music, animation, art, books, video, voice. It opens up new ways of learning, exchanging ideas, doing business, relaxing. It can be stimulating and exciting, and you can communicate with people all over the world. As more parts of our lives go online, there's all the more reason to stay logged in.

Still, it's a solitary pursuit—while your mind is engaged with the people and pleasures of the world online, you're not available to the people around you. To them, you're just absorbed in the screen and have no attention left for them. If you stay there for too long, your real world relationships can start to suffer, and it may become even more tempting to take refuge in your computer world.

Spending too much time online can even make you unavailable to yourself. You might lose track of time and spend hours or even whole days logged in without attending to your basic needs for food, water, and exercise. Keep it in balance. Take time to be with your partner, family, friends, and community. Set up your life so you can enjoy both worlds.

V

The Potential Risks of Electromagnetic Fields

Although there have been a number of studies, anecdotal accounts, and observations, we still don't know how radiation from our computers affects us. We do know:

- We are exposed to electromagnetic fields (EMFs) in the office from building wiring, lights, photocopiers, printers, computer monitors, and other sources. We're exposed to EMFs at home from electrical wiring, televisions, stoves, toasters, hair dryers, alarm clocks, and all sorts of appliances. Even outside, in both cities and rural areas, we are exposed to EMFs from electrical transmission lines and communications towers for cellular phones, radio, and television..

- EMFs are a possible influence in several health risks, from stress to miscarriage to cancer. However, we don't know how much risk these fields pose or what exposure levels might be dangerous.

- You can limit the possible effects of EMFs by prudent avoidance. Keep your distance from electrical devices and equipment. Turn off equipment when it's not in use. Consider electromagnetic emissions when purchasing equipment or when planning a new building.

CHAPTER

19

The Radiation Question

Because we spend much of our workday and sometimes even our leisure time in front of computer monitors, we tend to focus on them as our primary source of radiation, also called *electromagnetic fields*, or EMFs. However, exposure from computer monitors is part of the larger problem of exposure to electromagnetic fields in general, particularly *extremely low frequency* fields, called ELF, in the power line frequency range.

As more manufacturers provide low-emission monitors, concern is shifting to other sources of low frequency fields—building wiring, fluorescent lights, and other office equipment. Computer monitors are still a concern, but we must consider them as one of many sources of potentially harmful low frequency fields.

The Influence of Radiation

Radiation is energy in the form of electric and magnetic fields radiating out from an object. In nature, electromagnetic energy comes from the sun, bolts of lightning, atmospheric and solar disturbances, and the earth itself. These forces have influenced the evolution of human beings and of all life on Earth. Until recently, they were the only electromagnetic fields we were exposed to—the electromagnetic spectrum was virtually empty between the sun's high energy rays and the slow, steady pull of the Earth's magnetic field.

The transmission of electrical power in the late nineteenth century made possible the development of electric lighting, radio, television, telecommunications, radar, computers, microwave ovens, satellite dishes, cellular phones, and wireless computer networks, all operating on different frequencies with different intensities. In the span of a century, we filled the space around us with electromagnetic fields never before experienced.

Our bodies are always responding to electromagnetic energy. Our biological rhythms follow the cycles of light and dark, the 28-day lunar cycle, and the imperceptible daily shifts in the geomagnetic field. The way we behave is affected as well—long hours of darkness can bring on depression, and disturbances in the geomagnetic field (magnetic storms) have been associated with disturbances in behavior.

Only recently have we begun to discover and accept that we interact with man-made fields as well as natural ones. The mechanism and consequences of that interaction are matters of ongoing controversy, study, and debate.

Radiation in the Office

Wherever there is electrical power and equipment that uses it, there are electromagnetic fields. Power transmission lines and transformers, electric shavers, electric blankets, hair dryers, refrigerators, ovens, coffee makers, and power tools generate extremely low frequency fields and various higher frequency fields, as well.

Offices are filled with low frequency fields, generated by all kinds of electrical devices—lights, fans, computer equipment, typewriters, and office machines. Computer monitors are actually the fourth biggest source of ELF fields, behind fluorescent lights, photocopiers, and building wiring.[1]

Printers, computer equipment, and other office machines also emit radio frequencies. These fields are shielded by requirement of the U.S. Federal Communication Commission (FCC). The shielding is not for health reasons, but to prevent interference with other communication frequencies. Wireless computer networks use cellular, radio, or microwave frequencies to transmit information between terminals, replacing network cabling, but adding new fields to the office environment. Though the amounts emitted are considered small, their biological effects are unknown.[2]

Most of us can't feel or detect these fields directly, though some extremely sensitive individuals can. We may be aware that we feel tired, stressed, fatigued, or irritable when we're at work, but not know exactly why. Electromagnetic fields may play a part. Time, research, and experience will tell.

Radiation from Computers

Conventional computer monitors (video display terminals, or VDTs) emit electromagnetic fields from all ranges of the spectrum, from ELF to x-rays. They also give off energy in the form of static electric fields and high-pitched sounds. The

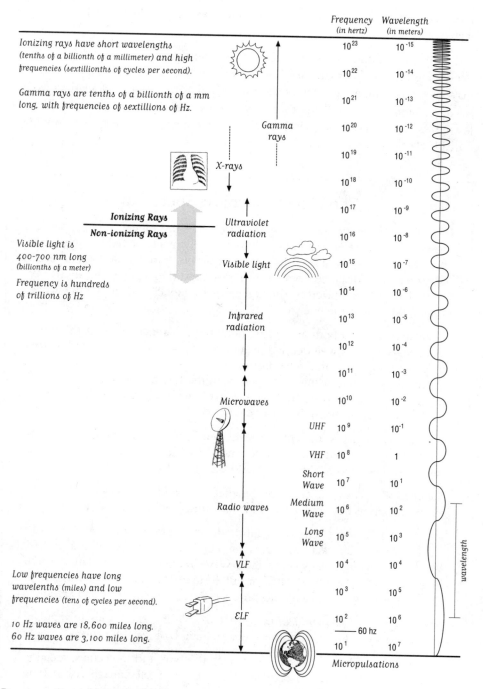

Ionizing rays have short wavelengths
(tenths of a billionth of a millimeter) and high
frequencies (sextillionths of cycles per second).

Gamma rays are tenths of a billionth of a mm
long, with frequencies of sextillions of Hz.

Visible light is
400-700 nm long
(billionths of a meter)

Frequency is hundreds
of trillions of Hz

Low frequencies have long
wavelenths (miles) and low
frequencies (tens of cycles per second).

10 Hz waves are 18,600 miles long.
60 Hz waves are 3,100 miles long.

Figure 19-1. The electromagnetic spectrum

fields are generated by the screen's cathode ray tube, which creates the screen image.

The strengths of the fields vary among different makes and models of VDTs, depending on how they are made and the quality of the components. Emissions may even vary among screens of the same model. In general, older screens emit stronger, more irregular fields than newer ones. The trend is toward affordable low-emission monitors as consumers demand them, and shielding technologies for cathode ray tubes improve.

The Electromagnetic Spectrum

The electromagnetic spectrum spans a tremendous range, from high energy cosmic rays to the almost imperceptible, steady magnetic field of the earth. Radiation moves away from its source in waves, and is described in terms of wavelength (distance from crest to crest) and frequency (oscillations per second, measured in Hertz). The higher the frequency and shorter the wavelength, the higher the energy.

The waves contain both an electric field and a magnetic field. At high frequencies, there is a well-defined relationship between the fields. At low frequencies, however, the relationship is not as clear. Fields can change instantaneously and within centimeters. In the low frequency ELF and VLF ranges, these fields appear to have distinct bioeffects, and are often considered separately in research.

Geomagnetic field. At the cellular level, our bodies are tuned to the micro-pulsations of the magnetic field generated by the earth itself, and may be sensitive to even its slightest fluctuations.

ELF and VLF. These fields create bioeffects in unknown ways. Certain frequencies, intensities, and waveforms have more effects than others.

Radio frequencies. Microwave, infrared, and some higher energy radio waves cause bioeffects from heat created by rotating or vibrating molecules. When very low frequency (VLF), radio wave frequency (RF), and microwave frequency (MWF) are modulated or pulsed in the ELF range—as most are in their applications—they seem to produce the same bioeffects as ELF fields.

Visible light and near/mid Ultraviolet (UV). We use these rays to regulate and coordinate almost all of our life-sustaining biological functions.

Ionizing rays. These rays split electrons off atoms and molecules, creating unstable, charged particles called ions, which cause cell damage by breaking biochemical bonds. The higher the energy, the greater the ability to ionize.

VDTs are now considered adequately shielded to contain radio frequencies, as well as minute emissions of infrared, ultraviolet, and x-rays. Static electric fields are reduced through proper grounding, and high-pitched sounds are reduced or eliminated through the use of higher quality flyback transformers. The most troublesome emissions are extremely and very low frequency fields (ELF and VLF) fields. These are difficult to contain, and may be more harmful than other fields, especially the magnetic fields. These fields are reduced through shielding or redesigning the deflection coils.

Flat panel displays typically have lower emissions than VDTs because they use less power and don't use a cathode ray tube to create the screen image. They do emit some fields, however. Liquid crystal displays (LCDs), in general, emit very weak fields, though some LCDs in portable computers can generate strong fields. Some backlit LCDs emit strong electric fields.[3] Plasma and electroluminescent displays generate low frequency electric and magnetic fields, similar to those of low-emission monitors.

ELF Magnetic Fields

The vertical deflection coils create ELF magnetic fields at about 50-90 Hz.

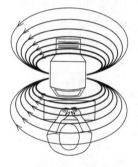

VLF Magnetic Fields

The horizontal deflection coils create VLF magnetic fields at about 10-30 kHz.

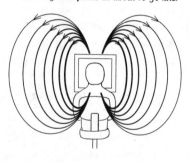

ELF and VLF Electric Fields

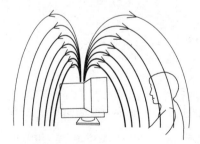

Static Electric Fields

High voltage static electric fields cause strong charges to build up between you and the screen, and deplete negative ions from the air.

Figure 19-2. Inside a video display terminal

The computer processor itself emits ELF and other fields. We haven't given these emissions much attention until recently; they are now starting to be addressed by organizations that develop emissions guidelines, such as the Swedish Confederation of Professional Employees (TCO).

The Nature of Low Frequency Fields

Our knowledge of how we interact biologically with low frequency fields is incomplete. We haven't been studying the issue for very long, and electromagnetic research is a complicated matter, involving biology, biochemistry, medicine, and physics, with a little politics thrown in.

Until the mid-1980s, many scientists believed that low frequency fields could not possibly be harmful. They don't affect cells and tissues by ionizing molecules and breaking biochemical bonds, the way x-rays and gamma rays do. They don't damage cells through heat, the way some radio frequencies and microwaves do. Yet studies on people living and working near power lines showed links between ELF fields and certain types of cancer, and prompted more researchers to explore the connections.

Most scientists currently agree that low frequency fields do have biological effects—particularly continuous ELF fields and weak, pulsed magnetic fields. They just don't know the extent of the effects, whether they're harmful or not, or why they occur. Some patterns are emerging, however.

ELF Magnetic Fields Have Biological Effects

Over the years, studies on cells, tissues, and animals have produced significant, yet inconclusive and sometimes contradictory results. Taken as a whole, they suggest that various ELF magnetic fields can:[4]

- Affect the growth of developing tissues

- Promote the growth of cancer cells

- Interfere with cell processes and functions

- Alter neurological functions

- Alter the production of neurohormones

- Affect the function of the pineal gland and its hormone, melatonin

- Influence the dopamine, opiate, and pineal systems, which in turn interact with the immune system

These various biological effects have potential both to heal and to promote disease, just as the use of drugs may have beneficial or harmful biological effects.

Magnetic Fields and Biological Systems

Low frequency magnetic fields may be acting on the pineal gland, suppressing its release of the hormone melatonin, which helps regulate many biological cycles, and may protect against breast, prostate, and skin cancer by inhibiting hormones that promote the growth of tumors. The fields may be acting through the retina, which sends signals to the pineal gland via the optic nerve and the hypothalamus (see Figure 16-1). The pineal gland may rely on both visible light and magnetic fields to regulate our biological functions.

The fields may also encourage breaks in cell membranes and interfere with communication between cells. This could change the behavior of hormones, antibodies, neurotransmitters, and molecules that promote cancer. The fields induce a stress response in cell, similar to that induced by heat. They also alter the flow of calcium ions between lymphocyte cells in rats and brain cell tissue in chickens. Calcium ion flow affects many biological functions, including hormone secretion and the actions of muscle, nerve, and immune cells.

Scientists are also investigating the possibility that low frequency magnetic fields influence the movements of magnetosomes, tiny magnetite particles in brain cells. Known to exist in some migratory birds, allowing them to navigate using the Earth's magnetic field, they were recently discovered to exist in humans as well. The movements of these particles in response to abnormal magnetic fields might cause intermittent breaks in cell membranes, which could alter the cells' chemical intake, which could lead to mutations and cancer.

There is also speculation that magnetic fields may increase the number of free radicals in tissue by slowing down their recombination rate. Free radicals are molecular fragments that try to join with other molecules, causing chain reactions that affect hundreds of molecules. Free radicals are considered harmful since their reactions can damage DNA and promote cancer.

The use of specific, pulsed magnetic fields for difficult-to-heal bone fractures or hip problems is now widely accepted. Currently, researchers are investigating whether the influence of certain fields on brain waves might aid in the treatment of epilepsy and Parkinson's disease.

In other cases, the fields cause breakdowns in cell functions or alter biological systems in ways that, in certain circumstances, might lead to certain diseases and conditions, such as breast cancer, brain tumors, childhood leukemia, immune system disorders, stress, sleep and mood disorders, and chronic depression. Some studies using fields similar to those from VDTs (weak, pulsed fields with a sawtooth waveform) showed increased resorptions and birth defects in rats. Research is underway to determine whether simulated VDT fields have the same effects on breast cancer cells as other fields do.

Scientists are testing several theories about how these fields cause biological changes, particularly the growth of cancer cells. They are finding that low frequency magnetic fields may be acting on the pineal gland and its hormone melatonin, cell membranes, and intercellular communication, movements of magnetite particles in brain cells, and the number of free radicals in tissue.[5]

How Can We Interpret the Results?

Low frequency magnetic fields act in unusual, often unpredictable ways. Slight variations in the fields can alter the results; even minute fluctuations in the geomagnetic field may make a difference. Effects vary with the frequency and strength of the fields, the shape of the waveform, the length of exposure, and whether the field is pulsed or continuous. Effects also vary among individuals— some cells, animals, and people seem to be more susceptible than others. Thus, we need to keep the results in context, and not extrapolate from one field to another, or from one species to another.

Determining the relationship between the *dose* (the amount and type of exposure), and the *response* (the biological or health effect), is not straightforward. With most chemical toxins, the dose-response is linear—the greater the dose, the greater the response. With magnetic fields, however, weaker fields sometimes have more effect than stronger fields. Effects may occur only from specific frequencies, or frequencies within a specific range (called *amplitude windows*). Effects are sometimes strongest just after the fields are turned on or off, so that changes in exposure level may be as significant as the length of time we are exposed. And because we don't know which aspects of the fields are acting on us, we don't yet have a solid definition of dose.[6]

Some scientists question whether the dose-response model is appropriate for research. A better approach might be to look at how the body is tuned to electromagnetic fields.[7] The body appears to tune itself to natural frequencies up to 30 Hz, and to pick up neighboring low frequency fields, which can interfere with the body's normal functioning. When higher frequencies are modulated in the ELF range—as most are when they are actually used, such as for microwave radar, AM and FM radio, and television signals—the body may respond to them biologically, as it does to ELF fields.[8]

For results to be widely accepted, they need to be reproduced several times. One of the difficulties here, especially with research on VDT fields, is that the fields are difficult to measure accurately and consistently. Changing a measuring point

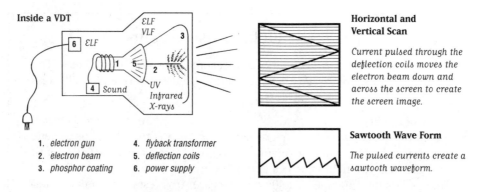

Figure 19-3. Emissions from video display terminals

by even a few centimeters can make a difference, especially with near fields. Not all researchers use the 'same measuring techniques or measure the same points. With such variation across studies, it's difficult to establish a baseline.

Standards for measuring emissions from VDTs are evolving. Measurement guidelines called MPR2, developed by SWEDAC, the Swedish Board for Technical Accreditations, have served as a *de facto* standard; a revised and expanded version of these guidelines, called MPR3, is expected to be approved in 1995. MPR3 could become a European standard, and eventually an international one. In 1994, the Institute of Electrical and Electronic Engineers (IEEE) approved its P-1140 standard, which provides comprehensive methods for measuring VDT emissions similar to those specified by MPR3. Limiting emissions is a separate issue from measuring them (see Chapter 21, *Protect Yourself*). MPR guidelines specify emissions limits, but the IEEE standard does not.

What Are the Implications?

We can't assume that biological effects observed in laboratory studies automatically imply health risks for people in everyday situations. Fields simulated in the laboratory may be different from those we actually experience, and not all the fields we are exposed to are the same. VDT fields are pulsed and have a sawtooth (jagged) waveform, while power line fields are continuous and have a sinusoidal (curved) waveform. Fields from office equipment and appliances all vary in frequency, waveform, and strength.

Still, changes at the cellular level may eventually manifest themselves as changes in our health. By noting tendencies in laboratory research, and putting them together with results from epidemiological studies, we can learn what types of effects are possible and what health effects to watch out for.

Magnetic Field Measurements

Magnetic field strength is commonly measured in units called Gauss. The magnetic field strengths we are exposed to most are described in milligauss (mG), one thousandth of a Gauss.

Many of the ELF magnetic fields of our own creation are much weaker than the earth's magnetic field—a significant difference is that the geomagnetic field is steady (DC), while many man-made fields are alternating (AC) fields. The geomagnetic field averages about 500 mG at 0 Hz, with daily fluctuations of less than 100 mG. The fluctuations are strongest for frequencies between 7 and 10 Hz.

Man-made fields as weak as a few milligauss have been shown to cause biological effects. Long-term exposure to weaker fields may be more harmful than short-term exposure to strong fields.

Appliances are for the most part not designed to contain electromagnetic fields, and many of them can generate strong ELF magnetic fields as well as higher frequency fields. Battery-operated appliances typically generate low strength fields, although this isn't always the case.

Field strengths typically drop off rapidly with distance, depending on the frequency and type of the field. Electric and magnetic field strengths diminish at different rates. Fields from appliances start dropping off almost immediately; fields from power distribution lines drop off after about 1 meter; and fields from power transmission lines drop off after about 10 meters.

In office buildings, measurements vary widely. A 1993 survey of 150 offices in Sweden found that background ELF magnetic fields averaged 0.7 mG, although a few offices had levels of 5 mG or more. In these offices, fields from computer monitors averaged 2.1 mG.[a] Offices can have ELF levels from the tens to hundreds of milligauss, and up to 3,000 mG near power conductors.[b]

a. *VDT News*, March/April 1994. 4.
b. *VDT News*, July/Aug 1991. 4.

How Much Exposure Is Considered Safe?

So far, no level has been proven absolutely safe or absolutely dangerous. Further, there's no consensus on whether our overall risk is high or low. The most common recommendation is an informal guideline called *prudent avoidance*—taking reasonable measures to protect ourselves from unnecessary exposure, while knowing that the potential for harm exists.

In general, weaker fields are thought to be more safe than stronger ones. Short-term exposure to strong fields, such as the few minutes it takes to photocopy a document, shave, or dry your hair, is considered less harmful than long-term exposure to weak fields, such as sitting close to a computer monitor all day or sleeping under an old electric blanket. Because of the unusual nature of the fields, however, these generalizations may not always hold true. We *may* be at less risk if we limit our average annual exposure to about 3 milligauss or below, and Robert Becker advocates keeping field strengths to 1 mG or less for continuous exposure to 60 Hz magnetic fields.[9]

The complexities and politics of electromagnetic research have hindered regulation, and so far no national government has established limits for exposure to low frequency magnetic fields at work or at home. Scientific studies have been inconclusive, and the political and economic implications of lowering emissions levels of the entire electric power infrastructure are vast.

Sweden recently considered but rejected setting exposure limits for magnetic fields. However, the Swedish National Safety Board continues to recommend reducing emissions from new power lines and power stations; locating new schools, day-care centers, and homes where exposure is less than 2 to 3 mG; and limiting exposure to strong fields in existing homes, schools, and work places.[10] A few other countries and some states in the U.S. regulate electric field strengths from power transmission lines, but not from distribution lines. A few states regulate their magnetic field strengths.[11] These regulations are primarily intended to prevent increases in field strengths, not to lower field strengths.

CHAPTER

20

Health Risks We Wonder About

Observations and anecdotal evidence about health effects from environmental hazards typically exist long before formal studies examine the association. This is true for radiation. Since the late 1970s, people have been concerned about whether computer monitors cause miscarriages, cancer, cataracts, skin rash, and stress. In the mid 1980s, some began to wonder whether radiation from computers had anything to do with new ailments such as chronic fatigue syndrome, and people started realizing that hypersensitivity to electromagnetic fields was not an imaginary allergy.

Proving an association between radiation and health problems is not a simple task. Isolating radiation from other factors is difficult, and isolating the effects of specific electromagnetic fields, such as those from computer monitors, is even more difficult. Inaccurate or inadequate measurement of fields for both the exposed group and the control group has been a drawback in many of the studies exploring the relationship between miscarriage and computer work.

Some ailments are relatively immediate, while others appear only after years of accumulated exposure. In general, health problems are often the result of several forces acting on us simultaneously and synergistically—the strength of our immune system, pre-existing conditions, stress levels, and exposure to environmental or occupational hazards.

The results of epidemiological studies on computer workers, electrical workers, and children living near power lines are far from conclusive. While the risks they do indicate are, for the most part, relatively low, some people *are* getting sick, and there's enough evidence to warrant caution. To be on the safe side, reduce your exposure to reduce your risk.

Miscarriage

We still don't know whether computer work increases the risk of miscarriage. A 1992 Finnish study, however, provides new insights. This was the first study designed specifically to assess the effects of electromagnetic fields from computer monitors on pregnancy. The results suggest that:[1]

- Working on a low-emission monitor (compliant with MPR2 emissions guidelines) probably does not increase your risk of miscarriage.

- Working on a high-emission monitor for more than 10 hours a week tends to increase your risk.

- Risk increases further from magnetic fields in the extremely low frequency (ELF) range than in the very low frequency (VLF) range. Risk increases with ELF fields greater than 3 mG.

- Risk tends to be greatest in the first trimester.

- The higher the emissions and the longer you are exposed, the greater the risk.

These findings bring us back to the problem of ELF magnetic fields in general. Exposure to ELF fields from power lines and older electric blankets has been shown to significantly increase the chance of miscarriage. Because the strongest fields in offices come from building wiring and other devices, some researchers feel we must consider these sources as well in our studies. Computer monitors are still sources of exposure, but may no longer be the primary suspects.[2]

This view gives us a different understanding of earlier pregnancy studies. These typically correlated the number of hours worked with risk of miscarriage and birth defects, and came up with inconclusive results. Some studies found no association between computer work and increased risk, while others did. Some increases were statistically significant and others were not. Researchers indicated that the increases in miscarriage could have been due as much to stress and other factors as to electromagnetic emissions from computer monitors.

In hindsight, some researchers feel that these studies may not have adequately measured exposure from either the monitors or other sources of electromagnetic fields in the office.[3] For example, a 1991 NIOSH study, which found no association between electromagnetic fields and miscarriage, didn't consider ELF magnetic fields because both the exposed group and the control group had the same exposure, possibly from the building wiring.

If you're worried about working on a computer when you're pregnant, keep in mind that risks come not just from the monitor, but also from exposure to ELF magnetic fields in general. If you have a low-emission monitor but are exposed to strong fields from the building wiring and a high-emission desk lamp, your risk may be higher. There are the usual factors to consider as well—high stress, lack of exercise, too much sitting, and a poor diet can all affect your pregnancy. Your best bet is to protect yourself from electromagnetic fields as much as possible before you get pregnant (or very early in the pregnancy), and take good care of yourself.

Other Reproductive Concerns

Whether computer work affects the male reproductive organs is largely unknown and unexamined. However, results of recent studies on male power line workers showed that their children had a greater number of birth defects than expected. Whether electromagnetic fields affect fertility in either women or men is unknown and has not been studied.

Over the years, many women have associated menstrual disorders and discomfort with computer work. The most common explanation is stress, but because electromagnetic fields are associated with stress, they could be an indirect influence.

Cancer

The connection between cancer and exposure to power line frequencies has existed for several years. In several studies since 1979, power line fields have been linked or associated with leukemia in children and adults, brain tumors, and breast cancer in both men and women.[4] Recent results have shown that the risk of cancers, particularly childhood leukemia, increases as the field strength increases.

We know less about the connection between cancer and exposure to emissions from computers. The only cancer study on computer workers completed to date found an increased risk of brain tumors in women, but not in men.[5] An investigation of breast cancer among women working at a telephone exchange in Australia found a higher rate of cancer, but did not identify a link between the cancers and either the computers or the physical environment.[6]

Cancer is increasingly a concern among office workers. Several cancer clusters, primarily brain tumors, among office workers have recently been reported in the United States (A cluster is defined as an unusually high number of people in the same workplace or neighborhood who develop similar illnesses. Concern about miscarriage and birth defects began with reports of clusters of adverse pregnancy outcomes from about 1979 to 1984.) Strong ELF magnetic fields from building wiring are the suspected cause, but brief investigations concluded that the cancers were probably not caused by the physical environment.[7] The issue is far from resolved.

Many children now spend a lot of time in front of computers from a very young age. Even babies and very young children like to watch animated stories on the screen. We don't know the effects of long-term exposure to computer monitor fields on children. We do know that certain cancers can develop in adults over years of accumulated exposure to strong ELF magnetic fields; that these fields tend to affect growing tissues; and that there is a strong association between power line fields and childhood leukemia. In view of this, it may be a good idea to protect children as much as possible from exposure to these fields.

In 1992, Sweden acknowledged the association between power frequency magnetic fields and cancer, especially childhood cancer, and advises that new schools, day-care centers, and homes be located where exposure does not exceed 2 to 3 mG.[8] In the U.S., a 1990 Environmental Protection Agency draft report acknowledged a possible but unproven link between electromagnetic fields and cancer. The report has not been finalized, and no action has been taken to regulate exposure.

Cataracts

Although cataracts can be caused by overexposure to mid-ultraviolet, microwave, and radio frequency fields, the general consensus is that electromagnetic fields from computer monitors do not cause cataracts. Some cases were reported among computer workers in the 1970s and early 1980s, when emissions from computer monitors were typically much higher than they are now, but a strong link between computer monitors and cataracts has not been generally accepted. Recent studies have not found higher rates of cataracts or other serious eye problems among computer workers.[9]

If you have a cataract and think it might have been caused or promoted by your computer work, ask your ophthalmologist to tell you where on the lens the cataract has formed. Radiation-induced cataracts form on the back of the lens capsule, the thin membrane surrounding the lens. Typically, cataracts develop in the lens itself.[10] If you were previously exposed to radar, radio frequencies, or microwaves, this may also be a factor. Also, don't spend a lot of time looking at the screen close up—fields are strongest right next to the screen and drop off rapidly with distance.

Stress

Electromagnetic fields are a known environmental stressor, and alter the levels of stress hormones in the blood.[11] Emissions from computer monitors and other sources in the office could therefore contribute to chronic stress, which is implicated in many health problems. High static electric fields and the related depletion of negative ions may also contribute to stress symptoms such as muscle fatigue, headaches, dizziness, nausea, and irritability.[12]

Skin Rash

Some people get skin rashes on their face, neck, and upper chest—the prime areas exposed directly to the monitor. Sometimes the rashes appear on areas that are covered by clothing. The most likely causes are stress, static electric fields (which attract dust and airborne particles to your skin), and electromagnetic fields. Recent research in Sweden has shown that:[13]

- If you work on a computer monitor for four hours or more at a time, you are twice as likely to get skin problems than if you work only one hour or less.

- You are even more susceptible if you already have environmental allergies such as asthma, and especially if you have a heavy workload and an unsupportive boss.

- You are more susceptible if you are exposed to background electric fields and ELF magnetic fields in the office in general.

Because we're not always aware of when we're exposed to strong magnetic fields, it may not be easy to find a correlation between the rash and exposure to EMFs. If you have a rash, see a physician. Try to recall when it started. Did the rash first appear after you started doing computer work for the first time, or when you switched to a different monitor? Notice when it gets better or worse. Does it go away when you've been away from the computer for a while, and return when you go back to it? Does it appear when you're under a lot of stress and disappear when the pressure eases?

Electromagnetic Sensitivity

Electromagnetic sensitivity is a relatively new condition found increasingly among computer workers and people living or working near power lines and communications towers (for cellular phones, radio and television, and other data transmissions).[14] It's an invisible condition that is frequently met with skepticism and disbelief. However, it is potentially debilitating and affects not only how you work in a high-tech office, but also how you function in daily life. Early intervention to reduce exposure to electromagnetic fields may prevent mild symptoms from getting worse, keep sensitive workers on the job, and ward off potentially high medical and disability costs.

Individuals report that electromagnetic sensitivity begins gradually, often with a feeling of vague heaviness in the abdomen, chest, or head. You may feel a minor irritation when working with a computer monitor, or a warm, burning sensation in the face, redness and prickling sensation on the skin, eye irritation, dryness in the nose or throat, or swollen mucous membranes.[15] People can experience a wide range of allergic and neurological symptoms, such as faintness, dizziness, giddiness, sleepiness, headaches, hyperactivity, irregular heartbeat, nausea, thirst, diarrhea, and sudden fatigue. Often, pre-existing allergies, environmental sensitivities, or chemical sensitivities get worse. Some people experience confusion, lack of concentration, depression, and memory loss. There may also be a connection between hypersensitivity and Alzheimer's Disease; early research suggests that exposure to EMFs may be an important contributing factor.[16]

As with any allergy, reactions to electromagnetic fields can be mild or severe. They're often set off by exposure to a new field, such as a new computer monitor or fluorescent lights. The triggering factor is not the same for everyone, but once people experience the symptoms, they become sensitive to many electromagnetic devices that had not caused them problems before—hair dryers, televisions, appliances at home, equipment at work, and even electronic control panels in automobiles. Many people are consistently sensitive to specific frequencies. Symptoms may come on unexpectedly, sufferers report, even when people in the neighboring apartment turn on their television.

Early symptoms are usually alleviated by turning off or moving away from the triggering device. For some people, however, the problem becomes progressively worse. Kathleen Hawk, a consultant to citizen groups and planners, describes her experience with electromagnetic sensitivity:

> I've always been sensitive to fluorescent lighting and electronic check-out equipment, but it wasn't until last year that I became sensitive to ordinary telephones. Gradually, I became sensitive to other sources. It was a rather slow process. My specific diagnosis is *otitis media* caused by abnormal electromagnetic frequencies. The very first sign is reddened skin, not just on the face, though it's certainly more severe there. In fact, those around me can see it before I become aware of the accompanying stinging, prickling sensation. The skin eventually peels like a sunburn.

> Often, I react, but am unable to determine a source. Last winter, every time I drove through a particular city neighborhood, I became almost too ill to drive. The dizziness and nausea would eventually leave as I drove out. Recently, I discovered that a medical clinic that uses x-rays had moved into that area. In traffic, someone using a cellular phone in a car next to mine will make me so ill I have to pull over. When I walk through a neighborhood near a cellular communications tower, I always react.

People with severe symptoms are advised to rely less on electrical devices, use shielded, grounded wiring, and avoid any source that may be aggravating their condition. Some sufferers have gotten relief through the therapeutic use of magnets, acupuncture, and other holistic methods.

Employers can help by increasing their awareness of the problem and taking action when employees report symptoms. The Ellemtel Telecommunications Systems Laboratory in Sweden provides a good example. Between 1988 and 1992, about 50 out of 1,000 employees developed electromagnetic sensitivity, reporting burning skin, dizziness, and nausea. Ellemtel responded by creating low-emission environments where many affected employees were able to continue working. They reduced exposure from equipment and wiring, shielded some offices and conference rooms, and provided some equipment-free offices with very low fields. Staff engineers developed several low-emission monitors and flat-panel displays as well as a non-electrical telephone receiver.[17]

Chronic Fatigue Syndrome

Chronic fatigue syndrome has afflicted many people in the electronics industry. In this industry, employees are surrounded by computers and monitors and other equipment in their offices and labs, and may even use more than one monitor regularly in their work. Whether or not their chronic fatigue is caused by electromagnetic fields is speculation, but the connection is worth exploring.

Symptoms are similar to those of electromagnetic hypersensitivity. Chronic fatigue begins with a flu, after which other symptoms set in. People have experienced fatigue, sore throat, tender lymph nodes, and mild fever, together with depression, lack of concentration, and mental confusion. Symptoms can last for months at a time. Exposure to electromagnetic fields seems to influence symptoms in some people, but not as strongly as it does in hypersensitive people. [18]

Hearing Discomfort

Some people have complained that high-pitched sounds from the computer monitor cause *tinnitus* (ringing of the ears), loss of balance, fullness in the ears, discomfort, pain, and stress. These sounds are in the range of 15.75 kHz, a frequency that has been shown to cause stress and lowered productivity.[19] Women and children tend to be more sensitive to these sounds than men. You can muffle high-frequency sounds by padding the flyback transformer inside the monitor (where they originate) or covering the back of the monitor, making sure not to block its ventilation. If that doesn't help, consider getting a monitor that doesn't create the sounds at all.

Some people are bothered by the constant hum of equipment, whether the sound is high-pitched or not. Pad or enclose offending equipment, or consider replacing it with quieter equipment. Power down equipment when you're not using it.

CHAPTER

21

Protect Yourself

Because there are no regulations regarding exposure to extremely low frequency (ELF) fields, you're on your own in deciding what your exposure limits are. Based on the information in this book and other sources, some of you may decide that ELF fields don't pose a threat, while some others may consider, at least for a moment, getting rid of your computers and changing careers.

Given the possibility of adverse health effects, it's probably not wise to continue the *status quo* and make no attempts to reduce your exposure. Nor is it possible to avoid exposure completely, given our dependence on electric power and the ubiquitous presence of electromagnetic devices. Many of these devices have become indispensable to us, and we would be hard-pressed to give them up. The transmission of electric power has brought us many benefits, but we can't ignore the potential risks.

The practical solution is to cut down on needless exposure. The easiest and cheapest way to reduce exposure is to distance yourself from sources of electro-magnetic fields and to power down equipment when you're not using it. When you buy new equipment or appliances, make low emissions and energy efficiency a priority. Your choices encourage manufacturers to create products that are safer for everyone.

Your course of action needs to balance three concerns—the benefits of your computer and other ELF-emitting devices, the amount of risk you're willing to accept, and the effort and expense required to reduce your exposure. Start by assessing the ELF fields in your immediate environment. The focus here is on the office, but you can apply the principles to other situations as well.

Assess Your Situation

Your overall exposure to electromagnetic fields depends on:

- How many electronic devices you use

- How long you spend using them or being near them, each day and over time (the effects are cumulative)

- The distance between you and the device

- What kind of fields they emit

- The strength of the fields

How Much ELF Are You Exposed To?

Think about other sources of low frequency fields in your environment, seen or unseen. Do you sit close to fluorescent lights or to the backs of other people's monitors, even if they're in a neighboring office? Is your office close to the building's main electrical switching equipment or power transformers? Do you live or work within a few hundred feet of power transmission lines? Do power cables run through the floor or ceiling of your office? Do you work in a computer lab or adjacent to one? Labs are often filled with unshielded equipment that could be exposing you to high fields.

If you spend a lot of time continuously surrounded by ELFs, your average exposure levels *could* be high, and you might want to reduce your exposure. You may also want to consider taking accurate field strength measurements to find the worst offenders.

How Much Risk Are You Willing to Accept?

Your answer to this question depends on how strongly you feel about the hazards of electromagnetic fields and how susceptible you think you are. If you are generally sensitive to chemicals and toxins, or if your family has a history of the conditions that seem to be worsened by electromagnetic fields, you may feel better in a low-emission environment.

If you want to have a child—whether you're female or male—you may be less willing to expose yourself to high fields. If you're pregnant, you may want to spend less time at your computer, at least for the first few months when the risk of miscarriage is higher.

If you have children, how much risk are you willing to let them take? Children are more susceptible to high emissions than adults. Teach them how to avoid high fields from computers, video games, and other devices they may use.

Measuring Low Frequency Fields

If you want a general idea of your exposure levels, you can buy or rent a gaussmeter. Choose the meter carefully, as they vary in sensitivity and in how they measure the fields. Use one that meets MPR2 or IEEE P-1140 requirements.[a] Take the measurements at the location(s) where you sit or spend the most time. Power on all equipment that is usually running, including monitors and lights near you.

Professional measurement of EMFs in your office will give you the most accurate assessment. Some power companies will measure fields for you at no charge, or you can hire a consultant to do it. Make sure the consultant is experienced and has good credentials.

Whether your office building has high or low field measurements, your overall exposure depends on the wiring configuration, placement of lights, where you sit in relation to sources of EMFs, and the length of time you are exposed.

Sometimes exposure from fluorescent lights is greater on the floor above them than in the room they're in. You might have a low-emission monitor but be sitting right next to a high-emission desk lamp. If your office neighbor has two or three monitors lined up along the wall adjoining your office, and you sit next to that wall, you're getting the strongest fields from all of those monitors, since emissions are stronger from the back than from the sides or front. Also, fields from neighboring monitors affect each other— measurements from a single monitor may be higher or lower when it's by itself or surrounded by other monitors.

One indicator of strong fields in your office is your own monitor—if it jitters erratically, it may be because of interference from the nearby lights or wiring. And if your monitor is being affected, so are you.

a. For a list of gaussmeters and the fields they measure, see *VDT News*, September/October 1994. For the most current list, send a self-addressed stamped envelope and $1 to VDT News, PO Box 1799, Grand Central Station, New York, NY 10163.

Choose Which Precautions to Take

The amount of time, effort, and expense you are willing to put into reducing your exposure may correspond with your degree of concern about the dangers. Choose precautions that are within your means and allay your fears. If you need to prioritize, start with the sources that are closest to you, are used the most, and have the highest emissions.

Behind nearly all the preventive measures are these basic guidelines:

- *Stay as far away from sources of electromagnetic fields as possible.* This involves not only how you set up your office, but how the building you work in is designed and laid out.

- *Don't expose yourself unnecessarily.* Limit the amount of time you spend around computers and electromagnetic devices in general, power down equipment you're not using, and cut down on the number of electronic devices you use. Remove high-emission devices from your office.

- *Use equipment and devices that have low emissions.* If this isn't feasible, shield those with high emissions.

Many of these changes are simple and cheap—they're mainly matters of planning and habit. Others, such as buying or modifying equipment, can cost tens, hundreds, or even thousands of dollars.

Some of the exposure you get is beyond your immediate control. You may want to work with your employer to find ways to reduce emissions in the workplace.

Table 21-1. Protecting Yourself from Low Frequency Electromagnetic Fields

What Helps	What Doesn't
Distance. Leave some distance between you and sources of electromagnetic fields. For computer monitors, keep about 2 feet from the front, 3 feet from the sides, and 4 feet from the back.	*Walls, ceilings, or petitions.* Solid walls and ordinary materials do not shield you from low frequency fields.
Turning off equipment. When electrical equipment is not in use, turn it off.	*Lead aprons.* Lead blocks x-rays, but not low frequency fields.
Knowledge. You can have your home or office measured for low frequency fields. Power companies often do these measurements for free.	*Glare filters.* These can block or reduce electric fields, but not magnetic fields.
Planning. If you're buying new computers, office equipment, or appliances, consider emissions ratings. For a new building, design the wiring and floor plan to minimize exposure.	*Screen savers or brightness controls.* If the monitor is on, you're still being exposed, even if the screen is blank.

Stay Away from Sources

You can significantly reduce your exposure simply by keeping your distance from sources of radiation.

- *Sit an arm's length or more from your monitor.* This distance is also good for vision and posture.

- *Stay 4 feet from the back and 3 feet from the sides of your own monitor and those of your neighbors.* Fields are stronger from the back and sides than from the front. Televisions share this emission pattern.

- *Sit at least a few feet from other sources of electromagnetic fields, such as fluorescent lights and power transformers or switching equipment.* Fields are strongest within a few inches of the source and drop off dramatically with distance.

- *Keep your distance even from equipment in adjacent rooms.* Magnetic fields pass through partitions, walls, and ceilings unless they are specially shielded, which is usually not the case.

Don't Expose Yourself Unnecessarily

In so many offices, we leave equipment on all the time—monitors, computers, printers, modems, photocopiers. This is not only expensive and a waste of energy, it also means electromagnetic fields are always present. Whenever a device is drawing power, it's emitting electromagnetic fields.

Turn off your equipment when you are not using it. You will not shorten the life of your monitor or computer by turning them on and off frequently. Current equipment can handle the power cycling. It will probably become technically obsolete long before you wear it out. Every time you power down equipment you aren't using, you drastically reduce your exposure to electromagnetic fields. When you leave it on, you expose yourself unnecessarily and contribute to environmental damage from the needless generation of electric power.

If you don't want to power your whole system down for short breaks, at least turn off the monitor, peripherals, and office lights. Turn the printer on only when you're ready to print. Save up your print jobs and do them all at the same time. If you're going to be at your desk, but don't need your computer for an hour or two, power it down. Use a power strip or some sort of master switch box to make powering down more convenient.

If you're buying new computer equipment, support the trend toward low power consumption and low emissions by choosing equipment that has either the U.S. EPA's Energy Star logo, or an environmental label from TCO, the Swedish Confederation of Professional Employees (TCO).[1] Equipment with one of these labels automatically powers down or consumes as little power as possible when you aren't using it, and returns to full power when you use it again. For example, the monitor powers back up and is ready to go when you press a key or move the mouse. Both the computer and the monitor must support the power-down feature for it to work.

Monitors with the TCO'92 label have the automatic power-down feature, and comply with the TCO's low-emission recommendations. Several manufacturers now offer products with the TCO'92 label, from 14 inch to 21 inch monochrome and color monitors. The TCO's efforts are part of a long-term program to develop ecologically sound, energy-efficient offices that integrate technology, people, and the environment. Called "6E," the program focuses on ecology, emissions (EMFs and chemical toxins), efficiency in design, economy, energy efficiency, and ergonomics. Monitors with the TCO'95 label comply with the other aspects of the 6E program.

Use Low-Emission Equipment and Appliances

Consider emission levels as a factor when you buy new products, and give preference to those with low emissions. Ask the sales representative or the manufacturer about electromagnetic frequency levels so they know you're paying attention. Appliances and office equipment other than monitors are not typically designed for low emissions, but this can change. With enough demand for low-emission products, manufacturers eventually respond so they don't lose business. There are precedents for this. When people became concerned about magnetic fields from electric blankets and actually stopped buying them, manufacturers developed blankets with significantly lower magnetic field emissions—though ironically, these blankets have higher electric fields, the effects of which are unknown. Finally, in response to increased public awareness, manufacturers significantly reduced emissions from computer monitors.

Use new technology with caution. Devices that use new technology haven't always been thoroughly tested for health effects, and we don't really know the consequences of using them. Be especially careful with devices you use right next to your body, such as cellular phones and some virtual reality headsets that use tiny CRT screens. You may want to think twice about using your laptop computer right in your lap.

Use a low-emission monitor or flat panel display

To get the lowest emissions possible from a monitor, use one that complies with current TCO or MPR guidelines. These monitors typically have high quality screen images as well as low emissions.

Flat panel displays usually have very low electric and magnetic fields, though some, because of backlighting and related circuitry, may generate electric fields that don't meet current MPR guidelines. Flat panels have only recently begun to be measured according to TCO or MPR guidelines, and measurements may not be readily available.

Monitors and flat panel displays should conform to FCC or equivalent regulations for radio frequency emissions.

Shield high-emission monitors

In general, smaller monitors have lower emissions than larger ones, and monochrome monitors have lower emissions than color ones, though this isn't always true. If you have a high-emission monitor—whether you know it from the manufacturer's specifications, a consultant's measurements, or your own hunches—you can have shielding retrofitted into the monitor or you can shield it externally. Sit a few feet away from the monitor, even if you shield it.

- Retrofit shielding can reduce both electric and magnetic fields. To get it done, you may have to send your monitor to the company providing the service.

- Specially designed glare filters that you put over the screen can reduce low frequency and static *electric* fields only (see Chapter 15, *Create a Visually Comfortable Environment*). *These filters do not block low frequency magnetic fields.* Read product literature carefully before you buy a glare filter and avoid buying products that do not specify exactly which fields they block. Some manufacturers claim their filters block all EMFs, which is currently not possible.

- Shielding magnetic fields requires a special metal alloy, such as mumetal. Some external magnetic shields use a metal band that attaches to the sides of the monitor.

- Any shielding you do should bring your monitor within current MPR guidelines, and preferably within TCO recommendations.

Shielding existing monitors can be expensive and inconvenient, though it's cheaper and creates less solid waste than buying a new one. The better solution is for manufacturers to shield monitors during production—it's cheaper, easier, and more effective. If shielding is part of the design, it can cost as little as one dollar to shield each monitor.[2]

Here are some other things to know about shielding:

- *You can't protect yourself by adjusting the monitor's brightness/contrast controls or using a screen-saver program.* These may affect power consumption, but they don't block electromagnetic emissions.

- *You can't block emissions with ordinary materials or blow it away with a fan.* In fact, the fan itself generates electromagnetic fields.

- *Lead aprons don't block low frequency electromagnetic fields.* They're designed for very brief use to block x-rays, which aren't considered a problem from computer monitors.

Control static electric fields

Most newer monitors and keyboards don't generate high static electric fields. Monitors that meet TCO or MPR guidelines generate no or very low fields.

If you notice that dust accumulates quickly on your screen, or if you actually feel a static charge on your equipment, you may have a problem. Ask your facilities department whether the equipment needs to be serviced, or call the manufacturer to find out what levels of static electric fields are considered normal. There are various ways to reduce static electric fields:

- *Make sure your equipment is grounded.* Grounded glare filters are a common way of reducing static electric fields. A grounding strip on your keyboard or an anti-static floor mat can also help, depending on how well you yourself are grounded. If the carpet seems to be generating static electricity, ask your facilities department whether it can be treated to reduce the effect.

- *Increase humidity.* Static electric fields are worse in dry air. Add moisture by using plants, aquariums, or humidifiers.

- *Add negative ions.* High static electric fields deplete negative ions. Many people find that ionizers significantly improve air quality, since they both generate negative ions and remove airborne dust and pollutants.

What About Unconventional Methods?

Some unusual protective devices have been developed outside the realm of traditional science. These are not widely distributed, but may be available in catalogs or at holistic health fairs or similar venues.

Many of these devices are intended to mitigate the effects of electromagnetic fields by protecting or strengthening the body's energetic pathways. Some are based on the theory that the body resonates with the Earth's natural electromagnetic fields. In this view, man-made fields override the natural ones and interfere with our normal, healthy state through their effect on the energetic pathways.

To evaluate the body's response to electromagnetic fields with and without the device, developers of these products have used various methods such as biofeedback, measuring the flow of energy through acupuncture meridians, and applied kinesiology (finding a person's energy level by testing muscle strength).

Here are a few examples of the types of products you might find:[3]

- Surge protectors and devices that use software technology to create coherent electromagnetic fields, which are claimed to neutralize fields from computer monitors and other sources.

- A pendant that contains a quartz crystal and several minerals arranged in a special pattern. This combination is claimed to keep your body tuned to the Earth's fields, instead of to the unnatural fields.

- A variety of other electronic devices, pendants, metal disks or plates, and products that use color in specific configurations.

Traditional science doesn't necessarily accept these types of products. They may seem strange, or they may appeal to you. They also may or may not be based on scientific principles. Before you buy anything, ask what the product is supposed to do, how it is supposed to work, and how it was tested. Then decide for yourself whether you want to give it a try.

TCO Recommendations

The limits are:

ELF magnetic fields. 2 milligauss at 30 centimeters (cm) in front of the screen

ELF electric fields. 10 volts per meter at 30 cm in front of the screen

VLF magnetic fields. 0.25 mG at 50 cm from any point around the monitor

VLF electric fields. 1 volt per meter at 30 cm in front of the screen

Static electric fields. 0 volts (+/− 500 volts).

MPR Guidelines

All readings at 50 centimeters (cm) in front of the screen. Limits are:

ELF magnetic fields. 2.5 milligauss

ELF electric fields. 25 volts per meter

VLF magnetic fields. 0.25 mG

VLF electric fields. 2.5 volts per meter

Static electric fields. 0 volts (+/− 500 volts)

Create a Low-Emission Office

Just as shielding an existing monitor is more expensive and more difficult than including the shielding from the start, it's much more difficult to shield an existing building than it is to design for low electromagnetic fields during construction. Shielding specific areas to reduce magnetic fields in large office buildings can cost hundreds of thousands of dollars.[4]

When designing a new building or remodeling an existing one, employers can create a low-emission office and save considerable future expense by following these guidelines:[5]

- Locate the main electrical switching equipment as far from work areas as possible, such as in the lowest basement level or outside the building.

- Locate electrical transformers for each floor near elevator lobbies. Use the adjacent areas for storage closets or low-use common areas.

- Install electronically ballasted fluorescent lights. Running two banks of lights on each ballast further reduces emissions.

- Design the office layout so that people spend the most time far away from electrical equipment and office machines that generate high fields.

- Evaluate emissions before purchasing new equipment, and choose low-emission monitors, photocopiers, printers, desk lamps, and so on.

VI

Appendixes

- Equipment Selection Guide
- Resources
- Notes

A

Equipment Selection Guide

Ergonomic Principles

"Ergonomic" is a popular marketing buzzword, but just describing a product as ergonomic doesn't necessarily mean it was engineered with human comfort and safety in mind. When you're shopping for equipment, furniture, or accessories, evaluate them according to true ergonomic principles. Look for these qualities:

- *Fit and comfort.* Any product should fit, be comfortable, and adapt to you and whatever task you're doing.

- *Function.* The product should do what it's intended to do, and do it well.

- *Ease-of-use.* The product should be intuititive and easy to use.

- *Adjustability.* This is especially important if the equipment is used by many people. Adjustments should require minimal effort.

- *Cost-effectiveness.* Take the time to evaluate products and buy the ones that suit your needs best for the lowest cost. Price is only one consideration—products that cost the least can turn out to be a waste of money in the long term if they aren't adjustable, easy to use, comfortable, or functional, and especially if they don't serve to prevent injury.

- *Environmental safety.* Choose products with low electromagnetic and chemical emissions, and products that are made from recycled and recyclable materials.

Many professional ergonomic consultants recommend that employers provide a variety of chairs, desks, equipment, and accessories so employees can select the ones that fit them best.

Hardware

Screens—Monitors and Flat Panel Displays

A high-quality screen is essential for reducing eyestrain and making computing more comfortable in general. Look for these features:

- Fast refresh rate for flicker-free, stable images (76 Hz or faster, with non-interlaced scanning)

- High resolution and high pixel density for sharp, clear text and images

- High-quality anti-reflective treatment

- Easy-to-read text

- Pleasing colors

- Separate controls for brightness and contrast

- Low electromagnetic emissions (meets or exceeds current TCO or MPR guidelines)

- Automatic power-down feature (meets TCO or U.S. EPA Energy Star guidelines; must also be supported by the system unit)

- Tilt and swivel mechanism (monitors and terminals)

Flat panel displays should be readable in bright light and at upright angles. Active matrix liquid crystal displays (LCD) are currently the most readable, followed by passive matrix LCDs with backlight. Magazines for computer users often follow developments in flat panel display technology.

Keyboards

If at all possible, try a keyboard before you buy it. If you can't do that, buy it, try it, and return it if you don't like it. Many companies have a return policy; others allow you to rent a keyboard for a month and apply the rental fee to the purchase price. Different designs appeal to different people. If one design doesn't work for you, don't hesitate to return it and try a different one. In general, look for a keyboard that:

- Fits your hands

- Promotes neutral wrist and arm position

- Has keys that are well-cushioned and easy to press

- Has tactile and audible feedback for keystrokes

- Allows you to redefine keys

- Has an optional alternate keyboard layout

- Has a separate numeric keypad that can be placed on either side of the keyboard

- Has optional footpedal support

Pointing Devices

Many types of pointing devices are available, including mice, trackballs, tablets, pucks, joy sticks, head wands, and mouth sticks. In general, use a pointing device that:

- Is comfortable and easy to hold, click, and drag

- Promotes neutral wrist and arm posture

- Has smooth, precise cursor control

- Has click-hold, cursor control, and other software options

- Accommodates right- and left-handed use

- Has optional footpedal support

Trackballs should have a large ball that can be used with the fingers or palm, not the thumb. No pointing device of any type should require you to use a strong pinch grip or to press hard.

Laptop and Portable Computers

Currently, few portable computers can be described as ergonomic. Many have small keyboards, trackballs with small balls, and non-detachable keyboards and screens. Try various models to find the most comfortable one for you, based on the previous suggestions for screens, keyboards, and pointing devices. A detachable screen that can be positioned separately is a plus. You may want to choose a lightweight, easy-to-carry portable computer that can also be used with a full-sized keyboard or screen, especially if have an RSI and prefer to type on an ergonomic keyboard.

Software

Though software ergonomics is an evolving field, ergonomic considerations are often an afterthought in software products. Asking for these features encourages software developers to make ergonomic design an integral part of their products:

- A well organized, consistent, and easy to use screen layout

- Icons and other items on the screen that are easy to see and select

- Menus items that are easy to access and select

- Colors that enhance meaning and readability

- Zoom feature and/or ability to change the character size

- Clear, readable text

- Keyboard shortcuts, macros, and word-prediction capability

- Minimal clicks, drags, keystrokes, and cursor movements

- Multi-tasking capability

Speech Recognition Systems

Speech recognition systems allow you to control your computer with your voice instead of, or in conjunction with, your keyboard. Some systems require specific hardware. The technology is improving all the time, and eventually inexpensive, easy-to-use, full dictation systems should become available.

There are basically two types of speech recognition systems. *Command control systems* are used for managing windows and files, selecting menu items and dialog box choices, clicking and dragging, creating text macros, and other software functions. *Full dictation systems* include command control functions and are used for word processing and entering text in various applications as well. Speech recognition systems have allowed many people with severe RSI or other disabilities to continue computing. In general, look for these features in a speech recognition system:

- Large pre-defined vocabulary (greater than 25,000 words)

- Large user-defined vocabulary (greater than 7,000 words)

- Compatible with all your applications

- Allows you to speak naturally, without modifying your normal speech patterns

For a listing of speech recognition products, see the *Onsight Ergonomic Products Resource Guide* or the *Typing Injury FAQ* online. The *sorehand* and *c+health* online newsgroups are good places to find out about people's personal experiences with various systems.

Furniture

Chairs

No single chair design is right for everyone. If possible, try a few chairs over a week's time, and choose the one that's the most comfortable. At the very least, try out a chair for several hours before you buy it. Look for a chair with these features:

- Fully adjustable height, backrest, armrests, and seatpan tilt
- Backrest and seatpan contours that fit the shape of your body
- Adjustment levers and controls that are easy to reach and use
- Stable five-pronged base
- Accommodates at least reclined and upright postures
- Optional headrest for very reclined postures
- Optional front support for forward postures

Work Surfaces

Most computer users need areas for computing, reading, writing, and using the telephone. Computer stands and desks should have these qualities:

- Adjustable height for keyboard and mouse, monitor, and writing materials
- Optional height adjustment for working in a standing posture
- Rounded edges
- Non-reflective surface
- Optional tilt for the writing surface
- Deep enough to keep monitor at arm's length
- Deep enough to give you substantial leg room
- Spacious enough to place the telephone and other materials within easy reach
- Enough storage and easy access to files and documents

Keyboard Trays, Monitor Stands, and Telephone Stands

Keyboard trays should fit both the keyboard and mouse, and be adjustable for height and tilt. The adjustment controls should not interfere with leg movements. Monitor and telephone stands should be adjustable, stable, sturdy, and easy to move.

Armrests, Wristrests, and Forearm Supports

All types of arm supports should have soft, padded surfaces, and be made of non-allergenic materials. Armrests and forearm supports should be easy to adjust, and forearm supports should move smoothly and easily. Wristrests should be deep and soft enough to support your wrists and protect them from hard surfaces and sharp edges. The height and length should be appropriate for the device with which you're using it.

Footrests

A good footrest is sturdy, lightweight, and large enough for your feet to move around. The platform should have an adjustable height and tilt.

Accessories

Gloves

Fingerless gloves, support gloves, and padded wrist-protector gloves should be comfortable, warm, and snug. They should *not* itch, chafe, fit tightly, or interfere with your dexterity.

Reading and Writing Accessories

Adjustable copyholders and slantboards make reading and writing more comfortable. Pen grips, fat pens, and pens with smooth-flowing ink can ease the strain of writing by hand.

Telephone Equipment

Telephone headsets should be lightweight, fit the head and ear comfortably, provide good sound quality, and have reliable connections.

Conventional telephone handsets should be lightweight and shaped to encourage a neutral wrist posture when holding the handset to your ear.

The keypad should be comfortable and easy to press. Make use of autodialing tools as much as possible.

Software for Injury Prevention

A variety of software, shareware, and freeware is available to help prevent RSI, stress, and eyestrain. These include:

- Self-monitoring software for taking breaks and pacing your typing speed
- Word-prediction software
- Macro packages
- File/window management software

Task Lights

Choose adjustable task lights with bulbs that aren't too bright, and can't be seen while you work. Any light bulbs you use, for task or overhead lighting, should have good color rendition and be free of flicker.

For good lighting, the placement of lights, the way the light interacts with the surfaces in the room, and the mix of daylight and artificial light are just as important as the type of fixtures and light bulbs used.

Glare Filters and Radiation Shields

A good glare filter eliminates glare and reflections without reducing the screen's readability, brightness, or contrast, and without distorting the image even at the edges of the screen. Take time to compare several filters.

Some glare filters reduce static electric fields and low frequency (ELF and VLF) electric fields. Glare filters do not block low frequency magnetic fields. To reduce ELF and VLF magnetic fields, you need a separate radiation shield. Any filter or shield that claims to block or reduce electromagnetic radiation should specify its effectiveness in reducing:

- ELF and VLF electric fields, also called E-fields

- ELF and VLF magnetic fields, also called H-fields

- Static electric fields

APPENDIX

B

Resources

Resource Guides

VDT News Product Directory

Published annually in the September/October issue of *VDT News*. Lists suppliers of ergonomic equipment, furniture, and accessories; low-emission monitors; magnetic field meters; professional services for ergonomics, eye care, and radiation; videos, software, and booklets; and trade associations, unions, and resource groups. *VDT News*, P.O. Box 1799, Grand Central Station, New York, NY, 10163. Phone (212) 517-2802. Fax (212) 734-0316.

CTD News Ergonomics Resource Guide

Extensive listing of equipment manufacturers, furniture suppliers, data entry accessories, educational references, publications, software, labor unions, government agencies, and ADA resources. Updated annually. *CTD News*, P.O. Box 239, Haverford, PA, 19042-0239. Phone (800) 554-4283 (U.S. and Canada) or (610) 896-2770. Fax (610) 896-2762.

Onsight Ergonomic Products Resource Guide

Descriptions and contact information for alternate keyboards, books, and videos, ergonomic furniture and products, information resources, Northern California suppliers, support groups, taped programs, speech recognition systems, and other resources. Onsight Technology Education Services, 1510 Eddy Street, Suite 1511, San Francisco, CA, 94115. Phone (415) 749-1983. Email *gkarp@sirius.com*. Compuserve *72212,3240*.

Back Designs Product Selection Guide & Catalog

Wide selection of ergonomic furniture and related products, and detailed description of how to choose them. Back Designs, Inc., 1045 Ashby Avenue, Berkeley, CA, 94701. Phone (510) 849-1923.

Microwave News 1995 EMF Resource Directory
>   *Microwave News*, P.O. Box 1799, Grand Central Station, New York, NY, 10163. Phone (212) 517-2800. Fax (212) 734-0316.

Directory of Human Factors/Ergonomics Consultants
>   Human Factors and Ergonomics Society, P.O. Box 1369, Santa Monica, CA 90406. Phone (310) 394-1811. Fax (310) 394-2410. Also publishes the ANSI standards on VDT workstations and many other papers.

International Directory of Occupational Safety and Health Institutions, Occupational Safety and Health Series, #66.
>   International Labor Organization (ILO), Geneva, Switzerland, 1990. Describes fields of competence for each agency. To order, contact ILO Publications Center, 49 Sheridan Ave., Suite SP, Albany, NY 12210 USA. Phone (518) 436-9686. Fax (518) 436-7433.

RSI Resources

Support Groups

Support groups are forming and changing all the time. Sometimes offered through clinics, groups are often organized by individuals who volunteer their time. Ask your health care provider or other RSI sufferers about support groups in your area. Listings of RSI support groups are provided in the *RSI Network*, the *CTS/RSI Association News*, and the *Onsight Ergonomic Product Resource Guide*.

Newsletters and Organizations

RSI Network
>   An online newsletter full of practical advice for RSI sufferers and current listings of RSI support groups. Caroline Rose, editor. *RSI Network* is distributed to many electronic bulletin board services and newsgroups.

CTS/RSI Association News
>   The Carpal Tunnel Syndrome/Repetitive Strain Injury Association newsletter. Stephanie Barnes, editor. CTS/RSI Association, P.O. Box 514, Santa Rosa, CA 95402-0514. Phone (707) 571-0397.

CTD News
>   Newsletter about workplace solutions to RSI and cumulative trauma disorders. Michael Gauf, editor. Center for Workplace Health, P.O. Box 239, Haverford, PA, 19041. Phone (800) 554-4283. Fax (610) 896-2762.

National RSI Foundation
> 200 South Desplaines Avenue, Chicago, IL 60661. Phone (800) END-RSIs or (800) 363-7747.

Compensation Alert
> Non-profit organization that encourages the exchange of information and resources between injured workers and the administrative systems that supply services to them (primarily for California). Provides a telephone answering service staffed by volunteers to assist injured workers with workers compensation and related issues. Publishes the *Comp Alert Newsletter*. Compensation Alert, 843 2nd Street, Santa Rosa, CA, 95404. Phone (707) 545-2266.

Online Newsgroups—Sorehand and c+health

Sorehand is an online newsgroup focused on the prevention and treatment of RSI. *c+health* is a moderated group for discussing all computer-related health problems. These are good places to find out about information resources not mentioned in this book or other resource guides, and to connect with other people in your country or local area. The *RSI Network* and *Typing Injury FAQs* (frequently asked questions) are posted regularly to both groups.

To subscribe to *sorehand*, send email to *sorehand@vm.ucsf.edu* with the message *SUBSCRIBE SOREHAND <your name>*. For example, if your name is John Doe, send the message SUBSCRIBE SOREHAND John Doe.

To subscribe to *c+health*, send email to *c+health@iubvm.ucs.indiana.edu* with the message *SUBSCRIBE C+HEALTH <your name>*.

Online Documents

An archive of files and documents related to RSI is available by anonymous FTP at *ftp.csua.berkeley.edu:/pub/typing-injury*, or on the World Wide Web (WWW) site *http://www.cs.princeton.edu/grad/dwallach/tifaq/archive.html*. Start with the *Typing Injury FAQs*. These FAQs are posted regularly to *sorehand*, *c+health*, *sci.med.occupational*, *comp.human-factors*, and other online newsgroups.

The *Medical Matrix*, a database of Internet resources for clinical medicine, is available on the WWW site *URL:gopher://una.hh.lib.umich.edu:70/00/inetdirsstacks/medclin:malet*. Resources are categorized by disease and specialty. For occupational and environmental medicine resources, see the section called "Specialty Categorized Information."

Government, Legal, and Other Services

JAN—Job Accommodation Network

A U.S. government service that provides information and consulting for individualized accommodation solutions for particular types of work. Also provides employers information on tax incentives that encourage the purchase of adaptive equipment and facilities. JAN also provides information on the ADA (Americans with Disabilities Act). 918 Chestnut Ridge Road, Suite 1, Morgantown, WV 26505. Phone (voice/TDD) (800) 526-7234, and (800) 526-2262 in Canada. ADA information (voice/TDD) (800) ADA-WORK (232-9675), (304) 293-7186, or (800) 526-2262 in Canada. Computer bulletin board (800) DIAL-JAN (342-5526).

EEOC—Equal Employment Opportunity Commission

Protects disabled workers against discrimination, and provides information on the ADA. 1801 L Street NW, Room 9024, Washington, DC 20507. Phone (800) 466-4232. TDD (800) 800-3302.

DREDF—Disability Rights Education and Defense Fund, Inc.

Provides information on the ADA. 2212 Sixth Street, Berkeley, CA 94710. Phone (510) 644-2555. Fax (510) 841-8645. TDD (510) 644-2626.

9to5, Association for Working Women

Works to protect the rights of working women, and researches and provides information on working conditions. Publishes pamphlets and fact sheets on various topics, such as electronic performance monitoring and fluorescent lighting. 238 West Wisconsin Avenue, Suite 700, Milwaukee, WI 53203. Phone (414) 274-0925. Job problem hotline (800) 522-0925.

NIOSH—National Institute of Occupational Safety and Health

Researches and provides information on workplace safety. Offers an onsite evaluation of working conditions to qualifying employers. Technical Information Branch, Mail Stop C19, 4676 Columbia Parkway, Cincinnati, OH, 45226. Information line (800) 356-4674.

London Occupational Safety and Health (LOSH)

A free health and safety resource center for questions about RSI. Publishes a booklet on RSI. 222–424 Wellington Street, London, Ontario, Canada, N6A 3P3. Phone (519) 433-4156. Fax (519) 433-2887.

London Hazards Centre

Provides information on occupational hazards. Publishes the book *VDU Work and the Hazards to Health*. 308 Gray's Inn Road, London WC1X 8DS, United Kingdom. Phone (44-71) 837-5605. Fax (44-71) 833-9956.

Stress Resources

Employee Burnout: Causes and Cures

This report on occupational stress is available from Northwestern National Life Insurance Company, P.O. Box 20, Minneapolis, MN 55440, phone (612) 342-7137. Part 1, *Employee Stress Levels*, presents the stress level research findings, and Part 2, *Addressing Stress in Your Organization*, presents cures for job stress and provides a test to identify workplace stress.

Developing an Action Plan to Manage Occupational Stress, Managing Client Aggression, and *A Supervisor's Guide to Identifying Stress Reactions*

These booklets, created by Comcare Australia, present a human resources rather than a medical approach to managing occupational stress. The booklets are available from Comcare Australia, GPO Box 9905, Canberra ACT 2601, Australia.

Promoting Health and Productivity in the Computerized Office

Edited by Steven Sauter, Marvin Dainoff, and Michael Smith.

Electromagnetic Sensitivity Resources

Organizations

Sensitive to a Toxic Environment, Inc. (The S.T.A.T.E. Foundation)

An organization for individuals with electrical and chemical sensitivities. Publishes the *S.T.A.T.E.ment Quarterly Newsletter,* several booklets on how to detoxify all aspects of your environment, and the *Highways to Health* resource catalog. P.O. Box 834, Orchard Park, NY, 14127. Phone (716) 675-1164. Fax (716) 675-7767.

The following organizations comprise an international consortium that provides information and educational materials on EMF hypersensitivity:

The EMR Alliance

Publishes *Network News,* a bimonthly newsletter providing information on EMF hypersensitivity and a communication link for hypersensitive individuals and activists worldwide. Also publishes the *EMF Grassroots Handbook,* a guide for EMF activists. 410 West 53rd Street, Suite 402, New York, NY 10019. Phone (212) 554-4073. Fax (212) 977-5541.

Ergotec Association, Inc

A human engineering non-profit association that communicates to the U.S. Congress the health hazards of electronic products, particularly computer products. Publishes the *Pollution Alert* newsletter, a pamphlet on electrical sensitivity, and the book *X-rayed Without Consent,* which analyzes scientific research done on computer EMFs and the role of EMFs in computer-related health problems, including RSI and eyestrain. P.O. Box 9571, Arlington, VA 22209. Phone and fax (703) 516-4576.

Residents Against the Towers (RATT)
Kathleen P. Hawk, 122 Thornwood Road, Butler, PA, 16001. (412) 287-5343.

ESN—Electrical Sensitivity Network
P.O. Box 4146, Prescott, AZ, 86302.

FEB—The Association for the Electrically and VDT-Injured
(Föreningen för el och bildskärmsskadade)
P.O. Box 15126, 10465 Stockholm, Sweden. Phone 46 8 7129065

The Association for the Electrically Oversensitive
(Föreningen för el overfölsömme)
Stubbanv. 2, 7037 Trondheim, Norway

The Electrically and VDT- Injured in Denmark
(El og billedskaermsskadede i Danmark).
Lunden 1, Alum, 8900 Randers, Denmark

Elektrosmog Selfhelp Group
(Selbshilfegruppe Elektrosmog, Bayreuth)
Ringau 1, D-95515 Plankenfels, Germany

Action Group for the Electrically Sensitive
(Arbeitskreis fur Elektrosensible e.V)
Aleestrasse 135, D-44793 Bochum, Germany

Clinics

Dr. William Rea, Environmental Health Center
8345 Walnut Hill Lane, Suite 205, Dallas, TX 75231. Phone (214) 368-4132.

Dr. Jean Monro, Allergy and Environmental Medicine Limited
Breakspear Hospital, Belswains Lane, Hemel Hempstead, Herts, HP3 9HP, England. Phone 01442-61333. Fax 01442-66388

Publications

The Electrical Sensitivity Handbook: How EMFs are Making People Sick is a comprehensive resource guide for people who have developed sensitivities and environmental illnesses from exposure to electromagnetic fields. By Lucinda Grant, Weldon Publishing, 1995. P.O. Box 4146, Prescott, AZ 86302.

Microwave News and VDT News cover this topic regularly. The January/February 1995 issue of VDT News has a special report on electromagnetic hypersensitivity that includes case studies and an overview of recent scientific research. P.O. Box 1799, Grand Central Station, New York, NY 10163. Phone (212) 517-2800. Fax (212) 734-0316.

Online Resources

The *c+health* newsgroup includes discussion of EMF sensitivities, and is a good place to find out about new online newsgroups devoted to this topic that may be forming.

On the WWW, *EMF-Link* contains general and technical information on the biological and health effects of electromagnetic fields. Part of Information Ventures, Inc's *EMF Clearinghouse, EMF-Link* is available on the WWW site
http://archive.xrt.upenn.edu:10000/0h/emf-link.html

Several highly informative documents are also available on the WWW site
http://www.isy.liu.se/~tegen/febost.html

EMF Emissions and Environmental Guidelines

TCO—The Swedish Confederation of Professional Employees
Promotes an integrated approach to technological development that focuses on the interaction of people, technology, and the environment. Develops test methods and emissions guidelines for computer equipment. Publishes the *Screen Facts* and *Screen Checker* booklets, the *Software Checker* booklet and diskette, and the *TCO Information Center Newsletter*. TCO Development Unit, S–11494 Stockholm, Sweden. Phone 46 8 782 91 00. Fax 46 8 782 92 07. TCO Information Center, 150 North Michigan Avenue, Suite 1200, Chicago, IL 60601. Phone (312) 781-6223. Fax (312) 346-0683.

EPA Energy Star Computers
Provides energy efficiency guidelines for computer equipment. U.S. Environmental Protection Agency Global Change Division 6202J, Washington, DC, 20460. Phone (202) 233-9114. Fax (202) 233-9578.

SWEDAC—Swedish Board for Technical Accreditation
Develops the MPR test methods and emissions guidelines for computer monitors. SWEDAC, Box 878, S–50115 Borås, Sweden. Phone 44 033 17 77 00. Fax 44 033 10 13 92.

IEEE—Institute of Electrical and Electronic Engineers
Developed the P–1140 *Standard Test Procedures for Measurement of Electric and Magnetic Fields from VDTs from 5 Hz to 400 kHs*. Currently in progress is the IEEE P-1140.1 project, *Standard Measurement Techniques for ELF and VLF*

Magnetic Fields and Electrical Fields from Desktop Computer Displays and Associated Desktop Devices. IEEE, 445 Hoes Lane, P.O. Box 1331, Piscataway, NJ 08855. Phone (800) 678-4333.

NEFTA—National Electromagnetic Field Testing Association
An international registry of independent professionals involved in EMF testing, consulting, mitigation, and research. G28-B Library Place, Evanston, IL, 60201. Phone (708) 475-3696.

Notes

Chapter 2

1. *Anthropometry for Designers*, NASA Reference Publication 1024, *Anthropometric Source Book*, Volume 1. Houston: National Aeronautics and Space Administration, 1978.

2. Grandjean, Etienne, *Ergonomics in Computerized Offices*. London: Taylor & Francis, 1987. 126.

Chapter 3

1. Eileen Vollowitz notes that vision and reach are actually more important than the chair in determining how you sit. As described by Michelle Bronsati, "Myth vs. Truth in Ergonomics" (an interview with Eileen Vollowitz, PT), *Advance for Physical Therapists*. King of Prussia, PA: Merion Publications, Inc., June 15, 1992. 14-15, 24.

Chapter 4

1. The body scanning techniques are loosely based on Jon Kabat-Zinn's body scan instructions in Full Catastrophe Living (New York: Dell Publishing, 1990) 75-93; Thich Nhat Hanh's meditation instructions throughout *The Sun My Heart* (Berkeley: Parallax Press, 1988); and suggestions from Wm Michael Smith, Ph.D., personal communication, 1992.

2. Choon-Nam Ong, "Ergonomic Intervention for Better Health and Productivity: Two Case Studies," in *Promoting Health and Productivity in the Computerized Office*. Edited by Steven Sauter, et al. London: Taylor & Francis, 1990. 25-26.

Chapter 7

1. Ramazzini, Bernardo, *The Disease of Workers*. Translated by W. Wright. Chicago: University of Chicago Press.

2. *Cumulative Trauma Disorders*. Edited by Vern Putz-Anderson. London: Taylor & Francis, 1988. 144.

3. U.S. Bureau of Labor Statistics, as quoted in *VDT News*, January/February 1995. 2; The *RSI Network* newsletter, issue 7, August 1992.

Chapter 8

1. Phil Balikian, Jay Himmelstein, Glenn Pransky, and William Morgan, "Medical Evaluation of the Patient with Persistent Upper Extremity Pain," *Cumulative Trauma Disability and Rehabilitation in the Workplace*. San Francisco: conference proceedings, December 9-10, 1992.

2. Rene Cailliet, *Soft Tissue Pain and Disability*. Philadelphia: F.A. Davis Company, 1991. 31-33, 164-165; David Simons and Janet Travell, *Myofascial Pain and Dysfunction, The Trigger Point Manual*. Baltimore: Williams & Wilkins, 1983. 13-16, 46-56.

3. Ruth Lowengart, M.D., *RSI Network* newsletter. Issue 9, December 1992.

4. Michael Patkin, "Neck and Arm Pain in Office Workers: Causes and Management," *Promoting Health and Productivity in the Computerized Office*. Edited by Marvin Dainoff, Stephen Sauter, and Michael Smith. London, New York, Philadelphia: Taylor & Francis. 209.

Chapter 9

1. Grandjean, *Ergonomics in Computerized Offices*. 151-153.

Chapter II

1. Linda Johnson, OTR, CVE, lecture. San Francisco: Cumulative Trauma Disability and Rehabilitation in the Workplace Conference, December 11, 1992.

2. Emil Pascarelli and Deborah Quilter, *Repetitive Strain Injury*. New York: John Wiley & Sons, Inc., 1994. 82. Richard Passwater, *The Antioxidants*. New Canaan: Keats Publishing, Inc., 1985. 23.

3. Elson Haas, *Staying Healthy with Nutrition*. Berkeley: Celestial Arts, 1992. 177, 166, 173.

4. Haas, 124-125.

Chapter 12

1. Cailliet, *Soft Tissue Pain and Disability.* 39, 41.
2. *The Americans with Disabilities Act, Your Employment Rights as an Individual With a Disability.* EEOC-BK-18, 1991. 2-3.

Chapter 13

1. Dr. James Sheedy, *VDT News*, November/December 1994. 1.
2. *VDT News*, March/April 1994. 12.
3. Edward Godnig and John Hacunda, *Computers and Visual Stress.* Charleston, Rhode Island: Seacoast Information Services, Inc., 1990. 35
4. Grandjean, *Ergonomics in Computerized Offices.* 20-21.
5. James Sheedy, "VDTs and Eye Problems," *Changing Technologies in the Workplace* conference proceedings. Los Angeles: California Policy Seminar, University of California, Berkeley, December 1-2, 1988. 46.
6. The Embudo Center, *Explorations of the Dark: Vision and the Non-Conscious*, Embudo, NM, 1991, p11.

Chapter 14

1. Penelope Ody, *The Complete Medicinal Herbal.* London: Dorling Kindersley Limited, 1993. 140.
2. Janet Goodrich, *Natural Vision Improvement.* Berkeley: Celestial Arts, 1985. 1-10; John Selby, *The Visual Handbook, The Complete Guide to Seeing More Clearly.* Shaftsbury, Dorset: Element Books Limited, 1987. x, 26-31, 73-76.
3. Joanna Rotté and Koji Yamamoto, *Vision, A Holistic Guide to Healing the Eyesight.* Tokyo and New York: Japan Publications, Inc., 1986, 1989. 55-72.
4. Grandjean, *Ergonomics in Computerized Offices*, 26.

Chapter 15

1. Grandjean, *Ergonomics in Computerized Offices*, 69-70.
2. *Screen Facts*, Stockholm: TCO (The Swedish Confederation for Professional Employees), 1991. 4, 5, 8.
3. *Screen Facts*, TCO. 6.
4. Jürgen Ziegler and Rolf Ilg, *Benutzergerechte Software-Gestaltung.* Edited by R. Oldenbourg Verlag. Wien: München, 1993. 57–67.
5. Douglas, Willard and Wolverton, B.C., "A Study of Interior Landscape Plants for Indoor Air Pollution Abatement," in the *Florida Nurseryman.* Lakeland, FL: January 1989. 9-14.

6. Liberman, Jacob, *Light, Medicine of the Future.* Santa Fe: Bear & Company, Inc., 1991. 40, 44.

7. Grandjean, *Ergonomics in Computerized Offices.* 42, 46.

Chapter 16

1. Roose, Diana, *Facts on Fluorescents.* Cleveland: National Association of Working Women. 1.

2. Liberman, *Light, Medicine of the Future.* 146.

3. Roose, *Facts on Fluorescents.* 3.

4. Liberman, 139-145.

5. Liberman, 53-63.

Chapter 17

1. "Employee Stress Levels," Part 1 of the report *Employee Burnout: Causes and Cures.* Minneapolis: Northwestern National Life Insurance Company (NWNL), 1992.

2. *Employee Burnout: America's Newest Epidemic.* Minneapolis: NWNL, 1991. 18. The average amount that an employer or insurer set aside for stress-related disability payments is $73,270, according to NWNL case records between 1982 and 1990.

3. *Employee Burnout: Causes and Cures*, NWNL. 11.

4. *VDT News*, March/April 1989. 8.

5. *Promoting Health and Productivity in the Computerized Office.* Edited by Marvin Dainoff, Steven Sauter, and Michael Smith. London: Taylor & Francis Ltd., 1990. 129–194. VDT News, ongoing coverage.

6. *VDT News*, Nov/Dec 1990. 6-7; Sep/Oct 1993. 2; Nov/Dec 1993. 12; Jan/Feb 1994. 5-6; *Stories of Mistrust and Manipulation: The Electronic Monitoring of the American Workforce.* Cleveland: 9to5, National Association of Working Women, 1990; *Computer Monitoring and Other Dirty Tricks.* 9to5, 1986; Forester, Tom and Morrison, Perry, *Computer Ethics.* Cambridge: The MIT Press, 1990. 150, 155-156; Garson, Barbara, *The Electronic Sweatshop.* New York: Simon & Schuster, Inc., 1988.

7. Östberg, Olov and Högberg, Yngve, "Perspectives on Ergonomics Issues in a VDT Office," in *Promoting Health and Productivity in the Computerized Office.* 139-140.

8. Everly, George Jr., and Girdano, Daniel, *Controlling Stress and Tension.* Englewood Cliffs, NJ: Prentice-Hall, 1986. 83.

Chapter 18

1. Paul Dennison and Gail Dennison, *Brain Gym, Simple Activities for Whole Brain Learning*. Ventura, CA: Edu-Kinesthetics, Inc., 1986. 31-31.

2. Nuernberger, *Freedom from Stress*. Himalayan International Institute of Yoga Science Philosophy Publishers, 1981. 139-146.

3. Worwood, Valerie Ann, *The Complete Book of Essential Oils and Aromatherapy*. San Rafael, CA: New World Library, 1991. 79, 80.

Chapter 19

1. *VDT News*, January/February 1992. 2.

2. Ratcliffe, Mitch, "How Safe Are Wireless Nets?" *MacWeek*, v5 n30, September 10, 1991. 1, 112.

3. *Screen Facts*, TCO, 1991. 27, 28.

4. For detailed reporting on current research, see Bette Hileman, "Findings Point to Complexity of Health Effects of Electric, Magnetic Fields," *Chemical & Engineering News* (C&EN), July 18, 1994. 27-33. See also "Health Effects of Electromagnetic Fields Remain Unresolved," *C&EN*, November 8, 1993. 15-29. For compilations of recent research papers, see *On the Nature of Electromagnetic Field Interactions with Biological Systems*, edited by Allan Frey, R.G. Landes Company, Medical Intelligence Unit, 1994. See also *Biological Effects of Electric and Magnetic Fields*, edited by David Carpenter, Academic Press, Inc., 1994. For an interpretive account of research done before 1990, see Robert Becker, *Cross Currents*, Los Angeles: Jeremy P. Tarcher, Inc., 1990.

5. Based on Allan Frey, ed., *On the Nature of Electromagnetic Field Interactions with Biological Systems*, and Bette Hileman, "Findings Pointing to Complexity of Health Effects of Electric, Magnetic Fields," *C&EN*, 18 July 1994, pp 27-33; "Health Effects of Electromagnetic Fields Remain Unresolved," *C&EN*, 8 Nov 1993, p 15. To follow developments in pineal research, see the *Journal of Pineal Research*. For a discussion of the functions of the pineal gland, see Jacob Liberman, *Light, Medicine of the Future*, pp 29-36.

6. Hileman, "Findings Point to Complexity of Health Effects of Electric, Magnetic Fields," *Chemical & Engineering News*. 33; Hileman, "Health Effects of Electromagnetic Fields Remain Unresolved," *C&EN*. 23-24.

7. Frey, *On the Nature of Electromagnetic Field Interactions with Biological Systems*. 4.

8. Becker, *Cross Currents*. 212.

9. Becker, *Cross Currents*. 271.

10. *Microwave News*, January/February 1995. 5.

11. Morgan, M.G., *Electric and Magnetic Fields from 60 Hz Electric Power*, Pittsburgh: Carnegie Mellon University, Department of Engineering and Public Policy, 1989. 31-32.

12. *VDT News*, July/August 1991. 4; March/April 1994. 4.

Chapter 20

1. *VDT News*, March/April 1992. 1; January/February 1994. 1.

2. Electric blankets as described in *Cross Currents*, page 215; power lines as reported in *VDT News*, March/April 1992, page 10; office EMFs as reported in *VDT News*, March/April 1994, pages 4, 13.

3. For a summary of pregnancy studies from 1984 to 1991, see *VDT News,* May/June 1991, page 6. For a review of 21 pregnancy studies, see Vincent Delpizzo, "Epidemiological Studies of Work with VDTs and Adverse Pregnancy Outcomes: 1984-1992," *American Journal of Industrial Medicine*, Vol 26, No. 4, October 1994, pages 465-480.

4. Frey, *On the Nature of Electromagnetic Field Interactions with Biological Systems*. 10-11.

5. *VDT News*, July/August 1992. 1.

6. *VDT News*, March/April 1993. 4.

7. *VDT News*, May/June 1993. 8; November/December 1993. 6; May/June 1994; 6.

8. *Microwave News*, January/February 1995. 4.

9. *VDT News*, January/February 1985. 7; November/December 1989. 2; May/June 1994. 15.

10. deMatteo, Bob, *Terminal Shock*. Toronto: NC Press Limited, 1985. 30.

11. deMatteo, *Terminal Shock*. 32-33, 82, 88.

12. deMatteo, *Terminal Shock*. 92.

13. *Research News*, No. 2, Swedish National Institute of Occupational Health, 1991. 1.

14. Becker, *Cross Currents*. 249-252; *VDT News,* July/August 1991. 14; January/February 1995. 1, 7-11; *Research News*, No. 1, Swedish National Institute of Occupational Health, 1991. 1.

15. *FEB Information Sheet*. The Swedish Association for the Electrically and VDT Injured. 2.

16. Maugh, Thomas II, "Studies Link EMF Exposure to Higher Risk of Alzheimer's," in *Network News*. National EMR Alliance, August/September 1994. 3.

17. *VDT News*, January/February 1995. 8-9.

18. Becker, *Cross Currents*. 252-253.

19. *VDT News*, September/October 1990. 5.

Chapter 21

1. Energy Star Computers, US EPA 6202J, Washington, DC 20460. Phone (202) 233-9114.

2. *VDT News*, July/August 1991. 5.

3. *Tools for Exploration* catalog, Vol 6 No 1, Winter/spring 1994/1995.

4. *VDT News*, May/June 1993. 9.

5. Based on measures taken by the World Bank to reduce exposure to EMFs in their new headquarters, scheduled for completion in 1996. As reported in *VDT News*, May/June 1993. 1.

Suggested Reading

Ergonomics and Occupational Health

Ergonomics in Computerized Offices
Etienne Grandjean, Taylor & Francis, London, 1987.

Promoting Health and Productivity in the Computerized Office
Steven Sauter, Marvin Dainoff, and Michael Smith, editors, Taylor & Francis, London, 1990.

VDT News
Louis Slesin, editor. Bimonthly publication on computer health and safety. P.O. Box 1799, Grand Central Station, New York, NY 10163.

Ergonomics, Work, and Health
Stephen Pheasant, Aspen Publishing, Inc., Gaithersberg, MD, 1991.

Computer Ethics
Tom Forester and Perry Morrison, The MIT Press, Cambridge, MA, 1990, 2nd edition 1994.

The Electronic Sweatshop
Barbara Garson, Penguin Books, New York 1988 (reprint), Simon & Schuster, Inc., 1989.

In the Age of the Smart Machine
Shoshana Zuboff, Basic Books, Inc., Publishers, New York, 1988.

The Overworked American
Juliet Schor, BasicBooks, HarperCollins Publishers, 1991.

Working Ourselves to Death
Diane Fassel, HarperCollins Publishers, New York, 1990, 1993.

The Reinvention of Work
> Matthew Fox, HarperCollins Publishers, San Francisco, 1994.

Love Your Job! Loving the job you have…finding the job you love
> Paul Powers and Deborah Russell, O'Reilly & Associates, Inc, Sebastopol, 1993.

The Nontoxic Home & Office
> Debra Lynn Dadd, Jeremy P Tarcher, Inc., Los Angeles, 1992.

The Green PC
> Steven Anzovin, Windcrest/McGraw-Hill, New York, 1993.

Office Hazards
> Joel Makower, Tilden Press, Washington, DC, 1981.

Office Work Can Be Dangerous to Your Health
> Jeanne Stellman and Mary Sue Henefin, Pantheon Books, New York, 1983.

Independence Day, designing computer solutions for individuals with disabiliy
> Peter Green and Alan Brightman, Apple Computer, Inc., Cupertino, 1990.

Mental and Emotional Health

Full Catastrophe Living
> Jon Kabat-Zinn, Delta Books, Dell Publishing, New York, 1990.

The Miracle of Mindfulness
> Thich Nhat Hanh, Beacon Press, Boston, 1987.

Healing and the Mind
> Book by Bill Moyers, Doubleday, New York, 1993. Video produced by David Grubin Productions, Inc. and Public Affairs Television, Inc.

Freedom from Stress
> Phil Nuernberger, Himalayan International Institute of Yoga Science and Philosophy Publishers, Honesdale, PA, 1981, 1990.

The Breath Connection
> Robert Fried, Insight Books, Plenum Press, New York and London, 1990.

Anatomy of an Illness
> Norman Cousins, Bantam Books, New York, 1979.

Visual Health

The Visual Handbook, the Complete Guide to Seeing More Clearly
> John Selby, Element Books Limited, Shaftsbury, Dorset, 1987.

Vision, a Holistic Guide to Healing the Eyesight
 Joanna Rotté and Koji Yamamoto, Japan Publications, Inc., Tokyo and New York, 1989.

Hypnovision, the New Natural Way to Vision Improvement
 Lisette Scholl, Henry Holt and Company, New York, 1990.

The Art of Seeing
 Aldous Huxley, Creative Arts Book Company, Berkeley, 1942, 1982.

Natural Vision Improvement
 Janet Goodrich, Celestial Arts, Berkeley, 1985.

Light, Medicine of the Future
 Jacob Liberman, Bear & Company, Inc., Santa Fe, 1991.

Health and Light
 John Ott. Ariel Press, Colombus, 1973, 1976.

Physical Health

The Alternative Health & Medicine Encyclopedia
 James E. Marti with Andrea Hine, Visible Ink Press, Detroit, 1995.

World Medicine, the EastWest Guide to Healing Your Body
 Tom Monte and the editors of EastWest Natural Health, G.P. Putnam's Son's, New York, 1993.

Stretching
 Bob Anderson, Shelter Publications, Inc., Bolinas, CA 1980. Stretching, Inc., Box 767 Palmer Lake, CO 80133.

Treat Your Own Neck and *Treat Your Own Back*
 Robin McKenzie, Spinal Publications Ltd, Waikanae, New Zealand, 1989.

Office Yoga
 Julie Friedeberger, Harper Collins Publishers, London, 1991.

Combined Tai-Chi Chuan
 Bow-Sim Mark, Chinese Wushu Research Institute, 1979. CWRI, 246 Harrison Avenue, Boston, MA, 02111.

The Eight Pieces of Brocade, Improving and Maintaining Health
 Yang Jwing-Ming, Yang's Martial Arts Association, 1988. YMAA, 38 Hyde Park Avenue, Jamaica Plain, MA, 01230.

Qigong for Health, Chinese Traditional Exercise for Cure and Prevention
Masaru Takahashi and Stephen Brown, Japan Publications, Inc, Tokyo and New York, 1986.

Chinese Health Balls, Practical Exercises
Hans Höting, Binkey Kok Publications, Diever, Holland, 1990.

Staying Healthy with Nutrition
Elson Haas, Celestial Arts, Berkeley, 1992.

Diet for a New America
John Robbins, Stillpoint Publishing, Walpole, NH, 1987.

Atlas of Human Anatomy
Frank H. Netter, CIBA-GEIGY Corporation, Summit, NJ, 1993.

Anatomy of Movement
Blandine Calais-Germain, Eastland Press, Inc, Seattle, 1993.

RSI

Repetitive Strain Injury, a Computer User's Guide
Emil Pascarelli and Deborah Quilter, John Wiley & Sons, Inc., NY, 1994.

The Hand Book, Preventing Compuer Injury
Stephanie Brown, Ergonome Incorporated, New York, 1994. 145 W. 96th Street, Suite 800, New York, NY 10025

Cululative Trauma Disorders, a Manual for Musculoskeletal Diseases of the Upper limbs. Vern Putz-Anderson, editor, Taylor & Francis, London, 1988, 1990, 1991.

The Carpal Tunnel Syndrome Book
Mark Pinsky, Warner Books, New York, 1994.

Carpal Tunnel Syndrome and Overuse Injuries
Tammy Crouch and Michael Madden, North Atlantic Books, Berkeley, 1992.

Listen to Your Pain
Ben E. Benjamin, Penguin Books, New York, 1984.

Soft Tissue Pain and Disability
Renee Cailliet, F.A. Davis Company, Philadelphia, 1988, 1991.

Chronic Muscle Pain Syndrome
Paul Davidson, Berkeley Books, New York, 1989.

Myofascial Pain and Dysfunction, the Trigger Point Manual
Janet Travell and David Simons, Williams & Wilkins, Baltimore, 1983.

Legal Issues

Your Rights in the Workplace
Dan Lacey, Nolo Press, Berkeley, 1991, 1992.

Worker Compensation Disability and Rehabilitation: An Alert to Claimants, the fraud of compulsory medical and vocational "rehabilitation" to end disability claims. William E Washburn, CEDI Publications, Arlington, VA, 1992.

Workers Compensation Claims Deskbook (California)
Gwen Hamptom, Workers Compensation Company, 1993. P.O. Box 11448, Glendale, CA, 91226.

Electromagnetic Radiation

The EMF Book
Mark Pinsky, Warner Books, New York, 1995.

EMF Handbook
Stephen Prata, Waite Group Press, Corte Madera, CA, 1993.

EMF in Your Environment
US Environmental Protection Agency, Office of Radiation and Indoor Air, Division 6603J, 402-R-92-008, Washington, DC, 20460, December 1992. Available from the US Government Printing Office, Superintendent of Documents, Mail Stop SSOP, Washington, DC, 20402-0328.

Microwave News
Louis Slesin, editor. Bimonthly publication on the effects of electromagnetic radiation. P.O. Box 1799, Grand Central Station, New York, NY 10163.

Cross Currents
Robert O. Becker, Jeremy P. Tarcher, Inc., Los Angeles, 1990.

Currents of Death
Paul Brodeur, Simon and Schuster, New York, 1989.

Bioelectromagnetics
Professional journal for researchers studying the effects of electromagnetic fields on biological systems. Published by Alan R. Liss, New York.

On the Nature of Electromagnetic Field Interactions with Biological Systems
Allan H. Frey, editor, R.G. Landes Company, Austin, 1994.

Index

About the Author

Joan Stigliani spent more than three years researching and writing *The Computer User's Survival Guide*. She discussed the issues with practitioners of traditional and alternative medicine; physical, occupational, and massage therapists; psychologists; researchers in ergonomics; research scientists; ergonomic consultants; equipment developers and suppliers; and computer users themselves to provide a comprehensive, integrated view of computer-related health problems.

Joan holds degrees in literature, linguistics, and education from the University of Michigan, as well as a certificate in technical writing from Middlesex Community College. She worked as a technical writer in the computer industry for seven years, and taught English as a second language before that. Over the last 15 years, she has practiced tai chi, aikido, yoga, and natural vision improvement.

She can be contacted by email at the address *joan@netcom.com*.

Colophon

Because a properly-equipped work environment is essential to the computer user's well-being, we are listing here the equipment that Joan used when writing this book:

Apple Macintosh IIci

Chair from Neutral Posture Ergonomics, Inc.

Maltron keyboard from PCD Maltron Limited

TurboMouse 4.0 from Kensington Microware Limited

21-inch low-emission grayscale monitor (meets MPR2 guidelines) from Radius, Inc.

Easy Access utility, part of Apple's System 7 software

LifeGuard 1.0.2 computer safety software from Visionary Software, Inc.

Automenus 1.1, shareware by Michael J. Conrad

Computer desk with lowered keyboard tray from Creative Computer Furniture (lowered more using woodblocks)

Writing desk

Slant board

Copy stand

Swing-arm, clamp-on task lights with 75-watt neodymium floodlamps, usually set up to reflect light from the walls, curtains, and ceiling for indirect lighting

Fingerless wool gloves by Linda Lorraine

MouseMitt padded wrist protectors from MouseMitt International

BioElectric Shield pendant

Edie Freedman designed the cover of this book, using 19th-century engravings from the Dover Pictorial Archive. The cover layout was produced using Quark XPress 3.3, in Emigre Matrix and Adobe ITC Garamond fonts.

The interior layout was designed by Nancy Priest and Marcia Ciro and implemented in FrameMaker 4.0 by Mike Sierra. The heading fonts are from the Matrix family and the text is set in ITC Garamond Light. The pen and ink drawings that appear in the book were created by medical illustrator Jaye Schlesinger. The artwork was scanned and manipulated in Photoshop, and the final layout was executed in Macromedia Freehand 5.0 by Chris Reilley.

INTERNET

Books from O'Reilly & Associates, Inc.

FALL/WINTER 1995-96

The Whole Internet User's Guide & Catalog

By Ed Krol
2nd Edition April 1994
574 pages, ISBN 1-56592-063-5

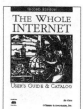

Still the best book on the Internet! This is the second edition of our comprehensive—and bestselling—introduction to the Internet, the international network that includes virtually every major computer site in the world. In addition to email, file transfer, remote login, and network news, this book pays special attention to some new tools for helping you find information. Useful to beginners and veterans alike, this book will help you explore what's possible on the Net. Also includes a pull-out quick-reference card.

"An ongoing classic."
—*Rochester Business Journal*

"The book against which all subsequent Internet guides are measured, Krol's work has emerged as an indispensable reference to beginners and seasoned travelers alike as they venture out on the data highway."
—*Microtimes*

"*The Whole Internet User's Guide & Catalog* will probably become the Internet user's bible because it provides comprehensive, easy instructions for those who want to get the most from this valuable electronic tool."
—David J. Buerger, Editor, *Communications Week*

"Krol's work is comprehensive and lucid, an overview which presents network basics in clear and understandable language. I consider it essential."
—Paul Gilster, *Triad Business News*

The Whole Internet for Windows 95

By Ed Krol & Paula Ferguson
1st Edition October 1995 (est.)
650 pages (est.), ISBN 1-56592-155-0

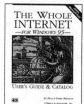

The best book on the Internet...now updated for Windows 95! *The Whole Internet for Windows 95* is the most comprehensive introduction to the Internet available today. For Windows users who in the past have struggled to take full advantage of the Internet's powerful utilities, Windows 95's built-in Internet support is a cause for celebration. And when you get online with Windows 95, this new edition of *The Whole Internet* will guide you every step of the way.

This book shows you how to use the Internet tools that are part of Windows 95 and Microsoft Plus!: Microsoft Internet Explorer (the World Wide Web multimedia browser included in Microsoft Plus!) and Microsoft Exchange, an email program also included in Microsoft Plus!. It also covers Netscape, the most popular Web browser on the market, and shows you how to use Usenet readers, file transfer tools, and database searching software.

But it does much more. Whether you own Microsoft Plus! or not, you'll want to take advantage of alternative popular free software programs that are downloadable from the Net. This book shows you where to find them and how to use them to save you time and money.

WebSite™

By O'Reilly & Associates, Inc.
Documentation by Susan Peck & Linda Mui
1st Edition May 1995
ISBN 1-56592-143-7, UPC 9 781565 921436
Includes two diskettes, 342-page book, and WebSite T-shirt

WebSite™ is an elegant, easy solution for Windows NT 3.5 users who want to start publishing on the Internet. WebSite is a 32-bit World Wide Web server that combines the power and flexibility of a UNIX server with the ease of use of a Windows application. Its intuitive graphical interface is a natural for Windows NT users. WebSite provides a tree-like display of all the documents and links on your server, with a simple solution for finding and fixing broken links. You can run a desktop application like Excel or Visual Basic from within a Web document on WebSite. Its access authentication lets you control which users have access to different parts of your Web server. In addition to Windows NT 3.5, WebSite runs on the current version of Windows 95. WebSite is a product of O'Reilly & Associates, Inc. It is created in cooperation with Bob Denny and Enterprise Integration Technologies, Inc. (EIT).

WebSite is for anyone who wants to publish information on the Web, including individuals, corporate desktop users, and small and medium-size businesses and groups. The intuitive nature of the software and the comprehensive, easy instructions in the book make WebSite a natural choice for a wide variety of users.

The Website package includes a 32-bit HTTP server, WebView,™ Enhanced Mosaic 2.0, and complete documentation.

Getting Connected:
Establishing a Presence on the Internet

By Kevin Dowd
1st Edition December 1995 (est.)
450 pages (est.), ISBN 1-56592-154-2

A complete guide for businesses, schools, and other organizations who want to connect their computers to the Internet. This book covers everything you need to know to make informed decisions, from helping you figure out which services you really need to providing down-to-earth explanations of telecommunication options, such as frame relay, ISDN, and leased lines. Once you're online, it shows you how to set up basic Internet services, such as a World Wide Web server. Tackles issues for the PC, Macintosh, and UNIX platforms.

Internet In A Box,™ Version 2.0

Published by SPRY, Inc. (Product good only in U.S. and Canada)
2nd Edition June 1995
UPC 799364 012001
*Two diskettes & a 528-page version of **The Whole***
***Internet Users Guide& Catalog** as documentation*

Now there are more ways to connect to the Internet—and you get to choose the most economical plan based on your dialing habits.

What will Internet In A Box *do for me?*

Internet In A Box is for PC users who want to connect to the Internet. Quite simply, it solves Internet access problems for individuals and small businesses without dedicated lines and/or UNIX machines. *Internet In A Box* provides instant connectivity, a multimedia Windows interface, and a full suite of applications. This product is so easy to use, you need to know only two things to get started: how to load software onto your PC and how to use a mouse.

New features of version 2.0 include:

- More connectivity options with the CompuServe Network.
- With Spry Mosaic and Progressive Image Rendering, browsing the Internet has never been easier.
- SPRY Mail provides MIME support and a built-in spell checker. Mail and News are now available within the Mosaic Toolbar.
- You'll enjoy safe and secure shopping online with Secure HTTP.
- SPRY News offers offline support for viewing and sending individual articles.
- A Network File Manager means there's an improved interface for dealing with various Internet hosts.

Connecting to the Internet

By Susan Estrada
1st Edition August 1993
188 pages, ISBN 1-56592-061-9

This book provides practical advice on how to get an Internet connection. It describes how to assess your needs to determine the kind of Internet service that is best for you and how to find a local access provider and evaluate the services they offer.

Knowing how to purchase the right kind of Internet access can help you save money and avoid a lot of frustration. This book is the fastest way for you to learn how to get on the Internet. Then you can begin exploring one of the world's most valuable resources.

The Mosaic Handbooks

Mosaic is the hottest new graphical interfaces to the Internet. These books describe how to navigate the World Wide Web using Mosaic's point-and-click interface and how to use Mosaic to replace some of the traditional Internet functions, like FTP, Gopher, Archie, Veronica, and WAIS. For more advanced users, the books describe how to add external viewers to Mosaic (allowing it to display many additional file types) and how to customize the Mosaic interface, such as screen elements, colors, and fonts.

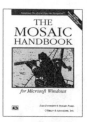

The Mosaic Handbook for Microsoft Windows

By Dale Dougherty & Richard Koman
1st Edition October 1994
230 pages, ISBN 1-56592-094-5
(includes Enhanced NCSA Mosaic V1.0 on two diskettes)

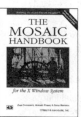

The Mosaic Handbook for the X Window System

By Dale Dougherty, Richard Koman &
Paula Ferguson
1st Edition October 1994
288 pages, ISBN 1-56592-095-3
(includes Enhanced NCSA Mosaic V2.4 on CD-ROM)

The Mosaic Handbook for the Macintosh

By Dale Dougherty & Richard Koman
1st Edition October 1994
198 pages, ISBN 1-56592-096-1
(includes Enhanced NCSA Mosaic V1.0 on diskette)

Web Design for Designers

By Jennifer Niederst, Edie Freedman & Kathy Peebles
1st Edition December 1995 (est.)
120 pages (est.), ISBN 1-56592-165-8

This book is for designers who need to hone their skills for the Web. It explains how to work with HTML documents from a designer's point of view, outlines special problems with presenting information online, and walks through incorporating images into Web pages, with emphasis on resolution and improving efficiency. Also discusses the different browsers available and how to make sure a document is most effective for a broad spectrum of browsers and platforms.

Managing Internet Information Services

By Cricket Liu, Jerry Peek, Russ Jones, Bryan Buus & Adrian Nye
1st Edition December 1994
668 pages, ISBN 1-56592-062-7

This comprehensive guide describes how to set up information services and make them available over the Internet. It discusses why a company would want to offer Internet services, provides complete coverage of all popular services, and tells how to select which ones to provide. Most of the book describes how to set up Gopher, World Wide Web, FTP, and WAIS servers and email services.

"*Managing Internet Information Services* has long been needed in the Internet community, as well as in many organizations with IP-based networks. Although many on the Internet are quite savvy when it comes to administering these types of tools, *MIIS* will allow a much larger community to join in and perhaps provide more diverse information. This book will be a welcome addition to my Internet shelf."
—Robert H'obbes' Zakon, MITRE Corporation

Using Email Effectively

By Linda Lamb & Jerry Peek
1st Edition April 1995
160 pages, ISBN 1-56592-103-8

When you're new to email, you're usually shown what keystrokes to use to read and send a message. After using email for a few years, you learn from your own mistakes and from reading other people's mail. You learn:

- How to organize saved mail so that you can find it again
- When to include a previous message, and how much to include, so that your reader can quickly make sense of what's being discussed
- When a network address "looks right," so that more of your messages get through the first time
- When a "bounced" message will never be delivered and when the bounce merely indicates temporary network difficulties
- How to successfully subscribe and unsubscribe to a mailing list

With first-person anecdotes, examples, and general observations, *Using Email Effectively* shortens the learning-from-experience curve for all mailers, so you can quickly be productive and send email that looks intelligent to others.

PGP: Pretty Good Privacy

By Simson Garfinkel
1st Edition December 1994
430 pages, ISBN 1-56592-098-8

PGP is a freely available encryption program that protects the privacy of files and electronic mail. It uses powerful public key cryptography and works on virtually every platform. This book is both a readable technical user's guide and a fascinating behind-the-scenes look at cryptography and privacy. It describes how to use PGP and provides background on cryptography, PGP's history, battles over public key cryptography patents and U.S. government export restrictions, and public debates about privacy and free speech.

"I even learned a few things about PGP from Simson's informative book."—Phil Zimmermann, Author of PGP

"Since the release of PGP 2.0 from Europe in the fall of 1992, PGP's popularity and usage has grown to make it the de-facto standard for email encryption. Simson's book is an excellent overview of PGP and the history of cryptography in general. It should prove a useful addition to the resource library for any computer user, from the UNIX wizard to the PC novice."
—Derek Atkins, PGP Development Team, MIT

Building Internet Firewalls

By D. Brent Chapman & Elizabeth D. Zwicky
1st Edition September 1995
544 pages, ISBN 1-56592-124-0

Everyone is jumping on the Internet bandwagon, despite the fact that the security risks associated with connecting to the Net have never been greater. This book is a practical guide to building firewalls on the Internet. It describes a variety of firewall approaches and architectures and discusses how you can build packet filtering and proxying solutions at your site. It also contains a full discussion of how to configure Internet services (e.g., FTP, SMTP, Telnet) to work with a firewall, as well as a complete list of resources, including the location of many publicly available firewall construction tools.

MH & xmh: Email for Users & Programmers

By Jerry Peek
3rd Edition April 1995
782 pages, ISBN 1-56592-093-7

There are lots of mail programs in use these days, but MH is one of the most durable and flexible. Best of all, it's available on almost all UNIX systems. It has spawned a number of interfaces that many users prefer. This book covers three popular interfaces: *xmh* (for the X environment), *exmh* (written with tcl/tk), and *mh-e* (for GNU Emacs users).

The book contains:

- A quick tour through MH, *xmh*, *exmh*, and *mh-e* for new users

- Configuration and customization information

- Lots of tips and techniques for programmers—and plenty of practical examples for everyone

- Information beyond the manual pages, explaining how to make MH do things you never thought an email program could do

- Quick reference pages in the back of the book

In addition, the third edition describes the Multipurpose Internet Mail Extensions (MIME) and describes how to use it with these mail programs. MIME is an extension that allows users to send graphics, sound, and other multimedia formats through mail between otherwise incompatible systems.

Marketing on the Internet

By Linda Lamb, Tim O'Reilly, Dale Dougherty & Brian Erwin
1st Edition Winter 1995-96 (est.)
170 pages (est.), ISBN 1-56592-105-4

Marketing on the Internet tells you what you need to know to successfully use this new communication and sales channel to put product and sales information online, build relationships with customers, send targeted announcements, and answer product support questions. In short, how to use the Internet as part of your overall marketing mix. Written from a marketing, not technical, perspective.

The USENET Handbook

By Mark Harrison
1st Edition May 1995
388 pages, ISBN 1-56592-101-1

USENET, also called Netnews, is the world's largest discussion forum, encompassing the worldwide Internet and many other sites that aren't formally connected to any network. USENET provides a forum for asking and answering technical questions, arguing politics, religion, and society, or discussing most scientific, artistic, or humanistic disciplines. It's also a forum for distributing free software, as well as digitized pictures and sound.

This book unlocks USENET for you. It includes tutorials on the most popular newsreaders for UNIX and Windows (*tin*, *nn*, GNUS, and Trumpet). It's also a guide to the culture of the Net, giving you an introduction to etiquette, the private language, and some of the history.

Smileys

By David W. Sanderson
1st Edition March 1993
93 pages, ISBN 1-56592-041-4

From the people who put an armadillo on the cover of a system administrator book comes this collection of the computer underground hieroglyphs called "smileys." Originally inserted into email messages to denote "said with a cynical smile" :-), smileys now run rampant throughout the electronic mail culture.

!%@:: A Directory of Electronic Mail Addressing & Networks

By Donnalyn Frey & Rick Adams
4th Edition June 1994
662 pages, ISBN 1-56592-046-5

The only up-to-date directory that charts the networks that make up the Internet, provides contact names and addresses, and describes the services each network provides. This is the fourth edition of this directory, now in a simplified format designed to allow more frequent updates.

The Computer User's Survival Guide

By Joan Stigliani
1st Edition October 1995
296 pages, ISBN 1-56592-030-9

The bad news: You can be hurt by working at a computer. The good news: Many of the factors that pose a risk are within your control.

The Computer User's Survival Guide looks squarely at all the factors that affect your health on the job, including positioning, equipment, work habits, lighting, stress, radiation, and general health. It is not a book of gloom and doom. It is a guide to protecting yourself against health risks from your computer, while boosting your effectiveness and making your work more enjoyable.

This guide will teach you what's going on "under the skin" when your hands and arms spend much of the day mousing and typing, and what you can do to prevent overuse injuries. You'll learn various postures to help reduce stress; what you can do to prevent glare from modern office lighting; simple breathing techniques and stretches to keep your body well oxygenated and relaxed; and how to reduce eye strain. Also covers radiation issues and what electrical equipment is responsible for the most exposure.

The Future Does Not Compute

By Stephen L. Talbott
1st Edition May 1995
502 pages, ISBN 1-56592-085-6

This book explores the networked computer as an expression of the darker, dimly conscious side of the human being. What we have been imparting to the Net—or what the Net has been eliciting from us— is a half-submerged, barely intended logic, contaminated by wishes and tendencies we prefer not to acknowledge. The urgent necessity is for us to wake up to what is most fully human and unmachinelike in ourselves, rather than yield to an ever more strangling embrace with our machines. The author's thesis is sure to raise a controversy among the millions of users now adapting themselves to the Net.

Linux Network Administrator's Guide

By Olaf Kirch
1st Edition January 1995
370 pages, ISBN 1-56592-087-2

Linux, a UNIX-compatible operating system that runs on personal computers, is a pinnacle within the free software movement. It is based on a kernel developed by Finnish student Linus Torvalds and is distributed on the Net or on low-cost disks, along with a complete set of UNIX libraries, popular free software utilities, and traditional layered products like NFS and the X Window System.

Networking is a fundamental part of Linux. Whether you want a simple UUCP connection or a full LAN with NFS and NIS, you are going to have to build a network.

Linux Network Administrator's Guide by Olaf Kirch is one of the most successful books to come from the Linux Documentation Project. It touches on all the essential networking software included with Linux, plus some hardware considerations. Topics include serial connections, UUCP, routing and DNS, mail and News, SLIP and PPP, NFS, and NIS.

---

sendmail

By Bryan Costales, with Eric Allman & Neil Rickert
1st Edition November 1993
830 pages, ISBN 1-56592-056-2

Although sendmail is used on almost every UNIX system, it's one of the last great uncharted territories—and most difficult utilities to learn—in UNIX system administration. This book provides a complete sendmail tutorial, plus extensive reference material. It covers the BSD, UIUC IDA, and V8 versions of sendmail.

"The program and its rule description file, sendmail.cf, have long been regarded as the pit of coals that separated the mild UNIX system administrators from the real fire walkers. Now, sendmail syntax, testing, hidden rules, and other mysteries are revealed. Costales, Allman, and Rickert are the indisputable authorities to do the text."
—Ben Smith, *Byte*

Networking Personal Computers with TCP/IP

By Craig Hunt
1st Edition July 1995
408 pages, ISBN 1-56592-123-2

If you're like most network administrators, you probably have several networking "islands": a TCP/IP-based network of UNIX systems (possibly connected to the Internet), plus a separate Netware or NetBIOS network for your PCs. Perhaps even separate Netware and NetBIOS networks in different departments, or at different sites. And you've probably dreaded the task of integrating those networks into one.

If that's your situation, you need this book! When done properly, integrating PCs onto a TCP/IP-based Internet is less threatening than it seems; long term, it gives you a much more flexible and extensible network. Craig Hunt, author of the classic *TCP/IP Network Administration*, tells you how to build a maintainable network that includes your PCs. Don't delay; as Craig points out, if you don't provide a network solution for your PC users, someone else will.

Covers: DOS, Windows, Windows for Workgroups, Windows NT, Windows 95, and Novell Netware; Chameleon (NetManage), PC/TCP (FTP Software), LAN WorkPlace (Novell), Super TCP, and Trumpet; Basic Network setup and configuration, with special attention given to email, network printing, and file sharing

---

TCP/IP Network Administration

By Craig Hunt
1st Edition August 1992
502 pages, ISBN 0-937175-82-X

TCP/IP Network Administration is a complete guide to setting up and running a TCP/IP network for administrators of networks of systems or lone home systems that access the Internet. It starts with the fundamentals: what the protocols do and how they work, how to request a network address and a name (the forms needed are included in an appendix), and how to set up your network.

Beyond basic setup, the book discusses how to configure important network applications, including sendmail, the r* commands, and some simple setups for NIS and NFS. There are also chapters on troubleshooting and security. In addition, this book covers several important packages that are available from the Net (such as *gated*). Covers BSD and System V TCP/IP implementations.

Learning the UNIX Operating System

By Grace Todino, John Strang & Jerry Peek
3rd Edition August 1993
108 pages, ISBN 1-56592-060-0

If you are new to UNIX, this concise introduction will tell you just what you need to get started and no more. Why wade through a 600-page book when you can begin working productively in a matter of minutes? It's an ideal primer for Mac and PC users of the Internet who need to know a little bit about UNIX on the systems they visit. This book is the most effective introduction to UNIX in print. The third edition has been updated and expanded to provide increased coverage of window systems and networking. It's a handy book for someone just starting with UNIX, as well as someone who encounters a UNIX system as a "visitor" via remote login over the Internet.

Learning Perl

By Randal L. Schwartz, Foreword by Larry Wall
1st Edition November 1993
274 pages, ISBN 1-56592-042-2

Learning Perl is ideal for system administrators, programmers, and anyone else wanting a down-to-earth introduction to this useful language. Written by a Perl trainer, its aim is to make a competent, hands-on Perl programmer out of the reader as quickly as possible. The book takes a tutorial approach and includes hundreds of short code examples, along with some lengthy ones. The relatively inexperienced programmer will find *Learning Perl* easily accessible.

Each chapter of the book includes practical programming exercises. Solutions are presented for all exercises.

For a comprehensive and detailed guide to advanced programming with Perl, read O'Reilly's companion book, *Programming perl*.

DNS and BIND

By Cricket Liu & Paul Albitz
1st Edition October 1992
418 pages, ISBN 1-56592-010-4

DNS and BIND contains all you need to know about the Internet's Domain Name System (DNS) and the Berkeley Internet Name Domain (BIND), its UNIX implementation. The Domain Name System is the Internet's "phone book"; it's a database that tracks important information (in particular, names and addresses) for every computer on the Internet. If you're a system administrator, this book will show you how to set up and maintain the DNS software on your network.

"At [418] pages it blows away easily any vendor supplied information, and because it has an extensive troubleshooting section (using nslookup) it should never be far from your desk—especially when things on your network start to go awry :-)"
—Ian Hoyle, BHP Research, Melbourne Laboratories

Practical UNIX Security

By Simson Garfinkel & Gene Spafford
1st Edition June 1991
2nd Edition expected January 1996 (est.)
512 pages, ISBN 0-937175-72-2

Practical UNIX Security tells system administrators how to make their UNIX system—either System V or BSD—as secure as it possibly can be without going to trusted system technology. The book describes UNIX concepts and how they enforce security, tells how to defend against and handle security breaches, and explains network security (including UUCP, NFS, Kerberos, and firewall machines) in detail. If you are a UNIX system administrator or user who deals with security, you need this book.

"Timely, accurate, written by recognized experts...covers every imaginable topic relating to Unix security. An excellent book and I recommend it as a valuable addition to any system administrator's or computer site manager's collection."
—Jon Wright, *Informatics* (Australia)

FOR INFORMATION: **800-998-9938**, 707-829-0515; INFO@ORA.COM; HTTP://WWW.ORA.COM/

O'Reilly on the Net—
ONLINE PROGRAM GUIDE

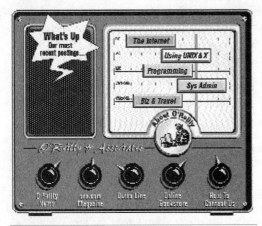

O'Reilly & Associates offers extensive information through various online resources. We invite you to come and explore our little neck-of-the-woods.

Ora-news

An easy way to stay informed of the latest projects and products from O'Reilly & Associates is to subscribe to "ora-news," our electronic news service. Subscribers receive email as soon as the information breaks.

To subscribe to "ora-news":

Send email to:
listproc@online.ora.com

and put the following information on the first line of your message (not in "Subject"):
subscribe ora-news "your name" **of** "your company"

For example enter:
```
mail listproc@online.ora.com
subscribe ora-news Kris Webber of
    Mighty Fine Enterprises
```

Email

Many customer services are provided via email. Here are a few of the most popular and useful.

info@ora.com
> For general questions and information.

bookquestions@ora.com
> For technical questions, or corrections, concerning book contents.

order@ora.com
> To order books online and for ordering questions.

catalog@ora.com
> To receive a free copy of our magazine/catalog, *ora.com*. Please include a postal address.

Online Resource Center

Most comprehensive among our online offerings is the O'Reilly Resource Center. Here, you'll find detailed information on all O'Reilly products: titles, prices, tables of contents, indexes, author bios, software contents, reviews...you can even view images of the products themselves. With GNN Direct you can now order our products directly off the Net (GNN Direct is available on the Web site only; Gopher users can still use **order@ora.com**). We supply contact information along with a list of distributors and bookstores available worldwide. In addition, we provide informative literature in the field: articles, interviews, excerpts, and bibliographies that help you stay informed and abreast.

To access ORA's Online Resource Center:

Point your Web browser (e.g., **mosaic, netscape,** or **lynx**) to:
http://www.ora.com/

For the plaintext version, **telnet** or **gopher** to:
gopher.ora.com
(telnet login: **gopher**)

FTP

The example files and programs in many of our books are available electronically via FTP.

To obtain example files and programs from O'Reilly texts:

ftp to:
ftp.ora.com

or **ftp.uu.net**
cd published/oreilly

Snailmail and Phones

O'Reilly & Associates, Inc.
103A Morris Street, Sebastopol, CA 95472
Inquiries: **707-829-0515, 800-998-9938**
Credit card orders: **800-889-8969** (Weekdays 6 A.M.- 5 P.M. PST)
FAX: **707-829-0104**

O'Reilly & Associates—
LISTING OF TITLES

INTERNET

!%@:: A Directory of Electronic Mail
  Addressing & Networks
Connecting to the Internet:
  An O'Reilly Buyer's Guide
Getting Connected (Winter '95 est.)
The Mosaic Handbook for
  Microsoft Windows
The Mosaic Handbook for
  the Macintosh
The Mosaic Handbook for
  the X Window System
Smileys
The Whole Internet User's
  Guide & Catalog
The Windows 95 Whole Internet
  (Fall '95 est.)
Web Design for Designers
  (Winter '95 est.)

SOFTWARE

Internet In A Box™
WebSite™

WHAT YOU NEED TO KNOW SERIES

Using Email Effectively
Marketing on the Internet
  (Winter '95 est.)
When You Can't Find Your
  System Administrator

HEALTH, CAREER & BUSINESS

Building a Successful Software Business
The Computer User's Survival Guide
Dictionary of Computer Terms
The Future Does Not Compute
Love Your Job!
TWI Day Calendar - 1996

AUDIOTAPES

INTERNET TALK RADIO'S
"GEEK OF THE WEEK" INTERVIEWS

The Future of the Internet Protocol
Global Network Operations
Mobile IP Networking
Networked Information and
  Online Libraries
Security and Networks
European Networking

NOTABLE SPEECHES OF THE
INFORMATION AGE

John Perry Barlow

USING UNIX

BASICS

Learning GNU Emacs
Learning the Bash Shell
Learning the Korn Shell
Learning the UNIX Operating System
Learning the vi Editor
MH & xmh: Email for Users &
  Programmers
SCO UNIX in a Nutshell
The USENET Handbook
Using and Managing UUCP
  (Winter '95 /'96 est.)
UNIX in a Nutshell: System V Edition

ADVANCED

Exploring Expect
The Frame Handbook
Learning Perl
Making TeX Work
Programming perl
Running LINUX
sed & awk
UNIX Power Tools (with CD-ROM)

SYSTEM ADMINISTRATION

Building Internet Firewalls
Computer Crime:
  A Crimefighter's Handbook
Computer Security Basics
DNS and BIND
Essential System Administration
Linux Network Administrator's Guide
Managing Internet Information Services
Managing NFS and NIS
Managing UUCP and Usenet
Networking Personal Computers
  with TCP/IP
Practical UNIX Security
PGP: Pretty Good Privacy
sendmail
System Performance Tuning
TCP/IP Network Administration
termcap & terminfo
Volume 8 : X Window System
  Administrator's Guide
The X Companion CD for R6

PROGRAMMING

Applying RCS and SCCS
C++: The Core Language (Winter '95 est.)
Checking C Programs with lint
DCE Security Programming
Distributing Applications Across DCE
  and Windows NT
Encyclopedia of Graphics File Formats
Guide to Writing DCE Applications
High Performance Computing
lex & yacc
Managing Projects with make
Microsoft RPC Programming Guide
Migrating to Fortran 90
Multi-Platform Code Management
ORACLE Performance Tuning
ORACLE PL/SQL Programming
Porting UNIX Software (Fall '95 est.)
POSIX Programmer's Guide
POSIX.4: Programming for
  the Real World
Power Programming with RPC
Practical C Programming
Practical C++ Programming
Programming with curses
Programming with GNU Software
  (Winter '95 /'96 est.)
Programming with Pthreads
  (Winter '95 /'96 est.)
Software Portability with imake
Understanding and Using COFF
Understanding DCE
Understanding Japanese Information
  Processing
UNIX for FORTRAN Programmers
UNIX Systems Programming for SVR4
  (Winter '95 /'96 est.)
Using C on the UNIX System
Using csh and tcsh

BERKELEY 4.4 SOFTWARE DISTRIBUTION

4.4BSD System Manager's Manual
4.4BSD User's Reference Manual
4.4BSD User's Supplementary Docs.
4.4BSD Programmer's Reference Man.
4.4BSD Programmer's Supp. Docs.
4.4BSD-Lite CD Companion
4.4BSD-Lite CD Companion: Int. Ver.

X PROGRAMMING

THE X WINDOW SYSTEM

Volume 0: X Protocol Reference Manual
Volume 1: Xlib Programming Manual
Volume 2: Xlib Reference Manual
Volume 3: X Window System
  User's Guide
Volume. 3M: X Window System
  User's Guide, Motif Ed.
Volume. 4: X Toolkit Intrinsics
  Programming Manual
Volume 4M: X Toolkit Intrinsics
  Programming Manual, Motif Ed.
Volume 5: X Toolkit Intrinsics
  Reference Manual
Volume 6A: Motif Programming Man.
Volume 6B: Motif Reference Manual
Volume 7A: XView Programming Man.
Volume 7B: XView Reference Manual
Volume 8 : X Window System
  Administrator's Guide
PEXlib Programming Manual
PEXlib Reference Manual
PHIGS Programming Manual
PHIGS Reference Manual
Programmer's Supplement for Release 6
Motif Tools (with CD-ROM)
The X Companion CD for R6
The X Window System in a Nutshell
X User Tools (with CD-ROM)

THE X RESOURCE

A QUARTERLY WORKING JOURNAL
FOR X PROGRAMMERS

The X Resource: Issues 0 through 15

TRAVEL

Travelers' Tales France
Travelers' Tales Hong Kong (11/95 est.)
Travelers' Tales India
Travelers' Tales Mexico
Travelers' Tales Spain (11/95 est.)
Travelers' Tales Thailand
Travelers' Tales: A Woman's World

O'Reilly & Associates—
INTERNATIONAL DISTRIBUTORS

Customers outside North America can now order O'Reilly & Associates books through the following distributors. They offer our international customers faster order processing, more bookstores, increased representation at tradeshows worldwide, and the high-quality, responsive service our customers have come to expect.

EUROPE, MIDDLE EAST, AND AFRICA
(except Germany, Switzerland, and Austria)

INQUIRIES
International Thomson Publishing Europe
Berkshire House
168-173 High Holborn
London WC1V 7AA, United Kingdom
Telephone: 44-71-497-1422
Fax: 44-71-497-1426
Email: itpint@itps.co.uk

ORDERS
International Thomson Publishing Services, Ltd.
Cheriton House, North Way
Andover, Hampshire SP10 5BE, United Kingdom
Telephone: 44-264-342-832 (UK orders)
Telephone: 44-264-342-806 (outside UK)
Fax: 44-264-364418 (UK orders)
Fax: 44-264-342761 (outside UK)

GERMANY, SWITZERLAND, AND AUSTRIA

International Thomson Publishing GmbH
O'Reilly-International Thomson Verlag
Königswinterer Straße 418
53227 Bonn, Germany
Telephone: 49-228-97024 0
Fax: 49-228-441342
Email: anfragen@ora.de

ASIA *(except Japan)*
INQUIRIES
International Thomson Publishing Asia
221 Henderson Road
#08-03 Henderson Industrial Park
Singapore 0315
Telephone: 65-272-6496
Fax: 65-272-6498

ORDERS
Telephone: 65-268-7867
Fax: 65-268-6727

JAPAN
International Thomson Publishing Japan
Hirakawa-cho Kyowa Building 3F
2-2-1 Hirakawa-cho, Chiyoda-Ku
Tokyo, 102 Japan
Telephone: 81-3-3221-1428
Fax: 81-3-3237-1459

Toppan Publishing
Froebel Kan Bldg. 3-1, Kanda Ogawamachi Chiyoda-Ku
Tokyo 101 Japan
Telex: J 27317
Cable: Toppanbook, Tokyo
Telephone: 03-3295-3461
Fax: 03-3293-5963

AUSTRALIA
WoodsLane Pty. Ltd.
7/5 Vuko Place, Warriewood NSW 2102
P.O. Box 935, Mona Vale NSW 2103
Australia
Telephone: 02-970-5111
Fax: 02-970-5002
Email: woods@tmx.mhs.oz.au

NEW ZEALAND
WoodsLane New Zealand Ltd.
21 Cooks Street (P.O. Box 575)
Wanganui, New Zealand
Telephone: 64-6-347-6543
Fax: 64-6-345-4840
Email: woods@tmx.mhs.oz.au

THE AMERICAS
O'Reilly & Associates, Inc.
103A Morris Street
Sebastopol, CA 95472 U.S.A.
Telephone: 707-829-0515
Telephone: 800-998-9938 (U.S. & Canada)
Fax: 707-829-0104
Email: order@ora.com

TO ORDER: **800-889-8969** (CREDIT CARD ORDERS ONLY); **ORDER@ORA.COM**